ADIVASI

OR

VANVASI

ADIVASI OR VANVASI

Tribal India & the Politics of Hindutva

KAMAL NAYAN CHOUBEY

VINTAGE
An imprint of Penguin Random House

VINTAGE

Vintage is an imprint of the Penguin Random House group of companies whose addresses can be found at global.penguinrandomhouse.com

Published by Penguin Random House India Pvt. Ltd
4th Floor, Capital Tower 1, MG Road,
Gurugram 122 002, Haryana, India

First published in Vintage by Penguin Random House India 2025

10 9 8 7 6 5 4 3 2 1

ISBN 9780143470489

Typeset in Adobe Caslon Pro by Manipal Technologies Limited, Manipal
Printed at Thomson Press India Ltd, New Delhi

www.penguin.co.in

To my father

Contents

Abbreviations

ABVKA:	Akhil Bharatiya Vanvasi Kalyan Ashram
ADC:	Autonomous District Council
AFSPA:	Armed Forces (Special Powers) Act
AIUFWP:	All India Union for Forest Working People
BAP:	Bharat Adivasi Party
BJP:	Bharatiya Janata Party
CFRs:	Community Forest Rights
CPI(M):	Communist Party of India (Marxist)
CSD:	Campaign for Survival and Dignity
DJS:	Dharma Jagran Samiti
DMK:	Dravida Munnetra Kazhagam
DNP:	Dudhwa National Park
FCA:	Forest Conservation Act
FD:	Forest Department
FRA:	Forest Rights Act
GoI:	Government of India
IDRF:	India Development Relief Fund

IFA:	Indian Forest Act
IFRs:	Individual Forest Rights
IGF:	Inspector General of Forests
ILO:	International Labour Organization
INC:	Indian National Congress
ITP:	Bharatiya Tribal Party
JFMC:	Joint Forest Management Committee
JMM:	Jharkhand Mukti Morcha
JPC:	Joint Parliamentary Committee
JSM:	Janjati Suraksha Manch
MoEF:	The Ministry of Environment and Forest
MoEFCC:	Ministry of Environment, Forest and Climate Change
MoPR:	Ministry of Panchayati Raj
MoTA:	Ministry of Tribal Affairs
NCST:	National Commission for Scheduled Tribes
NDA:	National Democratic Alliance
NFFPFW:	National Forum of Forest People and Forest Workers
NGT:	National Green Tribunal
NSCSTC:	National Scheduled Castes and Scheduled Tribes Commission
NTFPs:	Non-Timber Forest Produces
ORP:	Other Religion Peoples
OTFD:	Other Traditional Forest Dwellers
PAs:	Protected Areas
PESA:	Panchayat (Extension to Scheduled Areas) Act
PTGs:	Primitive Tribal Groups

PVTGs:	Particularly Vulnerable Tribal Groups
RSS:	Rashtriya Swayamsevak Sangh
SAs:	Scheduled Areas
STs:	Scheduled Tribes
SVD:	Samyukt Vidhayak Dal
TAC:	Tribal Advisory Council
TAMMKM:	Tharu Adivasi Mahila Mazdoor Kisan Manch
UCC:	Uniform Civil Code
UNDRIP:	United Nations Declaration on the Rights of Indigenous People
UPA:	United Progressive Alliance
VHP:	Vishwa Hindu Parishad
VKA:	Vanvasi Kalyan Ashram (short version of ABVKA)
WLPA:	Wild Life (Protection) Act

1

Introduction: The Uniqueness of the Vanvasi Kalyan Ashram

The Akhil Bharatiya Vanvasi Kalyan Ashram, hereafter referred to as the Vanvasi Kalyan Ashram or the VKA, was established in December 1952 and is the tribal wing of the Rashtriya Swayamsevak Sangh (RSS). It works in different tribal areas in India to propagate the ideals of the RSS and primarily focuses on enhancing Hindu values in the lives of tribal people. The VKA's work has created a strong base for Hindu right-wing politics in tribal areas and consequently, the Bharatiya Janata Party (BJP) has achieved electoral success in these areas, improved performance in the North-eastern states and successfully won many elections, including the legislative assembly election in Tripura. Political watchers say the VKA and its affiliate organizations are behind this success. RSS *shakhas* (cells) in Tripura rose from sixty in 2014 to 265 in 2018, and suggests that ideological indoctrination is both a reason and an outcome of elections.[1]

However, the opposition parties, particularly Congress leader Rahul Gandhi have constantly criticized the RSS and BJP for using the term *vanvasi* for tribals. For example, at a rally in Mahuva during the Gujarat Legislative Assembly election in 2022, Rahul Gandhi said that,

> The people of BJP don't call you adivasi. What do they call you? Vanvasi. They don't tell you that you are the first owners of Hindustan. They tell you that you live in the jungles, meaning they don't wish that you live in cities, that your children become engineers, doctors, fly planes, speak in English . . . [2]

Gandhi repeated this allegation several times in his speeches in tribal-dominated areas in Maharashtra, Rajasthan, Madhya Pradesh and Chhattisgarh. The RSS and BJP leaders criticized Rahul Gandhi for his comment, and senior leader Ram Madhav underlined, 'we call them vanvasis. We do not call them *adivasis* because adivasi means original inhabitants or aboriginals, which implies all others are from outside. But the *sangh parivar* (the RSS family, an umbrella term for Hindutva organizations spawned by the RSS) believes that we all are original inhabitants of this continent.'[3]

The identity of tribes has always been a contested issue not only in the political arena but also in academic and sociological writings. During colonial rule, the use of the term 'tribe' was initiated to describe a certain category of people in India. At the initial state, it was not clear what was the precise meaning of this term and how people would be included in this category, and sometimes 'tribe' and 'caste' were used interchangeably or as similar terms. However, it soon became clear that the term 'tribe' was used for those communities or groups that were different from the dominant section of the Indian society. In the book *The Aborigines 'So-called' and Their Future* (1943),

G.S. Ghurye justified describing tribes as Hindus, and used the expression 'backward Hindus' based on the observations of the Census Commissioners between the period 1891 and 1931, who felt tribes should not be described as animists. Ghurye's book was later published under a new title *The Scheduled Tribes*. In the book, Ghurye described tribes as 'backward Hindus' because there was so much similarity between the Hindu religion and the animistic tribal religion that they could not be distinguished from one another.[4] Several scholars have accepted that tribes are different from Hindus, but emphasized that there had been interactions between tribal societies and 'mainstream' civilization. N.K. Bose describes this process as a Hindu method of tribal absorption,[5] while D.D. Kosambi argues that the primary method of tribal integration into Hindu society was the adoption of technology.[6] Sociologists like Virginius Xaxa have emphatically rejected the argument that the tribes are 'backward Hindus'. He says that the categorization of tribes as Hindus leads to both conceptual and empirical difficulties. He accepts that there are some similarities between certain tribal practices and Hindu practices. Nevertheless, this cannot be a basis to declare them as part of the Hindu religion, because one can also find such similarities with other religions. For Xaxa, the autonomous identity of tribals is the most crucial.[7] Indeed, many diverse groups are included in the Constitutional category of scheduled tribes. While it is difficult to accept them as part of the Hindu religion, there are indeed many communities whose lifestyle and cultural values are closer to Hinduism.

The RSS and its tribal front, the VKA, always emphasized that tribals are naturally part of Hinduism. Later, they also invented the idea of Sanatan Dharma (a Sanskrit word meaning 'eternal religion') as an indigenous religion to engage with the tribal communities of the North-east. Certain tribal sects do not consider themselves as Hindus, because their mode of worship and other cultural values are different. But they can be considered as part of Sanatan Dharma which embraces all religions and sects that originated in India. In this sense, it excludes Christianity and Islam and accommodates all other tribal sects.[8] The RSS generally, and the VKA particularly, prefer the word vanvasi (inhabitant of forests) rather than Adivasi (original inhabitant) for tribals. The premise behind using the term vanvasi, is that the word adivasi, expresses a separation between people living in and around forests and the larger Hindu society. The term vanvasi or janjati underlines that these communities are part of the Hindu religion, and the unique primary feature of these communities is that they live in forest areas. The VKA uses this slogan as its motto: '*Tu Main Ek Rakt*' (You and I have the same blood). This slogan represents the unity between tribal communities and the rest of Hindu society, and attempts to establish a cohesive relationship between vanvasis and non-tribal groups living in villages and urban areas. The idea emerges from another basic slogan of the VKA—'*Vanvasi, Gramvasi, Nagarvasi, Hum Sab Bharatvasi*' (Forest dwellers, village dwellers and town dwellers, we are all Indians). It should be noted that the VKA does not work only for forest-dwelling communities; it has also expanded to village development and the rights of educated tribes.[9] Primarily, it still focuses on tribal communities living in forests or adjacent villages.

Vanvasi Kalyan Ashram: Need for Systematic Study

The VKA started at the local level in Jashpur town of Central Provinces (which became part of Madhya Pradesh in 1956 after its formation and now it is in Chhattisgarh). Till 1978, it worked in a few tribal pockets of Odisha, south Bihar (now Jharkhand) and some other places. However, after 1978, it extended its work in many other tribal areas and also developed different wings/departments to cover varied aspects or issues of tribal life. It started with opposing the increasing influence of the Christian missionaries in tribal areas and focused on the spread of Hindu values among janjatis/vanvasis. This book wishes to present an analytical study of the history, organizational structure, development and other facets of the work of the VKA. It aims to explore and present the works of the VKA in the areas of education, medical services, women empowerment and securing forest rights of forest-dwelling communities. It also focuses on the work of the VKA to spread Hindu values in tribal society and its opposition to 'foreign' religions—Christianity and Islam. Through the study of VKA, the book explores the different facets of the politics of Hindutva in tribal areas and the duality of the VKA, where its activists form other organizations and carry out more aggressive, controversial and polarizing work.[10]

Studies on the RSS have discussed the VKA marginally as if it's a cog in the wheel. There are many studies on the formation, expansion and work of the RSS. Many books have been written by the office-bearers, senior pracharaks (preachers) of the RSS or journalists who sympathize with the body. In all these books, one can find more or less positive descriptions regarding the RSS and its work and there is no separate or extensive description of the organization or the work of the VKA. For example, H.V. Seshadri, a former *sarkarayah* (general secretary) of the RSS, in his edited book *RSS: A Vision In Action* (1998*)* has not mentioned the VKA's work.[11] On the other hand, a senior office-bearer of the RSS, Sunil Ambekar, has mentioned the role of the VKA in a few sentences in his book *The RSS: Roadmaps 21*st *Century* (2019) to show the RSS's concern regarding the conversion of tribals. He writes,

> Conversion is a threat, particularly in tribal and underprivileged areas . . . The Sangh has expanded its footprints in these spheres. It is a high-priority focus. The Sangh runs a wide range of diverse programmes through its Vanvasi Kalyan Ashram, a social welfare organization dedicated to tribal people, and is headquartered in Jashpur Chhattisgarh.[12]

However, apart from these few sentences, he does not mention anything else regarding the VKA. Another RSS-related scholar Ratan Sharda gives a two-page introduction about the VKA in his book *RSS 360º: Demystifying Rashtriya Swayamsevak Sangh* (2018).[13]

Many independent researchers and scholars have studied the history of RSS and changes in its organization and strategies. Walter K. Anderson and Shridhar D. Damle in their book, *The Brotherhood in Saffron: The Rashtriya Swayamsevak Sangh and Hindu Revivalism* (1987) present an extensive study of the formation of the RSS and its ideological roots.[14] However, there is no description regarding the formation or working of the VKA. Similarly, in their second book, *The RSS: A View to the Inside* (2018) they focus on the works of the RSS in recent decades, also discuss the relationship between its different affiliate organizations, but they have again overlooked the role or importance of the VKA within the RSS or in tribal areas.[15] Noted journalist, Vijay Trivedi's book *Sangham Sharanam Gachchami*: *RSS Ke Safar Ka Ek Imandar Dastavej* (2020) presents an exhaustive study of the RSS, where he refers to the work of the VKA in the context of conversion and works in tribal areas. However, the VKA comes as a minuscule part of a larger story in his description.[16] Nilanjan Mukhopadhyay's scholarly book, *The RSS: Icons of the Indian Right* (2019) has presented a lucid biography and the ideological journey of many right-wing leaders including Keshav Baliram Hedgewar (1989–1940), Madhav Sadashiv Golwalkar (1906–1973) and Madhukar Dattatraya Deoras (1915–1996).[17] In this book one can find a lucid description of the lives of many Hindu right-wing leaders, but it does not provide any understanding of the VKA or personalities related to it. Indeed, there are many books on the lives of the RSS leaders, and most of these books are hagiographies.[18] In his famous study of the RSS, *The Hindu Nationalist Movement and Indian Politics: 1925 to the 1990s* (1996) Christophe Jaffrelot, discusses the VKA in a few pages, as a small part of a larger discussion, which barely introduces the organization. Similarly, in his edited volume, *Hindu Nationalism: A Reader* (2007) Jaffrelot, has compiled papers written by renowned scholars regarding the RSS and its different wings, but there is no separate chapter on the VKA except for a description in the introduction.[19] Pralay Kanungo's book *RSS's Tryst with Politics: From Hedgewar to Sudarshan* (2003) presents an engaging study of the RSS ideological core and its works but does not focus on the VKA.[20]

P.M. Joshy and K.M. Seethi have discussed the works of the VKA in the context of Hindutva and militarism in India in their book *state and Civil Society Under Siege: Hindutva, Security and Militarism in India* (2015). They have presented a deep analysis of the Hindutva politics and the emergence of militarism in India. These authors also mentioned VKA in a few paragraphs, which introduces VKA to the readers.[21] In the same way, Achin Vanaik has made passing remarks regarding the role of the VKA during his discussion on communalism in his book *Hindutva Rising: Secular Claims, Communal Realities* (2017).[22] Abhay Kumar Dubey and Badri Narayan have written scholarly works on the changes within the RSS in the last five decades and the grassroots work of the RSS, respectively. In his book *Hindu Ekta Banam Gyan ki Rajneeti* (2019), Dubey has underlined that the RSS has changed through internal debates in the last fifty years, but its critics are still battling the old RSS.[23] While Dubey does marginally discuss the work of the VKA, he does not present any systematic discussion on the organization, its work, or its changes. Similarly, Badri Narayan's book *Republic of Hindutva: How the Sangh Is Reshaping Indian Democracy* (2021) is based on extensive fieldwork, and in this book, he has focused on the strategies and work of the RSS at the grassroots, which profoundly influenced marginalized sections of society by its ideology. Narayan mentions some of the crucial work of the VKA in tribal areas of Uttar Pradesh and writes that 'the sangh believes in traditional ways of tribal living. Many tribal areas have acute water crises and the Vanvasi Kalyan Ashram in Sonbhadra has taken up a project to revive traditional sources of water to address the shortage'.[24] He also mentions the opposition to conversion and enhancement of Hindu values in tribals by the sangh and the VKA.

The VKA has been overlooked as an organization by scholars who have been studying tribal life and its issues. One can make a list of books, that claim to discuss different aspects and issues of the life and politics of tribal people, but they very conveniently overlook the VKA.[25] In this context, three recently published books on tribal issues could be mentioned: first, the Jagannath Amagudia and Virginius Xaxa edited book *Handbook of Tribal Politics in India* (2021) has thirty-one chapters but there is no chapter on the VKA. Second, Abhay Xaxa and G.N. Devi have edited an excellent book titled *Being Adivasi: Existence, Entitlements, Exclusion* (2021). It has also not included any chapter on the VKA and its impact on tribal life.[26] Interestingly, it seems that for many researchers of the tribal issues the VKA is a non-existent entity. Third, Varsha Bhagat–Ganguly and Sujit Kumar have edited a book titled *India's Scheduled Areas: Untangling Governance, Law and Politics* (2019). There are ten chapters in the book, which discuss different aspects related to Fifth Schedule areas. There are chapters which discuss the impact of Left extremism and the Pathalgadi movement in these areas. However, in this book too, there is no systematic discussion about the VKA.[27] In this context, one can consider two excellent monographs published in the recent past: first, Alf Gunvald Nilsen's book *Adivasis and the state: Subalternity and Citizenship in India's Bhil Heartland* (2018), which focuses on the state–society relations in the Bhil heartland, and in this context, it also analyses contemporary events and concerns. However, the VKA is absent in the analysis of the author. Second, author Rahul Ranjan's book *The Political Life of Memory: Birsa Munda in Contemporary India* (2022), focuses on the politics surrounding the figure of Birsa Munda in contemporary India, but he does not mention anything regarding the VKA's use of Munda.[28]

One can also find discussions on issues that are integral to the VKA's ideology, or work, in many papers and book chapters written by scholars like Amita Baviskar (2005) and Virgnius Xaxa (1999).[29] Amita Bavisakr has discussed the process of Hinduization in Madhya Pradesh, and Xaxa has focused on the idea of indigenous people. Both these issues are integral parts of the VKA's concern, but these scholars have not systematically analysed the work of the VKA. There are many studies of the VKA, which focus on the critical analysis of some aspects of the VKA, like education or 'Hinduization'. In this context the works of Nandini Sundar are noteworthy. In one of her famous papers titled 'Adivasi vs. Vanvasi: The Politics of Conversion in Central India' (2006), she presented a brief history of the VKA and analysed some of its works.

Similarly, in some other papers, she has mentioned the work of the VKA in the area of education or Hinduization of tribals or violence against Christian tribals.[30] However, Sundar does not focus on the changing nature of the VKA and she overlooks the expansion of the VKA's work in new areas, including its stand on tribal forest rights. Peggy Froerer's book *Religious Division and Social Conflict: The Emergence of Hindu Nationalism in Rural India* (2008) presents an ethnographic study in Chhattisgarh to understand the emergence of Hindu nationalism in rural India. However, in her study, she briefly mentions the VKA.[31] Angana P. Chatterji in her book *Violent Gods: Hindu Nationalism in India's Present; Narratives From Orissa* (2009) discusses the role of the VKA in her description of Hindu right-wing politics and anti-Christian violence in Odisha.[32] Tariq Thachil has presented an empirical study of social services and its impact on electoral politics in his book *Elite Parties, Poor Voters: How Social Services Win Votes in India* (2024), and he also focuses on the works of the VKA and its impact on elections.[33] Malini Bhattacharjee discusses RSS works in disaster relief in her book *Disaster Relief and the RSS: Resurrecting 'Religion' through Humanitarianism* (2019). In this context she also briefly discusses some aspects of the VKA's work. Similarly, Arkotong Longkumer has presented a study of the story of the RSS and its affiliates in the North-east region in his book *The Greater Indian Experiment: Hindutva and the Northeast* (2022). He discusses the role of the VKA, which gives an analytical understanding of its work in this region.[34] However, his study does not discuss the VKA's history or its work in other tribal areas. All the above-mentioned works do not present a comprehensive and systematic discussion on the history and changing nature of the VKA and it works.

Many activists of the VKA have written books/booklets about the works or certain activists related to the VKA. For example, in her booklet *Vanvasi Kalyan Ashram: Karya Parichay* (2011), Snehlata Vaid presents a lucid description of the different works and departments of the VKA. Similalry, Surya Narain Saxena's books *Vanvasi Kalyan Ashram: Kya Aur Kyun?* (1994) and *Wide Wings of Vanvasi Kalyan Ashram: A Tale of Service and Struggle* (2004) describe the purpose of the VKA. He has also compiled many VKA documents (memorandums etc.) in his book, which are helpful to understand the views of the VKA on certain issues.[35] A VKA activist Radhika Ladha has written a small biography of the founder of the VKA Ramakant Deshpande. The title of her book is *Vanyogi Balasahab Deshpande: Ek Prerak Zindgi* (2013) and it provides some crucial information about Deshpande's life and work. However, the book does not present a critical assessment of his work. One cannot get an understanding of the gradual evolution and expansion of the VKA. The VKA has published many reports regarding its aim and work. One such report is *Bharat Mein Janjatiyon Hetu ek Neeti Drishti-Patra* (A Vision Document for the janjatis of India, hereafter referred to as Vision Document) (2015), which describes the stand of VKA on several issues including, the Scheduled Tribes and Other Traditional Forest Dwellers (Recognition of Forest Rights) Act or the Forest Rights Act, 2006 (FRA), and the Panchayat (Extension to Scheduled Areas) Act, 1996 (PESA). This report presents the VKA's views regarding the different aspects of tribal life including governance, education, health and forest rights.[36] The VKA has published many books about its work and also publishes a monthly magazine, but usually, all of them are for internal circulation and avoid critical aspects.

Therefore, the present study makes a serious attempt to fill the vacuum in the existing literature of social sciences and provides a comprehensive understanding of the works of the VKA. Apart from presenting a historical and contextual understanding of the formation and expansion of the VKA, this study focuses on its work related to the rights of tribal communities over forest land and its resources. It is a wholesome story of the journey of the RSS ideology of Hindutva in tribal India through its tribal front, the VKA.

The Vanvasi Kalyan Ashram and Appropriation of the 'Progressive' Agenda

The VKA was formed to oppose the increasing influence on and proselytization of tribals by Christian missionaries through the use of 'wrong' means. From the beginning, it has focused on creating a system of schools to counter the educational works of the Christian missionaries. Simultaneously, it started *shradha jagran* (faith awakening) works among tribals through religious activities, which is still a predominant part of its functions. It then began work in medical services. 1978 was a watershed year in the history of VKA because it decided to spread its work to new areas like the North-east. Till then, its work was limited to certain pockets of Chhattisgarh, Jharkhand and Odisha. It also made serious attempts to focus on livelihood and forest rights-related issues of tribals.

Earlier, the VKA did not give due importance to the issue of tribal rights over forest land and its resources. There were few instances when its activists helped local communities against the forest department (FD), however it was not a part of the VKA's core agenda. But from the late 1980s, it started to focus on such issues and formed a *Hit Rakhsa Vibhag* (Interest Protection Department) in 1990. From then on, it took a strong stand on many demands that emerged from the 'Left'-oriented tribal movement. It is a well-documented fact that by the late 1970s, many grassroots movements emerged in tribal areas, which opposed displacement caused by mining and development projects, and demanded rights for tribals over forest resources. These movements resulted in the enactment of the PESA and the FRA. The PESA gives many crucial rights to scheduled tribes living in areas demarcated as part of the Fifth Schedule of the Constitution, while the FRA gives rights to the scheduled tribes and Other Traditional Forest Dwellers (OTFDs) over forest land and its resources. The VKA has continuously supported the proper implementation of both these laws. It opposes forced displacement and gives full support to the inclusion of new communities in the category of the STs after proper scrutiny, the inclusion of new areas in the Fifth Schedule of the Indian Constitution, the control of local communities over forest resources, and the protection of local communities from the arbitrary behaviour of the forest department etc. There are many examples where the VKA vehemently opposed dilution of the progressive provisions of PESA and FRA and it underlines that the VKA has moved from being only an organization for the spread of Hindu values, to one that demands the protection of tribal rights over forest land and its resources.[37]

It is true that through its mission of shradha jagran, the VKA has been popularizing Hindu religious characters like Ram and Sita among tribals. It has continuously emphasized the unbroken relationship between Hinduism and tribals. However, it is not a one-way street and the VKA has also started to celebrate many tribal festivals and tries to popularize their traditional handicrafts, folklore, etc., in different parts of the country. It has also adopted many tribal characters and celebrates their lives and struggle for the protection of tribal lifestyle and opposition of Christian missionaries. Interestingly, the VKA celebrates Birsa Munda's life and his challenges but focuses more on his struggle against Christian missionaries with an emphasis on his Hindu identity. There are many such tribal icons, whose struggle against the British has been popularized by the VKA, but all of them are presented as Hindu icons too.

The prominent aspect of the work of the VKA is that especially in the Northe-east region it has earnestly tried to present Sanatan Dharma as a broader and all-inclusive indigenous religion. In this region, the VKA does not claim that all tribals are Hindus. Rather, it makes a differentiation between those religions that have their roots in India, and those that came from a foreign land. Certainly, this differentiation has provided an opportunity to declare that tribal communities of the North-east are part of a large umbrella Sanatan Dharma. So, they should always resist the proselytization by the Christian missionaries. The VKA activists have been emphatically emphasizing the negative impacts of Christian missionaries on the culture and tradition of tribal communities.[38]

However, the VKA has strongly advocated the view in the other parts of the country that tribals are vanvasis and an integral part of Hinduism. Interestingly, it has also constantly emphasized on the sanctity of the culture and customs of tribal life. The RSS and BJP have supported the idea of a Uniform Civil Code (UCC) for the whole country, but the VKA opposed UCC for tribal communities. In fact, it urged tribal civil society organizations to approach the government and requested the government to adopt a more sensitive attitude towards the cultural rights of the tribals.[39] Indeed, its opposition compelled both central and different BJP ruled state governments to declare that the tribals would not be included in the UCC.

The sangh parivar (RSS family) and the VKA have always been against the beef-eating culture of tribals. When BJP leaders supported eating beef for electoral compulsions in states like Meghalaya, the VKA did not oppose it publicly. The VKA's activists never indulge in aggressive politics, so for issues like these, they form other organizations.

For example, to mobilize tribals for delisting, a separate organization, Janjati Surkasha Manch (JSM), was formed in 2006. Similarly, there are other organizations, such as Dharma Jagran Samiti (DJS), that focus on *ghar wapsi* (reconversion to Hinduism) of Christian tribals.

The opposition and resistance to the work of Christian missionaries have been the most prominent agenda and defining feature of the VKA. There are many examples where VKA activists (under the banner of other organizations) have mobilized tribals aggressively and communally. They have allegedly either actively participated in violence against Christian missionaries or created an environment of hate against them and the tribals who converted.[40] The VKA, as reported in the media, allegedly refers to Christian missionaries as their 'opposition' via publications, WhatsApp messages, Facebook, etc.[41]

The Vanvasi Kalyan Ashram: A Voice of Resistance or Supporter of Status Quo?

Should one treat the VKA as an organization that provides services for the betterment of the tribal people or is it an organization that works with the agenda of Hindutva and divides tribal society? It is noteworthy that in his later writings, Mahatma Gandhi arrived at the concept of *surajya*. It has its origin in 'Constructive Programme: Its Meaning and Place' (1941), which defines constructive programmes of non-government organizations as activities aimed at 'the construction of *poorna swaraj* (complete freedom) by truthful and non-violent means'.[42] Anthony Parel underlines that surajya represents swaraj (freedom) in its complete form, comprising (1) political swaraj (the sovereign state), (2) spiritual swaraj (ethically and spiritually motivated citizens) and (3) the array of very active non-violent and truthful non-government organizations. Parel underscores that the achievement of Gandhian surajya depends on the vital existence of non-coercive voluntary organizations. However, such organizations are not an alternative to the coercive state but complement the state. That is to say, the best state needs both non-coercive organizations of the civil society and the coercive organizations of the state.[43] The non-coercive organizations envisaged in the Constructive Programme are not political parties or anything remotely resembling them. Their object is not to struggle for political power and become part of a coercive political order. Their objective is to avoid coercive politics altogether. They only want to serve the public in specific areas of competence in the spirit of *seva* (service).[44] Is it plausible to consider the VKA as an organization working to establish surajya in tribal areas?

The VKA has done some commendable work in tribal areas by providing better education and medical facilities. It has also worked in several other aspects of tribal life, including forest rights. However, it is difficult to place VKA in the category of non-coercive organizations envisaged in the Constructive Programme based on the following reasons: first, its idea of seva is part of its larger agenda to counter Christian missionaries and spread Hindu values among the tribal population. Second, there are ample examples to underline its relationship with coercive political order. For instance, it has always supported coercive campaigns like Salwa Judum against the Maoists, which overwhelmingly caused suffering to tribals in the Bastar region of Chhattisgarh. Third, though it rejects the idea of a direct relationship with electoral politics, many examples underline its involvement with politics and electoral campaigns of the BJP in many tribal-dominated areas. Some studies have underlined that the seva of the different affiliated organizations of the RSS, including the VKA, have created a conducive electoral condition for the BJP.[45] Fourth, a crucial aspect of the VKA's work is the creation of a constant internal 'enemy' in the form of Christians and Muslims. It does not work to create poorna swaraj by truthful and non-violent means; rather there are ample examples, which show that its many members either support violent activities or actively participate in it.[46]

This study wishes to use and extrapolate Antonio Gramsci's analysis of the role of intellectuals in evaluating the function and work of the VKA. Indeed, Gramsci extends the Marxian notion that the state is a coercive instrument of the dominant class. He underlines that the process of domination is not achieved through coercion alone but also through the 'active' consent of the masses. His theory of state came out of a proper understanding of the relationship between the state and civil society. He also rejects the 'economism' of conventional Marxism in all its forms. He explains how both the state and civil society have played a constitutive role in creating/maintaining the ruling class hegemony.[47] Many civil society organizations use cultural metaphors to create an environment of consensus. The state accepts their specific demands on many occasions but they primarily become a tool to create consensus for state and capitalist systems. Indeed, the existence of political society i.e. military, police, and penal system of the state also plays an inactive but crucial role in the formation and continuation of the hegemony of the capitalist class.

In this context, Gramsci also discusses the role of intellectuals, some of them maintain the hegemony of the capitalist class, and some others create avenues of social change. Gramsci defines intellectuals broadly and underlines that all those persons are part of this category who do some organizational work in a broader sense. He argues that all human beings have rational or intellectual capacities but only a few work as intellectuals in society. He divided intellectuals into two parts: first, traditional, and second, organic. Traditional intellectuals are those who tend to go towards old historical situations. So, in the capitalist system, they always work to protect the existing system and oppose any change in this system. However, they do not consider themselves as part of the capitalist class and they are largely independent of social struggles and do not directly connect to a class or political discourse. As Gramsci underlines, 'they . . . put themselves forward as autonomous and independent of the dominant social group.'[48] Such intellectuals are often conservative and against systemic change. So, there is always a possibility that within a capitalist system, traditional intellectuals could emphasize certain values, that are not directly related to capitalism. Writing about the status of traditional intellectuals in India and China, Gramsci asserts that 'in both India and China the enormous gap separating intellectuals and people is manifested also in the religious field.'[49] It means that in both these countries one could find a difference between the traditional intellectuals and common masses regarding the nature and use of religion. On the other hand, organic intellectuals are necessary for all those classes aspiring for a new social system. They question the dominant frame of reference, the dominant assumption, and dominant policy trends and work to create awareness in the minds of the working class. They are organically tied to the classes and groups for whom stability is a state of emergency. Organic intellectuals create counter-hegemony against hegemonic ideas. They create awareness in the minds of exploited classes and mobilize them to demand new things from the capitalist state. The capitalist state accepts some of its demands to continue its hegemony.[50] Gramsci asserts that it is precisely in civil society that intellectuals both traditional and organic operate.[51]

By extrapolating such analysis of intellectuals, this study wishes to argue that VKA presents a mixture of tendencies presented by Gramsci's categorization of intellectuals. As an organization, it represents the features of both traditional and organic intellectuals, but in the last instance, the features of traditional intellectuals get prominence in its works. Several aspects of the works of the VKA create a façade of being a 'progressive' organization. They present it as an organization that embodies the features of organic intellectuals. The VKA has demanded radical steps be taken to ensure the rights of tribals and other forest-dwelling communities through its *Neeti Drishti Patra* (Vision Document) released in 2015. Its opposition to the dilution of the PESA and FRA compelled the government to change certain decisions. The VKA has also demanded many progressive measures to ensure the rights of tribal communities over forest land and its resources. Through its various service works, it has been trying to uplift the lives of the tribal communities in several parts of the country. The problem, therefore, is related to its denouncement of tribal people's mobilization against government policies. It made several demands via documents and press releases but never pressured governments through *dharna* (protests), demonstrations, etc.

The VKA implies traditional intellectuals and the following four points are significant: first, it has always tried to create a positive environment for the existing Indian state. It has never vehemently opposed policies of the Indian state, which created dispossession and displacement for the tribal people. Its opposition has been limited to the release of a memorandum and it has never mobilized people against state policies which caused displacement for the tribal people. Indeed, in most cases, it has created a conducive environment for the Indian state by totally negating activities that oppose mass mobilization. It never questioned the validity of the Centre or state governments (whether controlled by the BJP or otherwise), and created a positive image of the Indian state in the minds of adivasis.

Second, on many occasions, the VKA has criticized the violent methods of Maoists in questioning the legitimacy of the Indian state. It is essential to note that the VKA never openly questioned state violence against tribal people and allegedly supported the use of violence by the Indian state in the name of curbing the menace of Maoist violence. For example, writer Nandini Sundar says VKA supported the violent Salwa Judum campaign started by Congress leader Mahendra Karma and backed by the Chhattisgarh government of Raman Singh in 2005, which displaced thousands of tribal people.[52] The VKA organized many political meetings in support of Salwa Judum.[53]

Third, it is also a fact that no state government ever treated it as a challenge to their policies in tribal areas. The VKA has a very close relationship with BJP leaders and many tribal BJP leaders have worked as activists or as a pracharak (preacher or propagator of the cause) of the VKA. As part of the sangh parivar, both these organizations largely work with the same set of principles. However, it is interesting that the VKA developed good relations with many leaders in the Indian National Congress (INC). In the late 1940s, the then Central Provinces Chief Minister, Ravishankar Shukla, encouraged Ramakant Deshpande to work against Christian missionaries in tribal areas of what was then the state of Central Provinces.[54]

Fourth, though the VKA creates a conducive environment for the different policies of the Indian state and its development model, it considers itself as an organization autonomous from the Indian state or capitalist class and emphasizes its unique agenda. One can find a clear difference between the VKA's understanding of religion and its use and the understanding of religion by the common adivasis. Rather than accepting tribals in their original form, the VKA has consistently attached tribal communities to a mythological understanding of Hindu religious values. The VKA's vital and most important agenda is to spread Hindu religious values among tribal people and make them part of 'mainstream' Hindutva politics, which emphasizes the hegemony of Hindu religious values in the socio-cultural life of India. Indeed, the VKA has been trying to spread its ideology in tribal society through its service works in the areas of education, health, women empowerment, etc. However, its primary focus has been making adivasis part of the Hindu religion (it emphasizes that adivasis are Hindus and call them vanvasis). In other words, for the VKA, the traditional Hindu identity of tribals as vanvasis is the most vital aspect. It tries to prove that tribals have a relationship with Hindu mythological characters, opposes the conversion to Christianity and resists any attempt to declare them non-Hindu. In Northeast India, it uses the idea of 'Sanatan Dharma' as an indigenous religion because their many tribal communities are not ready to accept Hindu identity.[55]

Based on the above analysis, this study wishes to underline that the VKA works primarily as an organization of 'traditional intellectuals' in the Gramscian sense. It has indeed taken a strong stand for tribal rights and on many occasions severely criticized the BJP-led government at the Centre for diluting laws related to tribal rights. However, it has never tried to break the consensus about a neoliberal Indian state and development model. It has never given primacy to the demands of tribal forest rights and always primarily focused on its agenda of the creation of a Hindu society in tribal areas and resisted the work of Christian missionaries. Indeed, it has continuously tried to use the state to curb those elements that are obstacles to the construction of its ideal Hindu society. In the search for an ideal golden age of the unbreakable and seamless relationship between vanvasis and other Hindus, it uses the politics of Hindutva. It has tried to ensure that like-minded Hindutva political forces should control the state power. While the supporters of the Hindutva model have not always been able to control the state in India, the VKA has always been working in this direction.

Methodology and Framework of Chapters

This study is based on historical, empirical and comparative methods. These methods focus on the historical evolution and expansion of the VKA and explore the different aspects of the workings of the VKA. It also compares the work of the VKA with a tribal organization, which is influenced by the ideas of the Left. This study has used primary and secondary sources to understand the history and different works of the VKA. Many documents, press releases and booklets published by the VKA are used to analyse diverse facets of this organization. YouTube videos posted by the VKA and interviews with its various office-bearers have also been used as a source to develop a comprehensive narrative about the organization.

This study presents its arguments in the following chapters: The first chapter introduces and contextualizes the study within the larger framework of existing literature related to Hindutva politics and the works related to the RSS and underlines the purpose and uniqueness of this study. This chapter also proposes that the Gramscian idea of intellectuals could be used and extrapolated to analyse the role of the VKA in the tribal areas of India. The second chapter situates the VKA within the larger framework of the RSS and discusses the historical background in which the VKA was formed. The chapter also discusses the organizational structure, expansion and various facets of the works of the VKA. The third chapter of the book focuses on the

VKA's works related to the faith awakening, appropriation and Hinduization of tribal icons, the VKA's opposition to the idea of treating tribals as indigenous people of India, its opposition to proselytization and the use of the idea of Sanatan Dharma as an 'indigenous religion' to establish a strong connection with tribal groups in the North-east. The fourth chapter presents a critical study of the VKA's seva works in the areas of education, health, women empowerment, village development and urban awareness works regarding the lives of tribals and their cultural values. The chapter underscores that these works have created a positive environment regarding the VKA and helped spread its message in tribal areas, which ultimately created a solid base for Hindutva politics. The fifth chapter discusses the VKA's work regarding autonomous tribal life and forest rights and analyses the VKA's role regarding PESA and the FRA. The sixth chapter focuses on different issues related to tribal life and the VKA's stand on it. The chapter discusses the issue of delisting, Sarna Code (a demand for a separate religious identity for indigenous people in India's census), Left-wing extremism and the Pathalgadi movement, ghar wapsi and violence in tribal areas. In a separate section, the chapter analyses the role and the impact of the VKA on the electoral agenda and politics of the tribal areas. The last chapter presents the conclusion of the study and underlines the uniqueness of the work of the VKA and its impact in different tribal areas of the country.

Summing Up

Existing literature on tribal issues and/or RSS has not systematically focused on the politics of Hindutva in the tribal areas. The VKA has been the primary tool to expand the ideological basis of the RSS. The VKA has gradually expanded its works and adopted all crucial issues related to the tribal areas.

Though its aim was to enhance Hindu values in tribal areas and use education as its primary tool, it also expanded its work to medical services and women empowerment, etc. In the last few decades, it has started to focus on the issue of tribal rights over forest land and resources. The different chapters of the book will focus on the background of the formation of the VKA and the various aspects of its works.

2

Footprints of the RSS in Tribal Areas: Formation and Expansion of the Vanvasi Kalyan Ashram

The Rashtriya Swayamsevak Sangh (RSS) was formed in 1925 on Vijayadashmi. Its tribal wing, the VKA was formed in December 1952 and now works as the biggest tribal organization in the country. To comprehend the reasons behind the formation of the VKA it is imperative to understand the contexts, ideas and purposes which led to its formation. One cannot see the formation of the VKA in isolation and understand it only through the prism of the ideological moorings of the RSS. It is necessary to focus on the concerns of the leaders of the Indian National Congress to tribal politics in Bihar and Madhya Pradesh, which played a crucial role in the formation of the VKA. Ramakant Keshav Deshpande was the founder of the VKA, who dedicated his life to opposing Christian missionaries and the dispersion of Hindu values in tribal areas.[1] The VKA is a unique organization because it is an amalgamation of various state-level organizations.

This chapter presents the ideological background which led to the formation of the RSS. It analyses the emergence of the idea of Sangh Parivar, which includes different affiliated organizations of the RSS and positions the VKA within its larger framework. The chapter focuses on the political concerns within the INC (or Congress) that compelled leaders like Rajendra Prasad, Ravishankar Shukla, etc., to see the increasing influence of Christian missionaries with suspicion and concern. It also presents a brief biography of Ramakant Keshav Deshpande and deciphers the key factors of his life that led him towards the creation of a new organization—VKA. The chapter discusses the expansion, organizational structure and the different works of the VKA which evolved during the last seven decades.

RSS and Hindutva Politics: Situating the VKA within Sangh Parivar

The Sangh Parivar has used Hindutva as an integral concept of Hindu identity in its quest to create a Hindu *rashtra* (nation). In this process, many 'others' have been created by Hindutva forces within the country and outside the country. The idea of 'other' or 'enemy' has been playing the most central role in understanding the RSS on Hindu unity and solidarity. Furthermore, this idea of 'other' has been changing based on time and space. For example, Muslims have been termed as 'others' in most parts of the country, but in tribal areas Muslims turn into secondary enemies and Christians become the primary 'other' for Hindutva forces.

There are different kinds of analyses regarding the historical background of the emergence of the Hindu right wing, particularly the RSS in India. Scholars like Walter K. Anderson, Sridhar Damle, Bruce Graham, Thomas Bloom

Hansen and Christophe Jaffrelot, posit the beginning of Hindutva politics in the 1920s.[2] Other scholars like Partha Chatterjee, Vinay Lal, Ashis Nandy and Tapan Roychaudhuri underline that religious politics emerged as an integral part of nineteen century modern nationalist identity and blossomed in the first half of the twentieth century.[3] It is important to note that scholars like Jyotirmay Sharma have differentiated between the 'soft and hard version' of Hindutva. He includes thinkers like Dayanand Saraswati and Swami Vivekananda in the former category, and V.D. Savarkar and M.S. Golwalkar, in the latter.[4] A. Raghuramraju, on the other hand, questioned this kind of classification and tendency to link social reformers with the idea of Hindutva. It is true that Vivekananda and Dayanand Saraswati advocated Indian traditions and used them to criticize superstitions and belief systems of the time but they used Hinduism, rather than Hindutva, to propagate their ideas of humanism. The basic idea behind this argument is that Hindutva started with the writings of Savarkar who differentiated between Hinduism and Hindutva.[5]

It is also true that during the nineteenth century, a new middle class emerged in India, which initiated religious reform movements in the country. Many Hindu reformers underlined that the lack of unity in the religion made it vulnerable and they began to consider a version of modernity with 'indigenous' (Hindu Brahminical) roots. The Arya Samaj established by Dayanand Saraswati and the 'Sanatana Dharma Sabha' started the cow protection movement. In 1882, Dayanand Saraswati formed the first 'Gaurakshini Sabha' (Cow Protection Organization) in Punjab. It later grew in many urban centres and the cow became a symbol of unification.[6] It also enhanced the view, which considered Muslims and Christians as outsiders, while cow-worshipping

Hindus were glorified as the original inhabitants of India.[7] It could be argued this was the inception of religious nationalism in India.

For Aurobindo and Bankim Chandra Chatterjee, Hindu religious values were located at the centre of their idea of nationalism. For Aurobindo, nationalism was a religion and he emphasized that 'Indians were weak and unmanly and therefore required the "Kshatriya" impulse; they had grown feeble and had to appropriate the "shakti" of science.'[8] Bankim wrote 'Bande Matram', which became the most important slogan of the Indian freedom struggle. In his three historical novels—*Anandmath*, *Devi Chaudhurani* and *Sitaram*—he presented the theme of Hindu–Muslim antagonism.[9] These thinkers focused on Hindu traditions and values to develop their notion of nationalism. Most of them also vociferously criticized the negative aspects of Hindu society and only Bankim (in his later writings) presented a clear picture of the antagonism between Hindus and Muslims. Since they emphatically focussed on Hindu values, they became the icon of Hindutva politics, which emerged more systematically through the writings of Vinayak Damodar Savarkar and the formation of the RSS.

Savarkar (1883–1966) presented a systematic idea of Hindutva in his book *Hindutva: Who is a Hindu*, first published in 1923. He differentiated between Hinduism and Hindutva. He argued that he coined the word Hindutva to describe the political philosophy of the Hindu people, and Hinduism was only one aspect of Hindutva. The term Hinduism excluded other religions of the land of *Saptasindhu* (the land of the seven rivers)—Buddhism, Jainism and Sikhism. At the beginning of *Hindutva: Who is a Hindu*, Savarkar defines a Hindu as a,

> . . . person who regards this land of BHARATVARSHA, from the Indus to the Seas of his Father-Land as well as his Holy-Land that is the cradle land of his religion. To the converted Christians and Muslims, the Hindustan is the Fatherland as to any other Hindu. Yet it is not to them a 'Holy Land' too. Their holy land is in Arabia or Palestine. Their mythology and Godmen, ideas, and heroes are not the children of this soil. Their names and outlooks smack of a foreign origin, so their love is divided.[10]

Savarkar most explicitly presented the notion of Hindutva and created 'otherness' for the followers of Islam and Christianity. The members of both communities are outside the boundaries of the 'Hindu nation' and Savarkar primarily focused on the antagonistic relations between Hindus and Muslims locked in a life-and-death battle for centuries.[11] He cherished a nationalism based on the Hindu religion and the Hindu culture. As a propagator of Hindutva ideology, Savarkar underlines concerns about the impossibility of the coexistence of Hindus and Muslims. He accused Indian Muslims of being anti-Hindu and anti-India, with extraterritorial allegiance.[12]

Dr Keshav Baliram Hedgewar (1889–1940), who was an admirer of Sarvarkar's ideas, established the RSS in 1925, with the help of many like-minded people, including Savarkar's brother. The aim was to establish an organization to work for the awakening of Hindus for their religious interest and to serve the motherland. Indeed, like Savarkar, Hedgewar was also against the Gandhian idea of non-violence and felt that Gandhi's ideas were making Hindus weak and they benefitted Muslims. As a Congress worker, Hedgewar participated in the Non-cooperation Movement but felt cheated when Gandhi called it off after the Chauri Chaura incident of February 1922.[13] Further, the Moplah riots and other communal incidents affected him and he realized that to protect the interests of the Hindus, a separate organization was necessary.[14]

Savarkar's ideas influenced Hedgewar, but he was very cautious about protecting the structure of the RSS. Hence, as RSS chief (*sarsanghchalak*), he never participated in any activity, which could create suspicion in the minds of the colonial rulers about the work of the RSS. Even when he participated in the Civil Disobedience Movement and went to jail, he handed over the responsibility of the sarsanghchalak to another *swayamsevak* (volunteer). It is noteworthy that Savarkar severely criticized the RSS for its 'purely cultural' orientation. He publicly stated that '[t]he epitaph for the RSS volunteer will be that he was born, he joined the RSS and he died without accomplishing anything.'[15]

However, the second sarsanghchalak, M.S. Golwalkar (1906–1973), was also impressed by the ideas of Savarkar and asserted in his book *We or Our Nationhood Defined* (1939) that,

> The non-Hindu peoples in Hindusthan must either adopt the Hindu culture and language, must learn to respect and hold in reverence Hindu religion, must entertain no ideas but those of glorification of Hindu race and culture . . . in one word they must cease to be foreigners, or may stay in the country wholly subordinated to the Hindu nation, claiming nothing, deserving no privileges, far less any preferential treatment-not even citizen's right.[16]

Interestingly, writer and academic, Nilanjan Mukhopadhyay, notes that the book *We or Our Nationhood Defined* was the

English translation of G.D. Savarkar's book in Marathi titled, *Rashtra Mimansa*. G.D. Savarkar, also called 'Babarao', was V.D. Savarkar's brother, and Golwalkar translated it into English without crediting Savarkar and claimed in the preface of the first edition that the book was his 'maiden attempt'.[17]

Under the leadership of Golwalkar who was RSS chief from 1940 to 1973 (till his death), the RSS tried to expand its work and focused on reaching different sections of society through the creation of affiliates. Many affiliated organizations were formed under his guidance and leadership which include: Bharatiya Mazdoor Sangh (1955), Bharatiya Jana Sangh (1951), Akhil Bharatiya Vidyarthi Parishad (1949), Vanvasi Kalyan Ashram (1952), etc. Gradually, the number of affiliated organizations increased and now there are thirty-six fully affiliated organizations of the RSS. While more than a 100 organizations work with the RSS's help and guidance, they are not affiliated. Its fully affiliated organizations work in different spheres of society, like judiciary, public health, agriculture, social service, social unity, etc. The RSS pracharaks work and guide these organizations according to the RSS's policies and ensure the leadership's smooth control. In all these organizations, a person related to that area works as its chairperson. However, the role of *sangathan mantri* (the pracharak appointed by the RSS) is crucial in deciding its work.[18]

Following is the list of thirty-six important organizations affiliated to the RSS.

Table 1: Organizations where RSS Swayamsevaks are Active and Their Area of Work

	Organization	Area
1.	Akhil Bharatiya Vidyarthi Parishad	Students
2.	Akhil Bharatiya Adhivakta Parishad	Advocates
3.	Arogya Bharti	Public health
4.	Bharatiya Mazdoor Sangh	Labour
5.	Bharatiya Kisan Sangh	Farmers, agriculture
6.	Bharat Vikas Parishad	Social Service
7.	Bharatiya Itihas Sankalan Yojana	History
8.	Balagokulam	Children's Cultural Organization
9.	Bharatiya Sikhsan Mandal	Educationists
10.	Bharatiya Janata Party	Politics
11.	Deendayal Sodh Sansthan	All-round village development
12.	Gau Samvardhan	Cow Protection
13.	Gram Vikas	Overall village development
14.	Grahak Panchayat	Customer interest
15.	Kutumb Prabodhan	Family values and communion
16.	Kushth Rog Nivaran Samiti	Leprosy patients
17.	Kreeda Bharti	Sports
18.	Laghu Udyog Bharti	Small Industries
19.	National Medicos Organization	Doctors
20.	Akhil Bharatiya Sainik Seva Parishad	Ex-Serviceman
21.	Pragya Pravah	Academics and intelligentsia
22.	Rashtra Sevika Samiti	Women
23.	Rashtriya Sikhshak Mahasangh	Teachers

	Organization	Area
24.	Rashtriya Sikh Sangat	Religious solidarity
25.	Sahakar Bharati	Cooperatives
26.	Samajik Samrasta	Social Unity
27.	Sahitya Parishad	Literature
28.	Seva Bharati	Service
29.	Seema Jankalyan Samiti	Border Area Development
30.	Sanskar Bharati	Arts and artists
31.	Sanskriti Bharati	Sanskrit Language
32.	Swadeshi Jagran Manch	Development and Economy
33.	Akhil Bharatiya Vanavasi Kalyan Ashram	Tribal Welfare
34.	Vidya Bharati	Education
35.	Vishwa Hindu Parishad	Religion
36.	Vigyan Bharati	Science, scientists

Source: Thakur and Kranti (2015), in Anderson and Damle (2018), pp. 258–59.

All the aforementioned organizations were not formed simultaneously. Some of them formed just after Independence and some later on. All these organizations were formed to expand the works of the RSS in different sections of the society, for example, the Bharatiya Mazdoor Sangh operates among workers for their interests. Similarly, the Bharatiya Kisan Sangh works among farmers, expands the base of the RSS among them, protects the interests of farmers and mobilizes them around the larger agenda of the RSS. The Bharatiya Janata Party (BJP) is the political front of the RSS and was formed in 1980. Earlier, it was known as the Bharatiya Jana Sangh, which was merged with the Janata Party in 1977.

Since the Janata Party experiment failed, the RSS formed a new organization, the BJP, in 1980. The VKA was established in 1952 to oppose the works of Christian missionaries and spread Hindu values among tribal people.

Formation of the Vanvasi Kalyan Ashram: Fear of Separatism and the Desire for Hinduization

The formation of the VKA happened over concerns regarding the increasing activities of Christian missionaries in tribal areas. There was a fear that as the Muslim League started to demand a separate nation for Muslims, the Christian missionaries could instigate converted tribals to demand a separate nation-state for Christians. Indeed, the issue of conversion was prominent in many tribal areas, including Madhya Pradesh (then Central Provinces) even before Independence, with some princely states initiating enactments to ban conversion. These included the Raigarh state Conversion Act, 1936, the Surguja state Hindu Apostasy Act, 1945, and the Udaipur state Conversion Act, 1946.[19] What is interesting is that all these bills were introduced or passed primarily to ban the conversion of tribes to Christianity.[20]

During the national movement, proselytization by Christian missionaries emerged as one of the key contested issues and a matter of concern. Even Mahatma Gandhi, expressed his concern regarding conversion by Christian missionaries. In Bihar Notes (10 August 1925) he underlined that,

> Christian missionaries have been doing valuable service for generations, but in my humble opinion, their work suffers because at the end of it they expect the conversion of these simple people to Christianity . . . How very nice it would be if the missionaries rendered humanitarian service without the ulterior aim of conversion.[21]

After its formation, the RSS focused largely on the aspect of mobilizing Hindus against Muslims, its leaders expressed their concerns regarding the roles of Christian missionaries in tribal areas. However, they could not start systematic work in tribal areas before the early 1950s, but its leaders, particularly Golwalkar, always raised the issue of conversion of tribal people.[22]

During the late 1930s and 1940s, one can find two facets of the concerns among the Congress leaders related to the role of Christian missionaries: For some leaders like Rajendra Prasad, the key issue was to maintain the political popularity and acceptance of the Congress among tribals, but for some (like Ravishankar Shukla) the chief concern was the supposed separatist tendencies enhanced by Christian missionaries.[23] It is noteworthy that in the tribal belt of the Chota Nagpur[24] region of Bihar, the Jharkhand movement started to take shape by the late 1930s. The Adivasi Mahasabha[25] continuously raised the issue of a separate tribal province and became more prominent when Jaipal Singh Munda joined it and became its president in 1939. Jaipal Singh Munda was a famous hockey player, who was the captain of the Indian hockey team in the Amsterdam Olympics of 1927, where it won the gold medal. Thereafter, he was selected for the Indian Civil Services under the British India Government, but rather than joining it, he focused on different administrative works and teaching, before joining politics. Incidentally, when he returned to India, Rajendra Prasad asked him to work with the Congress. But after discussions with the then Bihar governor, Munda decided to work separately for adivasis.[26]

The Bihar Congress leadership was not happy with the growing influence of the Adivasi Mahasabha. Jaipal Singh Munda wrote to Rajendra Prasad on 16 January 1939, that 'I have now been recognized the natural leader of the Adivasis and I feel I must use all my weight to make the Adivasis work for their advancement within the national movement.' In the same letter, he emphatically argued that 'I have always felt that nothing should be done to weaken the nationalistic force and I am most concerned that the Adivasi movement should be within the major national struggle for an all-India struggle.'[27] In another letter written to Rajendra Prasad on 1 February 1939, Munda underlined that 'I have always been and shall remain an ardent lover of the Congress principles.' He criticized the Bihar government for overlooking the interest of adivasis.[28] Again, in his letter to Rajendra Prasad on 14 June 1939, Munda underlined that '. . . the aims and objects of the Adivasi Sabha . . . were in full harmony with the Indian National Congress'.[29] However, Rajendra Prasad was not convinced. He wrote to Munda on 3 July 1939 and mentioned, 'I do not know how the Adivasi Sabha can be said to be in harmony with the Indian National Congress when it thought fit to set up candidates against the Congress candidates.'[30]

Rajendra Prasad and other Congress leaders felt that the church was also helping the political activities of Jaipal Singh Munda and the Adivasi Mahasabha. Munda's biographer Ashwini Kumar Pankaj claims that due to instigation by Congress leaders, the issue of Christian and non-Christian also emerged in the Adivasi Mahasabha, which led to a split in the organization and a senior leader, Theble Uraon, formed a separate organization named 'Sanatan Adivasi Mahasabha'. Uraon had a close relationship with many Congress leaders. In 1940, when the Congress organized its annual session at Ramgarh, Jaipal Singh Munda claimed that it was a ploy by the Bihar Congress leaders to suppress his organization. A day before the Congress session, Uraon organized a meeting in Ramgarh and severely criticized Munda, asserting that he was not a representative of non-Christian tribals and should not mislead them with his separatist ideas. It is noteworthy that Congress leaders were against the Jharkhand movement. One argument was that the Bihar Congress leaders wanted non-tribal Bihar people to be dominant in tribal areas. This argument could be partially true, but it seems that the more credible reason for opposition to the Jharkhand movement was fear of separatism fuelled by the church and Christian missionaries.

Rajendra Prasad met a Catholic bishop in Ranchi in July 1939 and requested that the church keep a distance from politics and should not support any political party with separatist leanings. He wrote a letter to the bishop of Ranchi and requested him to keep away from the political activities of different organizations.[31]

There was concern that an organization like the Adivasi Mahasabha could create a feeling of separatism in the minds of tribal youths. The Congress leadership was also against the demand of Jharkhand. Gandhian leader, A.V. Thakkar, popularly called Thakkar Bapa, wrote to Rajendra Prasad on 8 March 1939 regarding the resolutions of the Adivasi Mahasabha conference held on 20 and 21 January 1939. He wrote, 'the chief and the first resolution is about the separation of Chota Nagpur from Bihar, to which we, of course, cannot agree.'[32] Thakkar Bapa suggested that Rajendra Prasad form a distinct organization to create confidence among the tribal people. On 27 March 1939, he wrote to Prasad, 'the Adivasi Sabha is a talking body or an agitating body. The committee that I propose is a silent constructive body of actual workers. Political work will not form part of it and it is expected to win the confidence of people, as you say, by its selfless work.'[33] He also urged Prasad that the Bihar provincial government should provide economic help to such organizations. Following his suggestions, a separate organization 'Admi Jaati Sevak Mandal' was formed. Thakkar Bapa had worked in tribal areas for many decades but did not directly advocate the spread of Hindu values in tribal society, but had deep suspicions about Christian missionaries who he thought could foster separatism in tribal areas. This feeling was prevalent among many Congress leaders as well, which played a crucial role in the formation of the VKA.[34]

In 1948, when the then chief minister of Central Provinces, Ravishankar Shukla, was on a visit to tribal areas of his state, he saw black flag protests and sloganeering by tribals for a separate Jharkhand state. Shukla thought it was a dangerous and divisive campaign propagated by Christian missionaries and was worried about the conversion of adivasis to Christianity and discussed his fears with Thakkar Bapa.[35] Bapa told Shukla that it was necessary to bring tribal people into the 'mainstream' to stop conversion and contain separatism. For this, he said, the help of nationalist organizations should be taken.[36]

Ramakant Deshpande and the Formation of the VKA

Ramakant Keshav Deshpande formed the VKA in December 1952 in Jashpur, now in Chhattisgarh (earlier part of Madhya Pradesh).[37] He was born in Amravati, Maharashtra, on 26 December 1913. His father, Keshvrao Deshpande, worked in the colonial government and was the jail superintendent in Amravati. His mother, Lakshmibai, was a homemaker, and his parents affectionately called him Bala Sahab.[38] Later, he became famous as Bala Sahab Deshpande among the workers of the VKA and RSS. Ramakant had three brothers, two elder and one younger. Both his elder brothers, Shridhar Rao and Neelkanth Rao, were advocates. His younger brother, Prabhakar Rao, went on to become an administrative officer.

Since his father had a transferable job, Ramakant studied at different places like Amravati, Akola, Narsinghpur and Nagpur, until matriculation. He completed his graduation in 1935 from Hislop College, Nagpur, and did his LLB and MA from Nagpur University in 1937 and 1939, respectively. He started his practice as an advocate in Nagpur and then moved to Ramtek Tehsil for work.

Ramakant Deshpande came in contact with the RSS in 1926 (a year after its formation) when he was a student in class six. While studying in Nagpur, he regularly met Keshav Baliram Hedgewar, the founder of the RSS. Influenced by Hedgewar, Deshpande decided to work lifelong for the RSS. When he was practicing law in Ramtek, he also became sarkaryavah of the Ramtek Tehsil. Like most of the RSS, Deshpande did not participate in the freedom movement.[39] However, according to his biographer, Radhika Ladha, he played a crucial role in protecting protestors from police firing in Ramtek Tehsil during the Quit India Movement. He shouted at police officers for planning to fire on protestors near the Tehsil Court, which, according to Ladha, forced an officer to hold fire. However, he was jailed for allegedly disrespecting the Union Jack, but was released after a few months due to lack of credible proof. After his release he married Prabhavati in 1943.[40]

Ramakant Deshpande's debut in working in tribal areas after Independence was a coincidence. His biographer K.D. Sapre has mentioned it was at Thakkar Bapa's suggestion that the Central Provinces chief minister appointed Deshpande as the regional director of the Tribal Welfare Department. Deshpande came to Jashpur in 1948 with his family, and for this challenging work was paid a salary of Rs 150 per month. Christian missionaries had established around a 100 primary schools in Jashpur, so Deshpande asked the government's permission to match the number. Thakkar Bapa promised to visit if Deshpande completed the establishment of the schools. Deshpande started work enthusiastically and established 100 schools near all the Christian missionaries' schools, recruited teachers based on their Brahminical outlook and physical strength and informed all the teachers that they were responsible for their self-protection.[41] The teachers were not very qualified; some educated only till the primary level. Deshpande also told different workers/teachers that tribals were pressurised to convert to Christianity and if they returned to their original faith, they would be freed from Christianity.[42] In this sense, he was preparing his co-workers to accept those who returned to Hinduism. The schools established by Deshpande, and the teachers, were allegedly pro-Hindu and anti-Christian.[43] Radhika Ladha claimed that he was influenced by three people/institutions—Hedgewar, the Ramakrishna Mission and Thakkar Bapa. [44]

Though Thakkar Bapa, a Gandhian, influenced him, Deshpande was not attracted to Gandhi's principle of non-violence. In fact, Christian missionaries complained that the teachers at Deshpande's school were threatening their teachers.[45] Radhika Ladha mentions an event that underlines Deshpande's faith in extreme nationalism, where he was not averse to using threats or force against those who were not ready to accept his version of nationalism. She writes,

> Due to the successful experiment of schools in Jashpur, Chief Minister Ravishankar ji had prepared an adult education plan. It was decided that apart from giving literacy, the people would be taught about history, religion, values of love for the nation, health, etc . . . However, Christian Fathers dissuaded the Christian tribals from participating in such activities. When Deshpande ji got information about it, he made a specific plan. He went to a Christian-dominated

> village, Patra Toli village. He told them during his address that "now our country is free and the government has started many programmes for the backward Vanvasis (forest-dwelling people), and we must respect them. I will say 'Jai Hind' and you people will repeat it." Nevertheless, when he received the answer of 'Jai Hind' by 'Jai Yeshu', he told them, "I will say 'Jai Hind' three times, and you have to repeat it, and if you do not do that, my young friends and I have sticks, and we will beat you with it, we will not spare anyone." After that, everyone repeated the slogan 'Jai Hind'. When it was necessary, Deshpande ji shows strength too.[46]

Ladha mentions other examples of Deshpande using the threat of violence to tackle his opponents. Deshpande's government school was working out of a *Guhdighar* (guest house), but Christian missionaries usurped it and started their school there. When Deshpande was informed, he called the guard of the building and the head of the missionary school, and told them that he was going to Goria (a village), and by the time he returned they should leave the Guhdighar, otherwise he would beat all of them with sticks. According to Ladha, the missionaries left the place.[47] Deshpande instilled fear.

It is clear from the above description that Deshpande had faith in extreme nationalism. He was ready to use force so that people would follow and respect the symbols related to it. He was prepared to use violent means for this purpose. Deshpande emphasized that he had no problem with Christianity and Jesus Christ. However, he was fiercely against the works of Christian missionaries, which according to him, represented Western imperialist interests. In 1951, he was suspended due to some complaints of misconduct and sent to Gadchiroli. After a year of investigation, it was found that all the complaints were false, and Deshpande was reinstated at his earlier post. He demanded that he must be posted in Jashpur so that people would realize that all allegations against him were false. The government accepted his demand. However, he realized that he could not work according to his vision and so, he resigned in May 1952. He realized that the government would not support him fully in his aim of actively propagating the values of the Hindu religion among tribal people.

After his resignation, he met the then *sarsanghchalak* M.S. Golwalkar of the RSS, who directed him to work in the tribal areas and spread the ideas of the body. In these tribal areas, Deshpande countered the influence of Christian missionaries and made space for RSS ideas. He formed the VKA on 26 December 1952 in Jashpur with the help of another *swayamsevak* (volunteer of RSS), Morubhau Ketkar. In its initial phase, the Maharaja of Jashpur, Vijaydev Bhusan Singh Judev, gave financial and moral support to this organization.[48] He donated a part of his old palace for the VKA to work out of and showed a great interest in its work. He later donated 125 acres of land to Ketkar towards the VKA.[49] Indeed, Ranjvijay Singh Judeo, scion of the former royal family of Jashpur and a BJP leader, claims that his grandfather Vijay Bhusan Singh Judev was not only the earliest patron of the VKA but even brainstormed with Deshpande to decide the name of the organization.[50] At the time of the formation, the VKA had no formal constitution, rule book, or documents. However, Deshpande and Ketkar were clear about their aim and ambition. Deshpande emphasized that 'we want such vanvasi leadership, which could establish unity among Hindus. We need to make a society that feels proud of its Hindutva. Our work is to create consciousness and prepare leadership'.[51] The VKA activists and its magazine *Van Bandhu* remembers Deshpande and Ketkar with reverence and describe them as Ram and Lakshman.[52]

Deshpande started the first school with a hostel under the banner of the VKA with only thirteen students, but gradually, more students joined the school. Deshpande included *Surya Namaskar* (sun salutation yoga sequence), physical work and training, recitation of the Ramayana and patriotic songs, in the daily routine of the school.[53] The VKA started its work to save vanvasis (tribals) from Christian missionaries and informally began shradha jagran from 1954. That year, another pracharak, Krishna Damodar Sapre, came to Jashpur. By this time, the number of students had increased to around forty and Sapre and others started a campaign to form a *bhajan mandali* (devotional songs' group) in the villages of these students. The VKA started to work more systematically for this purpose. To increase the feeling of devotion in students who were living in the VKA hostel, the Maharaja of Jashpur took them to the Kumbh Mela at Prayag. In 1959, Deshpande planned to organize *yagnas* (systematic Hindu ritual, an act of devotion, worship, offering in fire with Vedic mantras) to make tribals devout. During these yagnas, many other cultural programmes were organized where tribes displayed their dances, etc. In a sense, it was an attempt to familiarize them with Hindu rituals and in turn know tribal cultural practices.[54]

On Ram Navami, 1963, RSS sarsanghchalak Golwalkar, inaugurated the new building of the VKA in Jashpur.[55] Golwalkar's speech on this occasion also underlines the essential vision of the RSS behind the VKA. Golwalkar told the gathering that,

> Since our vanvasi brothers live in forest and mountain areas, they are cut off from Hindu society. Their life is full of different kinds of deprivations. They are facing horrible poverty. They don't have any education or medical facility. Their life is full of miseries. They are living in the condition of starvation.

> Still, they are very simple-minded. We have overlooked the miseries of our people. Foreign missionaries took the benefit of this situation, and by using schools, hostels, and hospitals, they converted them to Christianity and made them traitors and rebels. Even in their deprived situation, the vanvasis are not ready to leave the religion of their ancestors. They have pure character and pure hearts. They are like Shiva. So, we should immediately start working for their service with full devotion. Kalyan Ashram is working for this purpose. We are expecting cooperation from everyone . . . [56]

Golwalkar praised the working of the VKA school and hostel but also suggested that the VKA should focus on medical services and thereafter, the VKA established an ayurvedic hospital. Gradually, the VKA extended its work to provide medical facilities to the vanvasis. In 1967–68 an eminent person from Mumbai (then Bombay) gave Ramakant Deshpande a proposal of financing the establishment of big hospital. However, Deshpande declined the offer because he thought that the VKA's primary work was faith awakening and social service, and for this it would reach villages through small dispensaries. He thought critically ill people could be sent to Ranchi.[57]

In its early history, the VKA developed a very cozy relationship with the Indian National Congress government in MP, which was more or less like the relationship of Christian missionaries with the British. Many prominent right wing Congress leaders and government officials helped the VKA with funds and other logistical support. The VKA formally announced that it did not depend on the government for financial help and always tried to portray itself before the ruling party's officials and politicians, as a non-political organization that was doing good work in education, health and women empowerment in tribal society. In this phase, it never overtly emphasized its relationship with the RSS but did speak about the relationship in its internal documents and leaflets.[58]

Post-Emergency Era and the Expansion of the VKA

Till the late 1960s, the work of the VKA was centred mainly in Jashpur, but in a crucial meeting in 1968, it decided to expand outside Jashpur. The senior workers in this meeting underlined that in the tribal areas of Bihar and Nagaland, Christian missionaries were creating separatist feelings in the minds of tribals. So, they decided to extend the work of the VKA in the Gumla district of the Bihar and Sundargarh district of Odisha.[59] However, it did not extend beyond these and other places till 1978. Indeed, Golwalkar did not have a very clear political understanding regarding the issues of tribals and many times he also gave statements that could be construed as 'immature', 'controversial', and even 'humiliating' for the tribals.[60] For example, in 1969, when Golwalkar was asked if *samskaras* (values) could be imparted to the nomadic tribes, he gave a controversial reply: 'If we could domesticate even the wild animals roaming the jungles, can we not persuade our people to take the better and more stabilized ways of life? Certainly, we can, provided we display the human touch.'[61] In February 1973, Golwalkar expressed his views to journalists about reservations for the scheduled castes and scheduled tribes and said, 'we are opposed to continued special privileges based on caste only, as it would create vested interests in them in remaining as a separate entity. It would harm their integration with the rest of the society'.[62] All such statements underline that Golwalkar perpetuated old ideas. After his death in 1973, Madhukar Dattatraya Deoras (popularly known as Balasaheb Deoras) became sarsanghchalak of the RSS. He took many bold steps to make the RSS more inclusive and expand its affiliates' work in different parts of the country.[63] He also expanded the VKA in other tribal areas of the country.

In 1975, Emergency was imposed in the country and the RSS and its tribal wing, the VKA, were shut down. Ramakant Deshpande and many other workers of the VKA were arrested and the work of the VKA was stopped due to the ban on the RSS. When the Emergency was revoked, the VKA restarted its work and Deshpande tried to systematize it. It should also be noted that by this time the Jana Sangh had been merged with the Janata Party and after the 1977 general election, the Janata Party formed the government at the Centre and the VKA received respect and recognition for its work from the government. In 1977, the VKA completed twenty-five years of its formation and a big programme was organized in Jashpur, which was attended by then prime minister Morarji Desai.[64] Notably, the VKA benefited from the presence of the former members of the Jana Sangh in state governments from 1977–79 in fundraising and the VKA's work spread more extensively after the Emergency.

As mentioned earlier, before 1978, the work of the VKA was limited to some regions of Chhattisgarh (then Madhya Pradesh), Jharkhand (then Bihar) and Odisha. After the Emergency (1975–77), the then sarsanghchalak, Balasaheb Deoras, began work on his expansion plan for the RSS in different areas and sections of the country.[65] Deoras decided that the RSS would extend its work to the marginal sections of Hindu society.[66] The extension of the work of the VKA was part of Deoras' larger plan. The VKA targeted those tribal areas where Christian missionaries worked, including the North-east states and it was decided by the Deoras that a senior pracharak would be appointed as full term sangathan mantri (Organization Secretary) of the VKA. The sangathan mantri is an important position and the RSS central leadership appoints it in all its affiliated organizations, which are collectively called Sangh Parivar. The sangathan mantri works as a bridge between the central leadership and the affiliated organizations. It tries to ensure that the affiliated organization works according to the larger framework of the RSS without contradictions. The VKA organized a three-day meeting in Jashpur from 15 to 17 August 1978 to consider its expansion in other areas. Apart from senior VKA activists, RSS activists, including sarsanghchalk Deoras, attended the meeting.[67]

Both Deoras and VKA president Deshpande, evaluated the works of the tribal wing of the RSS and underlined the critical purpose behind its expansion. In his speech to the meeting, Deoras expressed his satisfaction with the VKA's work in Bihar, Madhya Pradesh and Odisha and welcomed the decision of the workers to expand its work in all tribal areas of the country. He informed them that the RSS would provide workers for the expansion of the VKA. Deoras underscored that 'there are many affiliated/connected organizations to the RSS, but if someone asks me which organization is closest to the Sangh (RSS), I will take the name of Vanvasi Kalyan Ashram (VKA)'. He also expressed hope that 'in the beginning, the workers from the Sangh will go the Kalyan Ashram, and later the workers from Kalyan Ashram will come to the Sangh'. He argued that the work of the VKA is essential and without the empowerment of the vanvasis, the nation cannot be decisive. He emphasized the necessity of protecting vanvasis from the conspiracies of Christian missionaries and the influence of Muslims and Naxals. He also stressed the need to protect vanvasis from Hindu businessmen, contractors and mine owners, who are ruthlessly exploiting tribal society.[68]

In this meeting, like Deoras, Deshpande also underlined the danger of the increasing influence of the Christian missionaries, Muslims, and Naxals. Deshpande emphasized the difficult living conditions of the vanvasis, who were struggling for food, water, medical facilities, education, etc. However, he asserted that the most significant danger came from the Christian missionaries, who use all means, including fear and inducement, to convert them to Christianity. Deshpande told workers that they (missionaries) took the land of the vanvasis and turned them into bonded labour. He also stressed other dangers for tribal society in the form of self-seeking businessmen and contractors from Hindu society.[69] It was also accepted in the meeting that since tribal communities were diverse and their socio-economic conditions differed, it was necessary to develop an organization according to local needs. The top leadership of the RSS and VKA accepted that the support and participation of the local people—both tribals and non-tribals—was necessary for the expansion of organizations. So, it was decided that local organizations would be formed in different states and registered separately.

Organizational Structure of the VKA and Relationship with the RSS

After the 1978 meeting, the VKA started to expand by forming local organizations in different tribal areas of the country. In the North-east, an organization was formed in Assam called, 'Kalyan Ashram Assam'. In Nagaland, a separate local organization, 'Janjati Vikas Samiti' was formed, while in Uttar Pradesh, the 'Seva Samarpan Sansthan' was formed. It is noteworthy that all local organizations are not based in states only and in many states, there is more than one local organization. For example, in Madhya Pradesh, one organization works in the Mahakaushal area,[70] called 'Vanvasi Vikas Parishad', based in Jabalpur. MP also has another organization, 'Vanvasi Kalyan Parishad, Madhya Bharat'. Similarly, in Maharashtra, four local organizations work and the central organization of the VKA specifies the area of their work. All these provincial or local organizations are separately registered; their budgets and auditing are also unrelated.[71]

Table 2: Name of the State-Level Affiliates of the VKA

SN.	Name of Organization	State/Union Territories
1.	Kerala Vanvasi Vikas Kendra	Kerala
2.	Vanvasi Seva Kendram, Tamil Nadu	Tamil Nadu
3.	Vanvasi Kalyan, Karnataka	Karnataka
4.	Vanvasi Kalyan Parishad, Telangana	Telangana
5.	Andhra Vanvasi Kalyan Ashram	Andhra Pradesh
6.	Vanvasi Vikas Samiti, Chhattisgarh	Chhattisgarh
7.	Vanvasi Vikas Parishad, Mahakaushal	Madhya Pradesh
8.	Vanvasi Kalyan Parishad, Madhya Bharat	Madhya Praesh
9.	Vidarbh Vanvasi Kalyan Ashram	Maharashtra
10.	Devgiri Kalyan Ashram	Maharashtra
11.	Vanvasi Kalyan Ashram, Paschim Maharashtra	Maharashtra
12.	Vanvasi Kalyan Ashram, Konkan	Maharashtra
13.	Vanvasi Kalyan Ashram, Goa	Goa
14.	Vanvasi Kalyan Ashram, Dadra and Nagar Haveli	Dadra and Nagar Haveli
15.	Janjati Kalyan Ashram, Gujarat	Gujarat
16.	Vanvasi Kalyan Parishad, Rajasthan	Rajasthan
17.	Vanvasi Kalyan Ashram, Delhi	Delhi
18.	Vanvasi Kalyan Ashram, Haryana	Haryana
19.	Vanvasi Kalyan Ashram, Punjab	Punjab

SN.	Name of Organization	State/Union Territories
20.	Himgiri Kalyan Ashram, Himachal Pradesh	Himachal Pradesh
21.	Seva Prakalp Sansthan, Uttarkhand	Uttarakhand
22.	Seva Samarpan Sansthan, Kanpur	Uttar Pradesh
23.	Vanvasi Kalyan Ashram, Goraksh Prant	Uttar Pradesh
24.	Vanvasi Kalyan Ashram, Bihar	Bihar
25.	Vanvasi Kalyan Kendra, Jharkhand	Jharkhand
26.	Giri Vanvasi Kalyan Parishad, Dumka	Jharkhand
27.	Vanvasi Kalyan Ashram, Odisha	Odisha
28.	Vanvasi Kalyan Ashram, Andaman	Andaman and Nicobar Islands
29.	Poorvanchal Kalyan Ashram, Dakshin Banga	West Bengal
30.	Vanvasi Kalyan Ashram, Uttar Banga	West Bengal
31.	Sikkim Kalyan Ashram, Sikkim	Sikkim
32.	Kalyan Ashram, Assam	Assam
33.	Kalyan Ashram, Dakshin Assam	Assam
34.	Kalyan Ashram, Meghalaya	Meghalaya
35.	Arunachal Vikas Parishad, Arunachal Pradesh	Arunachal Pradesh
36.	Janjati Vikas Samiti, Nagaland	Nagaland
37.	Kalyan Ashram, Mandipur	Manipur
38.	Kalyan Ashram, Mizoram	Mizoram
39.	Kalyan Ashram, Tripura	Tripura

Source: Discussion with Girish Kuber, 'Hit Raksha Vibhag Pramukh' (President, Interest Protection Department) VKA, New Delhi, 25 July 2021.

In the resolution during registration, these organizations mention that they are affiliated with the VKA and follow its directions and suggestions. The VKA can appoint the sangathan mantri for all these state-level organizations. The VKA has a precise mechanism to control and coordinate with local or state-level organizations and some national office-bearers or senior workers also attend the working committee meetings of state-level organizations. At the national level, the VKA develops its position on different issues after discussion with local affiliated organizations.

There are forty members in the All India Executive of the VKA. Before 1978, the structure was not fixed. Since the works of the VKA were limited to certain tribal districts, its founder-president Ramakant Deshpande used to run the organization with the help of some senior pracharaks of the RSS and other dedicated workers of the VKA. In 1978, the RSS decided to provide more pracharaks to the VKA to spread its work in other tribal areas of the country and the structure of the VKA took a more formal and systematic shape. For the last four decades, the RSS has appointed an organization secretary, who is the link between the RSS and the VKA. Apart from the organization secretary, the VKA selects a president, who selects office-bearers after consultation with senior RSS and VKA leaders.[72] There is no election for the organization secretary, president or other office bearers. Their selection is based on consultation within the organization and the decision of the RSS (in the case of the organization secretary and president) and organization secretary and president (in the case of other office-bearers) is considered as final. They take a decision whether they want to make the process consultative or not. As far as state-level organizations are concerned, there is an election of the state-level working committee and other office-bearers according to the respective organization's constitution. In such an election, the central leadership of the VKA plays a crucial role. If the central leadership does not agree, no person can be elected as the office-bearer of a state-level organization. Indeed, such 'elections' are nothing but appointments of office-bearers through consultation with local activists by the central leadership.[73]

However, there is an important aspect of the organization system of the VKA. Certain organizations are not officially affiliated with the VKA (or RSS), and though they work on the larger agenda of the VKA, their working pattern has been more aggressive. A more interesting point is that the activists of the VKA have been playing a central and active role in such organizations, for instance, in the 'Janjati Surkasha Manch' (JSM) and the 'Dharm Jagran Samiti' (DJS). JSM has been working for the delisting (from the list of scheduled tribes) of those tribals who converted to Christianity or Islam, and DJS is dedicated to the cause of ghar wapsi. The JSM and DJS are believed to have been formed for more aggressive and controversial work and it allows the VKA to maintain the image of an organization dedicated to the protection of the interests of tribals. The message is loud and clear that even if the VKA is opposing the works of the Christian missionaries, it has been doing it through constructive works.[74]

Like the RSS sarsanghchalak, the VKA's president is selected for life (or till they want to continue). The president of the VKA is respected in the Sangh Parivar. The first president of the VKA was Ramakant Keshav Deshpande, who formed the organization and worked as its president till 1995. Deshpande was called 'vanyogi' by the VKA and RSS activists and after his death Jagdev Ram Oraon became the president and held the post for twenty-five years till his death on 15 July 2020. After him, Ramchandra Kharadi became the national president of the VKA.[75]

The VKA has many wings (*prabhag* or *aayam*), which deal with different issues related to the life of tribal people in India. Different writers or office-bearers related to the VKA have presented different accounts of the work of the VKA. Snehlata Vaid describes the work of the VKA in the following points: Education, medical/health, women's work, sports, faith awakening, interest protection, urban work, urban contact wing, vanvasi contact wing, publicity, village development and work in the North-east.[76] The head of the 'Hit Raksha Vibhag' (Interest Protection Wing) has underlined that the VKA divides its work into three categories and different wings/departments fall under them: first, organizational works, which focuses on work among youths, women, urban areas and emphasizes the recruitment of new people in the organizations; second, service, which includes education, health, village development and interest protection; third, faith awakening (shradha jagran), which focuses on the spread of Hindu values, issues related to conversion and awareness about tribals' cultural values.[77] It is important to note that there is a clear overlap between the works of different wings/departments because all of them are working to spread certain core ideas of the VKA. Apart from the organization secretary, president and other office bearers, the head of all wings and some senior members are part of the national executive of the VKA.

The national leadership of the VKA also organizes an annual meeting of all state-level organizations to discuss various issues. Usually, every year, this meeting is organized in Jashpur in February and the organization secretary and general secretary of each state-level organization participate. They discuss their previous years' activities in tribal belts and their impact at the ground level and inform each other regarding the work of different wings (like education, health, etc.) in their respective areas.

The VKA office-bearers and senior activists also visit different tribal areas throughout the year. The annual February meeting also essentially decides about their work and responsibility in the coming year. This meeting also considers the previous year's budget and decides about the more significant agenda of the coming year and the budget. If a particular state organization is economically weak, then the national-level organization provides its economic resources. On many occasions, fundraising drives are organized in big cities to help the comparatively weak state-level organizations. For example, Kolkata is the primary source of funding for the many state-level organizations of the North-east region. The VKA not only takes funds in cash, but also in-kind donations to hostels or schools.[78] Though state-level organizations are registered separately, they are an integral part of one national organization, which is how the workers see their affiliation. The state-level organizations work according to the more significant decisions taken by the central leadership of the VKA.

The RSS does not interfere in the day-to-day activities of its affiliate organizations, including the VKA. The RSS appoints the organization secretary and sends a senior person in all affiliate organizations. It can change the organization secretary, and generally, one can find such changes in affiliate organizations. However, knowledge of a particular area/subject is necessary to work in an affiliate organization and so there is a tendency/convention, to give the responsibility of the organization secretary of an affiliate organization to a senior pracharak, who has some expertise in that area/subject. For example, the present organization secretary of the VKA, Atul Jog, has worked in the North-east for more than two decades. But it's not a norm. A senior pracharak, Bhaskar Rao, became organization secretary in 1984, but before that he never worked in the VKA. The RSS also sends some pracharaks from one affiliate organization to another. All affiliate organizations of the RSS work according to the larger framework given by the central leadership of the RSS. However, in situations of disagreements and conflicts between the affiliate organizations, the RSS leadership always tries to resolve such situations by giving directions depending on the socio-political scenario.[79]

It is also true that many affiliates of the RSS work simultaneously in a particular area. For example, both the VKA and the Vishwa Hindu Parishad (and many other affiliates) work independently of each other, since their work and goals are different. However, there is always a possibility of an overlap and if a problem emerges, high rank office-bearers try to resolve it. Interestingly, the VKA office-bearers always emphasize that their organization has nothing to do with politics and that it is a mere 'coincidence' that the BJP exploits their developmental work in tribal areas.[80]

Ramakant Deshpande declared in the early years of the formation of the VKA that the dependence on financial help from the government only weakened the core of the organization. Though it did not refuse financial help from different government departments, the VKA gave more importance to collecting money from the people, primarily from the business class, in smaller urban areas. With the spread of the RSS, at both national and international levels, the affiliated organizations have become more capable of collecting money from diverse sources. The organizations of non-resident Indians like the India Development Relief Fund (IDRF) in the United States and the 'Hindu Swayamsevak Sangh' in the UK, among others, provide financial help to the activities of RSS and the VKA. However, not all these organizations and their members are necessarily supporters of the RSS.[81] There is no denying that the formation of BJP-led governments at the Centre and in different states created a conducive atmosphere for the RSS and its affiliate organizations. They have been able to work smoothly and the government machinery helps them along. Many wealthy people help RSS-affiliated organizations to establish a good working relationship with the BJP-ruled governments. Indeed, in the VKA, there is a separate *prabhag* (wing/department), called Urban Work which collects funds from urban areas.[82]

There is no doubt that the VKA has successfully expanded its work, particularly in the last four decades with grassroots organizations in tribal areas. And while there are tribal areas where VKA is absent, it certainly does diverse work and makes a considerable impact on the lives of tribal people.[83] As mentioned, the VKA has a federal structure, and many state-level organizations are affiliated with it. The structure is not federal in the true sense because though state-level organizations can do some minor work on their own, they cannot make any critical decisions without the consent of the central leadership of the VKA. These state-level organizations only help the VKA expand its work.

Summing Up

The VKA was formed to oppose the work of Christian missionaries. Most importantly, many leaders in the INC were concerned with the work of the missionaries and they feared that they could create separatism in tribal areas. They helped and encouraged Ramakant Deshpande to start his work against Christian missionaries. Later, Deshpande formed the VKA after a consultation with the then RSS chief, Golwalkar. The VKA started work in areas of education, health, women empowerment, etc., and has gradually expanded its works in new areas and tried to mobilize tribal communities against Christian missionaries. Here, it should also be noted that the

VKA has largely used the aggressive idea of nationalism, which has often focused on a certain portrayal of the works of the Christian missionaries and tribals who adopted Christianity. At the grassroots level, some of its activities related to shradha jagran allegedly tried to create a sense of fear among minority Christian tribal groups in tribal areas.[84] However, the VKA has also used shradha jagran education, health, women empowerment, etc., to enhance its reach and impact in tribal society. The next chapter will engage with the VKA's work related to shradha jagran, its opposition to proselytization and the notion of the indigenous people and its extension to the North-east region of the country.

3

The Core Pillars of the Vanvasi Kalyan Ashram: Spread of Hindu Values, Opposition of 'Adivasi' and Proselytization

The VKA has been doing extensive work in education, health, interest protection[1] and village development in tribal regions in India. Like other organizations, the VKA has certain core principles, which decide its overall character and purpose. Indeed, since its inception, the VKA has defined its future path based on these very core principles. As discussed in the previous chapter, the fundamental reason for the formation of the VKA was a fear among senior Congress leaders regarding the increasing influence of Christian missionaries in tribal areas. After its formation in December 1952, the VKA focused on these critical principles: first, Hindu traditions, values and lifestyle should get prominence among the tribal population of the country; second, rejection of the idea of treating tribals as 'adivasi' or indigenous people of India, because it makes all other communities outsiders; third, since tribals are Hindus, their conversion to any other religion should be vehemently resisted. It is noteworthy, that when VKA started its extension plan in the North-east region of the country, it created a binary between religions that came from outside (like Christianity and Islam) and indigenous religions, and used the idea of Sanatan Dharma as an umbrella concept to include different tribal groups under its banner.

This chapter aims to evaluate debates within the VKA on these three basic principles. The first section of the chapter focuses on shradha jagran, which is organizing functions celebrating both Hindu and tribal festivals, visiting Hindu pilgrimages, etc. The second section also discusses the VKA's unique method to celebrate the lives of many tribal figures, popularize them among tribals and non-tribals and promote Hindu values. The second section discusses the debates on treating tribals as adivasis or indigenous people of the country. It underscores that the VKA prefers the word 'vanvasi' or tribal to the term 'adivasi' because the latter divides tribals and non-tribals. The third section critically examines the debates related to conversion and the continuous opposition by the VKA against the proselytization of tribals to Christianity. The fourth section discusses the extension of the VKA's work in the North-east and underlines the appropriation of some key figures, who opposed the activities of Christian missionaries and argued for a separate cultural identity of tribal groups.

Faith Awakening and Spread of Hindu Values: Its Background and Some Tools

Shradha jagran teaches tribals Hindu traditions and rituals and inspires them to adopt these religious and cultural norms. It has been an integral part of the work of the VKA since its formation. When Ramakant Deshpande started working as a government official in Jashpur, he established schools with teachers who followed the traditional Hindu lifestyle. Indeed, as discussed earlier, the then Chief Minister of Central Provinces (later Madhya Pradesh), Ravishankar Shukla, appointed him to counter the increasing influence of the Christian missionaries.[2] After he established the VKA, Deshpande systematically tried to spread Hindu values among tribals and VKA began Shradha Jagran from 1954 onwards. The VKA also started bhajan mandalis in the same year, in the villages of tribal students residing in VKA hostels. Deshpande and his senior colleagues emphasized the organizing of religious functions (recitation of Bhagwad Gita, Ramcharitmanas, etc.) in tribal villages to teach them about Hinduism. From the beginning to now, the VKA workers try to correlate tribal traditions with Hindu mythologies and present tribals as an integral part of the larger Hindu religious framework. It is clear from the many books/booklets published by the VKA that there has never been any confusion regarding the 'core' work or 'soul' of the VKA. Radhika Ladha describes the continuous quest of Deshpande to spread Hindu values among tribals. She writes,

> In 1959 the idea of organizing Sahatrachandi Yagna and Rudra Yagna came into the mind of Bala Sahab (Deshpande). He said that 'it would increase social harmony in the area and awaken sleeping faith and power.' So, this year (apart from Yagna, as mentioned earlier), Vishnu Yagna was also organized. Thousands of devotees came to see the Yagna. The Karpatri Ji Maharaj delivered his preachings. The Vanvasi saint of the Jashpur area, Gahira Guruji, was also invited . . . these Yagnas led to the spread of the name of Kalyan Ashram in different areas.[3]

In 1963, on *Ram Navmi* (a Hindu festival that celebrates the birth of Ram), RSS sarsanghchalak Golwalkar came to Jashpur to inaugurate the VKA's new hostel building. He was accompanied by seers and they distributed Hindu religious texts to the local people. Golwalkar emphasized that tribals were an integral part of Hindu society and praised the work of the VKA's schools/hostels in spreading education and religious values.[4] It indicates that the RSS leadership was clear from the beginning that the primary work of the VKA was related to faith awakening.[5] Indeed, this understanding has been continuously present in the minds of the office-bearers and senior activists of the VKA and a senior activist emphasized that 'giving knowledge about Hindu traditions and rituals to vanvasis is necessary because different forces, particularly Christian missionaries, are continuously working to cut them off from their actual identity i.e. Hindu identity'.[6]

With the expansion of the works of the VKA, the faith awakening works are also extended to new areas. The VKA has established 'Ramayan Mandali' (Ramayan reciting groups) and bhajan mandali in many tribal villages to spread Hindu religious values. The local traders and sadhus played a vital role in extending the VKA's spiritual awareness works. Traders provided economic resources to spread Hindu religious-cultural values in the tribal areas.[7] In its faith awakening programmes, the VKA always considers tribals as Hindus (particularly those tribals who do not live in the North-east region of the country) and expresses its concern over the alleged activities of Christian missionaries to distort the culture and tradition of vanvasis. Ramesh Babu, the president of the Akhil Bharatiya Shradha Jagran branch of the VKA, writes,

> The traditional religious culture of the tribal society is an integral part of the Sanatan culture of India. From time

> immemorial, their lifestyle has been based on the Vedas, and they are the spine of Sanatan Dharma . . . they have imbibed the actual meaning of the hymn of Atharva Veda, which tells that 'earth is my mother and I am the son of the earth' (Mata Bhumi Putrohamprithiviya) . . . However, specific disruptive forces are presenting the diversity of Indian society as difference . . . they are working for the division in the society . . . these anti-social elements are working on the direction of foreign forces . . . they are anti-social and anti-national too.[8]

Indeed, the VKA began other works (like education, health services, etc.) to strengthen its work of shradha jagran or Hinduization of the tribals. Ramesh Babu underlines that Swami Aseemanand played a crucial role in making shradha jagran a separate department in the VKA. In the North-east region of the country, the VKA tried to mobilize those communities, who were against conversion to Christianity by using the idea of Sanatan Dharma (eternal religion).[9]

The VKA tries to inculcate Hindu religious values in the hearts and minds of tribal people by enabling them to travel to religious places, particularly the Kumbh Mela. The Mahakumbh is a very auspicious religious occasion for Hindus, which is organized every twelve years. The former ruler of the princely state of Jashpur (who gave land to Ramakant Deshpande and Morubhau Ketkar to establish an ashram in Jashpur) wanted to give tribals an opportunity to travel to other Hindu religious places and foster their ties with Hinduism. The VKA adopted this idea and organizes a visit to the Kumbh for hundreds of tribals in Prayagraj (and other places like Nashik, Ujjain and Haridwar). In 2019, the Ardh-Kumbh (or Semi Kumbh), was organized in Prayagraj, which happens once in six years. The VKA organized a tribal gathering in Prayagraj and ensured that tribals also came to the Kumbh and took a dip in the Sangam (confluence of rivers Ganga, Yamuna, Saraswati). It also organizes many exhibitions that impart knowledge about the rich culture of tribals to people from different parts of the country. It also invited Bhagat-Baiga priests and bhajan mandalis to exhibit the cultural diversities of tribals to Hindus. Earlier the VKA had done the same things in 2016 at the Ujjain Kumbh, and tribals or vanvasis from different parts of the country participated in it.[10] The VKA also runs a weekly bhajan mandali and *satsang* (religious discussion) in 5,800 villages.[11]

The VKA has supported the Shabri Kumbh in the Dang district of Gujarat since 2006, which was different from the traditional Kumbh of Haridwar, Prayag, Nashik and Ujjain. The local people believe that Shabri, the famous tribal character of the Ramayana, belonged to the Dang district, and she met Ram and Laxman at this place. Thousands of vanvasis and hundreds of Hindu saints came to a religious meeting where they opposed conversions. Similarly, at Beneshwar in Rajasthan, at the confluence of three rivers, Som, Bhati and Jakham, each year from January to February a Magh Mela is organized where many tribals participate since it is important for them.[12] The former president of the VKA, Jagdev Ram Oraon, conceptualized the idea of an annual Rohtasgarh pilgrimage, which started in 2006. This annual pilgrimage has been organized to celebrate the grand history of the Oraon tribe, who according to some accounts ruled here and fought against Muslim rulers.[13] For the VKA, all such activities are important because they enhance the influence of Hindu values on tribal life.

The VKA has continuously tried to establish different Hindu deities, particularly Ram, as an integral part of the tribal tradition and social ethos. Many VKA activists often claim with pride that the members of their organization played a crucial role in the demolition of the Babri Masjid on 6 December 1992.[14] In the 1990s, the VKA organized village-level programmes at numerous tribal-dominated villages of Jharkhand, Chhattisgarh and Odisha to show the video recording of police action against *karsevaks* (volunteers) in October 1990 and the demolition of the Babri Masjid. It also made arrangements to screen Ramanand Sagar's *Ramayana* serial in these villages.[15] The key purpose behind such activities was to create a sense of belonging with Hinduism in the minds of tribal youth.

Through different articles in its magazine, *Van Bandhu*, pamphlets and social media platforms (Facebook and WhatsApp messages) the VKA emphasized the relationship of Ram with the tribal society. According to Vikas Markam, an active member of the VKA, Ram spent ten out of fourteen years of his vanvas (forest exile) in the tribal areas of Chhattisgarh. Local people, including tribals, believe that Ram ate *ber* (Indian Jujube) offered by Shabri at the Shivnarayan temple in the Ramgarh area of Surguja district.[16] Legend goes that she offered the fruit after tasting them to ensure they were of good quality. The members of the Sawar–Sawra tribe claim that they are descendants of Shabri. Markam claims that the vanvasis of these regions have deep faith in Ram. Indeed, in exaggerating the relationship between tribal and forest-dwelling society, he emphasized the unbreakable relationship between Ram and tribal people, who use the name of 'Sitaram' in their daily life and include the word 'Ram' with their names. He also claims that in the rural tribal areas of Chhattisgarh, people use the term 'Ram–Ram' to greet each other. They offer the first part of their crop to Ram and start the measurement of their crop by using the terms Ram, don (two), teen (three), etc. The recitation of *Ramcharitmanas* (an epic poem composed by the sixteenth-century Indian poet Tulsidas) is a popular practice in rural tribal areas, who also use the phrase *Ram Naam Satya Hai* (the name of Ram is the truth) during cremation. He underscores that tribal people living in forest areas worship Ram and Janki as their gods.[17] During the time of COVID, the VKA collaborated with many organizations and held a three-day online discussion on Ram, at which many famous personalities related to the RSS delivered lectures.[18] The VKA also focuses on establishing the importance of other Hindu gods (like Shiva, Parvati, Krishna, etc., in tribal society) and uses these figures in many festivals of tribal communities.[19]

It is noteworthy that the VKA has not imposed all Hindu festivals and traditions on the tribal people. It also celebrates some tribal festivals, and it has tried to normalize many Hindu festivals in these areas.[20] For example, on 8 October 2019, celebrations related to Karma (a popular festival among tribals and it is related to the harvest and tribute to the Karam or Haldu tree) were organized in the VKA office of Jashpur and many office-bearers participated in it. The VKA has started a separate department named Lok Kala to wean away tribal youth from Bollywood or Western music and popularize tribal folk songs instead. It uses festivals like Karma for this purpose.[21]

The VKA has also opposed the proposal of a Uniform Civil Code (UCC) for tribal communities though the UCC has been a core agenda of the RSS and the BJP. They have emphasized that the UCC fosters unity and integration in a true sense. Both organizations have always alleged that the absence of the UCC has been giving undue advantage to minority communities, particularly Muslims. It is also true that when Atal Bihari Vajpayee formed the National Democratic Alliance (NDA) in 1998, the BJP declared that it would not emphasize this issue. However, it never totally abandoned the issue and when Narendra Modi became the prime minister in 2014, the BJP brought it back to the fore. BJP leaders have been arguing that due to vote bank politics, the Congress and other non-BJP parties have opposed the UCC.[22] However, the VKA has opposed the imposition of the UCC on tribal communities because these communities are diverse and the UCC would negatively impact their rights to live according to, and follow, their customs and traditions.[23] The views of the VKA played an important factor in the exclusion of tribals from the Uttarakhand UCC Act.[24]

It is evident from the above description, that the VKA accepts and celebrates many tribal festivals and rituals. The VKA consciously tries to present itself as an organization that has complete respect for the diversity of tribal society and wishes to make the whole process of Hinduization of tribal communities more dialogical and non-coercive. However, there's a contradiction here. Though the VKA opposes UCC for tribal communities, it is not ready to accept the demand for the Sarna Code (a proposal to create a separate religious category for adivasis in India's census) by certain tribal communities. Similarly, there are organizations run by senior activists of the VKA, which indulge in aggressive mobilization against converted tribals and also conduct ghar wapsi.[25]

Hinduization of Tribal Icons: Creating Legitimacy for the VKA's Work

The VKA celebrates the life of many tribal freedom fighters, most of whom have been unknown or less known to the larger society. These tribal figures were never connected with the VKA or the RSS in their lifetime. It is interesting that in presenting the strife of these tribal fighters, the VKA focuses on their struggle against British or Muslim rulers, and underlines that these icons had great regard for Hinduism. In most of the cases, they are seen to be struggling against the proselytization of tribals by Christian missionaries. It tries to appropriate non-tribal saints or leaders who worked in tribal areas and spread the values of Hinduism, or opposed the work of Christian missionaries. The VKA has also appropriated and popularized many tribal icons and used them to further its ideology and increase its influence and legitimacy in many tribal areas.

Some of the key tribal figures whose struggles have been celebrated by the VKA include Birsa Munda, Sant Gahira Guru, Raghoji Bhangre, Nilamber-Pitamber, Tilka Manjhi, Budhu Bhagat, Telanga Kharia, Baba Bhagirath Hansda, Sido-Kanhu, Jatra Tana Bhagat, Rani Durgavati etc.[26] The RSS and the VKA used the same strategy in the North-east too. They invoked the local sixteenth-century scholar and reformer, Shankardev, to spread the RSS brand of nationalism. They consolidated the figure of Gopinath Bardoloi as a 'freedom fighter' and presented him as a 'Hindutva hero because he fought against Mohammad Ali Jinnah, who had attempted to incorporate Assam into East Pakistan. Similarly, they appropriated Manipur prince Tikendrajit Singh who fought the British in 1889 and U. Tirot Sing Syiem in Meghalaya, a Khasi chief, who fought the British in the eighteenth century. In Arunachal Pradesh, the VKA presented Talum Ragbo, the main organizer of the indigenous religion Donyi Polo, as a tribal hero.'[27]

Though the VKA has started to celebrate many tribal freedom fighters or historic characters, two of them—Birsa Munda and Rani Gaidinliu—are more important for the spread of its ideas and its goal of opposing Christian missionaries. Both have been continuously projected by the RSS and VKA, as heroes who fought against colonial rulers and Christian missionaries. Through popularizing their lives, the VKA has been trying to achieve the idea of faith awakening among tribals.

Birsa Munda: A Tribal Freedom Fighter

Birsa Munda (1874–1900) was a legendary freedom fighter who revolted against the colonial rulers. He was born on 15 November 1875 in Ulihatu (present-day Khunti district in Jharkhand). His father Sukhram Munda had four children, including Birsa. He was sent to a German missionary school in Chaibasa but was expelled from the school because he protested Father Notrott's objectionable comments against tribals. After his expulsion, he went in search of a livelihood and converted to Roman Catholicism, but remained Christian only for a short period. Gradually, he became closer to Anand Panre[28] who was a leader of the Sardari Ladai or Sardari agitation, an agrarian movement. The movement emerged due to the restrictions imposed on the traditional rights of the tribal groups. Birsa was hugely influenced by Anand Panre and began practicing Vaishnavism and participated in the Sardari agitation. Later he developed his own religion, known as Birsa Dharam, and its followers described themselves as Birsaites. This religion was influenced by his personal experience as a Christian and a Vaishnavite.

Many of Birsa's teachings were influenced by Vaishavism, such as vegetarianism, wearing the *janeu* (sacred thread), adhering to cleanliness, etc. He declared himself as Birsa Bhagwan and many adivasis were attracted to his religion. Birsa and his followers opposed the exploitation of tribals by the colonial rulers and zamindars and treated Christian missionaries as stooges of the colonial rulers. He mobilized adivasis against outsiders, and his political ideas and popularity became a threat to British officials, missionaries and zamindars. Birsa is portrayed in many books as a figure who was against British rule and the colonization of tribal society. He led a guerrilla war against the British from 1897–1900 and was arrested in February 1900 and killed in prison on 9 June

1901. Birsa's revolt led to the legislation of the Chota Nagpur Tenancy Act (CNTA), which ensured certain crucial rights of local communities over forest resources.[29]

The VKA's description of Birsa Munda emphasizes his opposition to Christian missionaries, their agenda of proselytization and the influence of Vaisnavism on his ideas. Thus, for example, an article published in *Van Bandhu* presents the following account of him:

> For some time, he received education from the German Mission School of Chaibasa. Nevertheless, he could not tolerate the mockery of tribal culture in the school. So, he also started to mock Christian priests and their religion . . . then, Pracharak of the Christian religion expelled him from the school . . . Then a new turn came in the life of Birsa, and he came in contact with Swami Anand Panre, and from him, he knew about the Hindu religion and the characters of the Mahabharata.[30]

However, noted anthropologist K.S. Singh and famous litterateur Mahashweta Devi underlined that Birsa's demand to give land to adivasis was the foremost reason behind leaving his school.[31] Indeed, Mahashweta Devi shows that Birsa was disenchanted with both Christianity and the preachings of Anand Panre. There is no doubt that the representation of Birsa as a person who fought against the conversion of tribals into Christianity is very convenient for the agenda of the VKA. They accept and propagate his sermons to illustrate that all of them are part of Sanatan Dharma. For example, the VKA released a message in 2020, on the death anniversary of Birsa Munda on 9 June, which depicted him as Bhagwan (god) Birsa Munda. Birsa was depicted with a sacred thread and the message with the picture was as follows:

> Today foreigners have extended their web (of false works), and it has become sin to claim to be a Hindu . . . due to the glorification of Ravana and Mahish whole forest area is confused. By destroying the purity of service, it has become a religion to cut your sacred hair (Choti). Persons living in mountains and forests are asking in impatient voices . . . dear Birsa, do we not have any religion . . . and no relationship with Ram, Hanuman, and Shiv.[32]

The VKA propagates eleven sermons of Birsa, which present him as a staunch supporter of Hinduism. Following are the key points of his sermons known as Birsaiat:

1. God, i.e. Singboga is one
2. Serve the cow and be kind to all creatures
3. Do not use any intoxicant
4. Do not eat impure food
5. Always keep your household clean and keep a plant of tulsi in your courtyard
6. Respect elders and keep a distance from bad people
7. Keep belief in your religion and unbroken faith on your ancestors
8. Always be united
9. Do payer of Singboga every Thursday and do not plough on that day
10. Do not forget the tradition of religion and culture; doing so erases the identity of our society
11. Do not get trapped in the optical illusion of Christianity[33]

The VKA, which always celebrated Birsa Munda, welcomed the decision of the Modi government to celebrate his birth anniversary as Janjatiya Gaurav Divas. The similarity between his religion and Hinduism, and his opposition to Christian missionaries, has made him more useful for the VKA. Using Birsa's ideology, the VKA tries to establish the legitimacy of Hindu values in tribal life and underline that even the greatest tribal icon was against the proselytization agenda of Christian missionaries.

Rani Gaidinliu: A Tribal Icon from the North-east

VKA activist Jagdamba Mall's biography revers Rani Gaidinliu and says she was born under auspicious signs.[34] Gaidinliu was born on 26 January 1915 in Lungkao, a Rongmei village in the Tamenglong district in Manipur. When she was a teenager, Rani Gaidinliu met Haipou Jadonang, who wanted to establish a Naga Raj (a regional sovereign government) and thus threaten the British colonial order. According to a predominant narrative, the relationship between Jadonang and Gaidinliu was akin to an older brother and younger sister.[35]

In 1931, the British captured and hanged Jadonang after implicating him on false charges of human sacrifice. Gaidinliu, his close collaborator, was then captured by the British in 1932 and sentenced to life imprisonment. She was just seventeen. In 1937, when Rani Gaidinliu was in Shillong jail, Jawaharlal Nehru heard of her and her struggle. In 1938, an article appeared in an American periodical called 'The Living Age', in which Nehru republished an essay he had contributed to the All India Congress Committee newsletter, called 'Gaidinliu Ranee'. In his article, he praised Gaidinliu for her brave struggle against the colonial rulers. He wrote, 'a day will come when India also will remember her and cherish and bring her out of her prison cell'.[36]

Nehru constantly tried to ensure the release of Rani Gaidinliu which eventually happened in 1945. In 1952, she was finally allowed to return to her home village of Lungkao in Manipur, after about twenty years in exile. There she was active in local affairs and launched her vision to unite the Zeliangrong people. The community includes the tribes, Zeme, Liangmei, and Rongmei and are scattered in Assam, Manipur and Nagaland. Gaidinliu wanted to create a Zeliangrong homeland. This idea clashed with the Naga National Council (NNC) vision of Naga sovereignty. While NNC largely wanted independence from India, Gaidinliu's agitations focused on the creation of a Zeliangrong homeland (a separate state) within the Indian union.[37] Gaidinliu was also against the conversion of tribal communities to Christianity. So, to protect the non-Christian identity of tribal communities and to push for a separate state within India, she organized the Heraka movement. She went underground in 1960 with the formation of the Zeliangrong government of the Rani Party. During this time she was popularly known as Amuipui (our mother). She taught her army cadres to 'love their religion, culture and preserve their traditional and customary practices'.[38] She went underground for six years and during this time she gave shape to the tribal religion known as Heraka. Since both Gaidinliu and the RSS were opposed to Christian missionaries, she was drawn to the RSS in the post-1966 era.

After her surrender in 1966, the RSS and the VHP tried to connect with her and the Heraka movement. According to Jagdamba Mall, Gaidinliu's greatest achievement was to establish a close relationship with the 'greater Hindu society', which included the Bharatiya Vanvasi Kalyan Ashram, Vishva Hindu Parishad, Rashtriya Swayamsevak Sangh, Rashtra Sevika Samiti and Vidya Bharati. When invited by these organizations to participate in their national programmes, she said she vehemently opposed the terrorism of the church. According to researcher and author Arkotong Longkumer, many books and articles about Rani Gaidinliu were written by

Hindu right-wing sympathizers that portray her as a Hindu freedom fighter.[39]

In 1979 she was invited to the Second World Hindu Conference, organized by the Vishva Hindu Parishad. This conference was organized at the time of Mahakumbh from 24 to 26 January 1979 at Prayag. She also went to Varanasi and visited the Kashi Vishwanath Mandir.[40] Gaidinliu never claimed to be a Hindu, but on many issues, she took a stand that validated the demands of the RSS and the VKA. Like the VKA president Ramakant Deshpande, she also opposed the visit of Pope John Paul II in 1986. Interestingly, Jagdamba Mall claims that she wrote a letter to the central government and demanded that 'Hindu Samaj' (society) must be permitted to build a Ram temple.[41] RSS intellectuals, including Jagdamba Mall, have tried to present her as a Hindu: 'Imagine a scenario where a Naga child would ask about Rani Gaidinliu and the parent would reply: She is Rani Gaidinliu. She is Hindu, an Indian freedom fighter.' Honoured with a Tamrapatra and the Padma Bhushan, Rani Gaidinliu opposed Naga separatist organizations and church proselytizations.[42] While it is true that the VKA uses the term Sanatan Dharma to describe all non-Christian and non-Muslim groups as part of a larger indigenous religion, for common Indian Hindus, there is no clear distinction between Hinduism and Sanatan Dharma. When in September 2023, Dravida Munnetra Kazhagam leader Udhayanidhi Maran criticized Sanatan Dharma,[43] the media described it as a criticism of the Hindu religion and not a criticism of all religions that originated in India.

It is obvious from the description of both tribal icons that neither presented themselves as a follower of Hinduism. Whereas Birsa adopted some crucial Hindu ideas and rituals, Gaidinliu constantly participated in the programmes of the RSS and its affiliates and supported them on several issues, including the Ram Janmabhoomi movement. The VKA portrays them as part of the larger Sanatan Dharma, and since they were against proselytization, the VKA adopted their views to give greater validity to its works.

Indeed, one can make an extensive list of figures whom the VKA now celebrates, including forgotten ones. The VKA describes all these figures as Hindu leaders and always depicts them as freedom fighters, social workers or spiritual gurus influenced by Hinduism. The other aspect is that it clearly overlooks, or sometimes depicts negatively, people who do not fit in its 'Hindu agenda'. Jaipal Singh Munda is an example. Munda played a significant role in the Constituent Assembly of India and continually raised pertinent questions about the rights of the tribal people, but the VKA never honours him.[44] On the other hand, the VKA celebrates the birth anniversary of the former MP and Congress leader Kartik Oraon because his works and ideas suit them. Kartik Oraon demanded the delisting of those tribals from the list of STs who converted to Christianity or Islam.[45]

The VKA and the Concept of Indigenous People

The VKA's fundamental slogan is *'Tu Main Ek Rakt'* (You and I have the same blood), which expresses the inseparability of the tribal population from the other sections of Hindu society. As mentioned in chapter one, INC leader Rahul Gandhi has been continuously arguing that the RSS and BJP do not call tribals, adivasis, because they want to keep them as vanvasis. However, the VKA has been arguing that tribals are an integral part of Hindu society, and calling them adivasis would imply separatism. Since most of them have been living in the forest, the VKA uses the term vanvasi and for them, it is not a derogatory term, but a revered one because Lord Ram and many saints etc., lived in the forest. Though the RSS and VKA use the term janjati in their publication, they have been vehemently against the use of the term adivasi. The Sangh Parivar, including the VKA, rejects the idea that Aryans came to India from outside.[46]

In an important anecdote, former Rajya Sabha MP Tarun Vijay describes an interesting incident:

> [W]hen Atal Bihari Vajpayee was Prime Minister the Ministry of Tribal Affairs was formed as a separate ministry. Some officers suggested the name Adivasi Kalyan Mantralay for this ministry. However, Atalji knew that I worked in Vanvasi Kalyan Ashram. So, in the evening he discussed this issue with me. I told him everything related to this issue and emphasized that in the Indian Constitution, Baba Saheb has not used the term adivasi, but accepted the term tribes.[47]

In this context, it is important to consider the debates on the indigenous people of India and the VKA's views on the issue. The VKA has taken a clear and strong stand on the issue of declaring the tribal population of the country as indigenous people. It is crucial to understand the development of the concept of indigenous people at the international level, and the key concerns and objections of the VKA. In recent decades, in anthropology, the use of the term indigenous people has increased, and international organizations have also started to use this term in their deliberations. In fact, 1993 was declared as the 'International Year of Indigenous People'. In 1957 the International Labour Organization (ILO) used this term and passed Convention 107, which protected indigenous people, tribal and semi-tribal communities in independent countries and emphasized their 'progressive integration' with national communities. Eventually, in the 1980s, the thinking about indigenous people's rights changed and the ILO Convention 169 charted in 1989 expressed a new framework for their rights. It primarily focuses on three points: Indigenous people are those who were living in a country or particular area before its colonization; second, they were pushed to the margin after the colonization by people outside; and third, rather than following the larger institutions of the society they are living their socio-economic and cultural life through their institution.[48] In September 2007, the UN accepted the Declaration of the Rights of Indigenous People, which emphasized that political, economic and social structures, and cultural and spiritual traditions, should be protected. In addition, their rights to land and resources should be recognized.[49] It accepts their rights to self-determination and autonomy in managing internal and local affairs.[50] In the Indian context, adivasi (original dwellers) has been used synonymously with indigenous people. Thus, the people coming under the category of ST are considered adivasis. Indeed, the term had been used by many leaders in the colonial period too.[51]

The VKA has consistently opposed the idea of indigenous people. In 1999 it submitted a memorandum to the then prime minister Atal Bihari Vajpayee stating its objections to the idea of indigenous people and the draft of the United Nations Declaration on the Rights of Indigenous People (UNDRIP), passed in 2007.[52] The key difference between the ILO Convention 169 and UNDRIP is that the former is legally binding and the latter is not. India has not ratified the ILO Convention 169.[53] At the beginning of the memorandum, the VKA congratulates Vajpayee for appointing a cabinet minister for tribal affairs for the first time after Independence. It also expresses its hope that the government will focus on the development of vanvasis (tribals), and take strong steps to curb the nefarious anti-national works of agencies (here the indication is towards Christian missionaries)[54].

The VKA accepts the progressive elements of the draft of the UNDRIP (most of them included in the final UNDRIP). For example, apart from the right to self-identification, the VKA accepts the individual and community rights given by the draft of UNDRIP. It also underlines that there is nothing to disagree with all articles related to life sources of livelihood and identity maintenance, and cultural and educational rights of the children, positive measures for promoting the political, economic, social and spiritual interests of the indigenous people.[55] However, it makes a strong reservation over the definition of the ideal of indigenous people. According to the VKA, it can harm the national interests of India and create a sense of separatism in the minds of the tribal people. Following are the key points related to its reservation:

First, there is no clear definition of who comprise indigenous people. Though certain thinkers focused on colonization, if one follows this logic, there would be no indigenous people in European countries because they never faced colonization. The VKA claims that Christian missionaries have popularised the word indigenous people in India. Many representatives who attended international conferences related to the concept and definition of indigenous people were financed by Christian missionaries.[56] They accepted that from a historical and anthropological point of view, tribal groups are the indigenous people of India from prehistoric times with distinct social, economic, political, and territorial identities. The VKA underlines that since tribal representatives were sponsored and tutored by the church, they have regularly followed that line in subsequent meetings of the working groups (formed to consider different aspects of the concept of indigenous people) and at forums of the UN. The VKA argues that this submission was false and was based on the assumption that tribals were victims of the colonization of Aryans.[57]

Second, since population is migratory, it is impossible to say which group is indigenous. The VKA memorandum quotes eminent anthropologist Dr K. Suresh Singh to support this claim. Singh edited a monumental ethnographic study of Indian people and argued that it is not possible for some communities to be more indigenous than others.[58]

Third, The VKA suggests that the idea of self-determination can be used in different tribal areas to enhance the feeling of secession and in this context, it mentions that '[T]here is a long-standing demand of the greater Jharkhand. Gondwana is the next target of the divisive forces. It is unlikely that these separatist movements may pose any formidable challenge but we have to guard against any move by the people claiming to be indigenous for destabilization of the country'.[59] In this sense, the VKA underlines that this term would be detrimental to national integrity and security.[60]

Fourth, it emphasizes its earlier stand that vanvasis are an integral part of mainstream society.[61]

Apart from submitting the memorandum to the government of India, the VKA has continuously been emphasizing that the idea of indigenous people is an imperialistic construct. Moreover, Christian missionaries and many foreign organizations directly or indirectly support this idea. The VKA termed 9 August, International Day of the World's Indigenous Peoples, as part of an international conspiracy to create secessionist feelings in the minds of Indian tribals. On 9 August 1982, the Working Group of Indigenous Peoples organized its first meeting. However, in an article published in *Van Bandhu* (the monthly journal published by the VKA), Laxman Raj Singh Markam 'Lakshya' argues that on 9 August 1610, the British army won its bilateral war against the indigenous peoples of the USA. It allowed Christian missionaries to expand their religion in new areas. Lakshya also underlines that in the UN, Christian forces decided to celebrate 9 August as International Indigenous Peoples Day to celebrate the victory of the British in the British–Powhatan war on that date in 1610. He emphasizes,

> Today in India tribals 'blindly' follow others and celebrate International Indigenous Peoples Day. However, on this day, the indigenous people of the USA remember the genocide of innocent persons in their community. Should we forget the oppression of tribal people in our country by European colonial powers? Should not we celebrate the important days related to Birsa Munda or any other tribal hero?[62]

The VKA's arguments against using the concept of indigenous people for tribals in India have found partial support from scholars, who disagree with using the concept of indigenous people in its literal sense in India. G.S. Ghurye underlined that this term (adivasi) was used in the colonial period for imperialist politics.[63] Andre Beteille points out that there has been a long history of cultural exchange between adivasis and other castes, so there are many theoretical and practical difficulties in distinguishing them.[64] Virginius Xaxa argues that in India, the communities identified as STs were not necessarily settled first in that particular geographical region and many non-tribal groups settled there before them. For instance, the Naga settled in India in the first millennium BCE, and many non-tribal communities settled before them in different parts of the country. Xaxa also underlines that earlier, colonial administrators used adivasis to describe tribals in isolated situations. However, later, many Indian tribal communities adopted the adivasi identity.[65] In the Indian context, the communities included in the category of ST claim that they are adivasis and have become a source of political mobilization in many parts of the country. However, it should be noted that there are many forest-dwelling communities, that are not part of the ST category, but they claim that they are adivasis.[66] Amita Baviskar has argued by citing the experience of the Narmada Bachao Andolan that the claims of indigeneity and indigenous (adivasi) rights played a role in the mobilization of adivasi communities and also provided support for their demands.[67]

The VKA's position on the term adivasi is fraught with many contradictions. The Vajpayee government adopted a 'self-definition' of indigenous people that 'all citizens are sons and daughters of the soil'.[68] The purpose behind this assertion was to negate the claim that adivasis are the only indigenous people in India. However, in practice, the VKA is not ready to accept this position and it uses the term indigenous according to its convenience. For the RSS and VKA to be fully Indian and indigenous is to be Hindu (or the follower of Sanatan Dharma). The VKA uses this idea to differentiate between tribals who are Hindu (or non-converted) and those who adopted Christianity or Islam.

It is also crucial to note that the VKA and other RSS affiliates desist the use of the term adivasi, and apart from vanvasi, they also use the term janjati. However, BJP leaders, including Prime Minister Narendra Modi, have frequently used the term adivasi, dropping vanvasi after Rahul Gandhi's criticism. Interestingly, Modi announced a Pradhan Mantri Janjati Adivasi Nyaya Maha Abhiyan (PM JANMAN) on 15 November 2023. The total outlay of the PM JANMAN would be Rs 24,104 crore and it would focus on providing basic amenities to adivasis. Interestingly, PM JANMAN uses both janjati and adivasi terms, which shows that Modi was trying to negate the accusation of Rahul Gandhi regarding the use of the term vanvasis for tribals. When in 2021, the Modi-led government decided to celebrate Birsa Munda Jayanti as a national event, the term coined for the occasion was 'Janjatiya Gaurav Divas'. The government desisted from using the term vanvasi. To counter Rahul Gandhi's allegations on the term adivasi, the Modi government used the term deliberately.[69] It is also clear that though the VKA prefers the term vanvasi or janjati, even mainstream political actors of the BJP have adopted the term adivasi.

The Opposition of Christian Missionaries

The conversion of tribal people to Christianity has always been a very central issue for the VKA and other affiliated organizations of the RSS. They have been emphatically arguing that Christian missionaries are using fraudulent means to convert innocent tribal people to Christianity. However, many scholars believe this to be a more complex issue. Apart from exceptions, like Ghurye, who termed tribals as backward Hindus, the 'mainstream' scholarship on tribal society has always underlined the distinct identity of tribal communities. It has been argued that both Hindus and Christians have converted tribals to their respective faiths.

Virginus Xaxa argues that in the colonial period, the tribes were identified as those who did not adhere to religions such as Hinduism, Christianity, Islam, etc. The dimension of caste assumes a central place in the religious tradition of Hinduism, and it became a basis for differentiating between Hinduism and tribes.[70] After Independence, there has been no unanimity on the characteristics to define tribals. The category of STs includes a wide range of groups and communities who are different on many accounts including language, technology, geographical locations, ecological settings, etc.

Scholars believe that Christian missionaries have used some fraudulent methods to convert tribal people to Christianity.[71] Indeed, the accusation of forced and fraudulent conversion as a stick with which to beat Christian organizations is an old one. Even in the pre-Independence period such accusations emerged, which had significant support within the Congress too. Nandini Sundar accepts that there was perhaps some truth in the charge and informs that in the 1940s, the well-known proponent of adivasi isolationism, Verrier Elwin, opposed such activities of Christian missionaries in Mandla. He supported the demands of organizations like the Gond Seva Mandal and the Arya Dharam Seva Sangh, to shut down mission schools in Mandla.[72] Simultaneously, such scholars have also underlined that the employment of unfair, unethical and illegal means has not been the dominant method of conversion used by Christian missionaries. The more common methods have been developmental and social services-oriented works, which include education, health, medicine, legal aid, agricultural credit, etc.[73]

Indeed, it has been argued by some scholars that Hindu groups have also been continuously converting tribals to their religion. According to such an argument, a continuous process of transformation from one religion to another among tribes in India began even before colonial rule, but conversion gained attention only with the advent of colonial rule. Hinduism expanded in tribal areas through both forcible and peaceful absorption of tribal people into Hindu society.[74] It is argued that until the nineteenth century, there was a frictionless coexistence between tribes and non-tribes. After that, due to the spread of railways and roads, non-tribal people moved to tribal areas and started to exploit tribals. They also compelled them to accept their cultural traditions and values.[75] D.D. Kosambi considers the adoption of technology in Hindu society by tribes to be a major method of integration.[76] N.K. Bose talks of the Hindu method of tribal absorption which takes place mainly under the system of caste-based organization of production founded on reciprocity.[77]

Several scholars have noted that Hinduism appropriated many local tribal practices like the worship of animals, trees, Mother Goddesses, and connected them with similar Hindu practices.[78] It has been emphatically argued that modernization, the reach of the post-colonial state, media, government schools and market forces increased the influence of Hindu values in tribal areas. state practices like the census that record adivasis as Hindus are major enablers in their conversion to Hinduism, and indeed, the decennial census has long been a battlefield for identity assertion.[79] However, state practice is contradictory because judicial pronouncements on adivasi personal law distinguish them from Hindus.[80]

Abhay Kumar Dubey has questioned the tendency to treat adivasis and Hindus as entirely different categories and supports the argument that historically with the development of civilization and growing interaction with Hindus, a part of the tribal community developed a close relationship with Hinduism. He asserts that anthropologists like B.K. Roy Burman, Verrier Elwin, etc., attempted to classify tribal populations in certain categories and accepted that at least one section of the tribal population had been accommodated in Hinduism. Dubey asserts that when VKA started its work in tribal areas, it found a favourable ground to expand its influence.[81]

However, the VKA (and the Sangh Parivar) vehemently opposed the idea that tribals and Hindus be treated as two distinct categories. The tendency among the Hindu right to conceive and identify tribes as Hindus is based on the observation made many years ago by G.S. Ghurye, a noted sociologist, and the Niyogi Commission report, that endorsed the observation made by Ghurye. He used the expression 'backward Hindus'.[82]

As discussed in the previous chapter, the opposition to the works of Christian missionaries in tribal areas was the foremost reason behind the formation of the VKA. With its formation, the VKA started to demand a curb in what was deemed anti-national and the conversion activities of Christian missionaries. Due to the pressure of the VKA and other right-wing forces, the Ravishankar Shukla government of Madhya Pradesh formed a commission chaired by a retired justice of the Nagpur High Court, Dr Bhawani Shankar Niyogi. Its mandate was to probe the charges that Christian missionaries were using fraudulent means to convert people to Christianity. Ramakant Deshpande and other RSS persons actively supported the work of the Niyogi Commission and ensured that the commission get all necessary information. In its report, the commission underlined that with Independence, American missionary evangelization had increased, which involved both coercion and inducement. The commission recommended different kinds of control over the activities of missionaries, particularly their attempts to convert people. It also suggested that Indian churches establish a 'United Independent Church in India without being dependent on foreign support'.[83] The commission's report provided solid proof to the VKA regarding the wrong means used by Christian missionaries to convert tribals and senior VKA activist, K.D. Sapre, underlined the close connection between the Niyogi Commission members with the RSS office-bearers and the help provided to the commission by them, most prominently by Deshpande.[84]

The VKA has been continuously demanding a stringent anti-conversion law to stop the alleged 'forced conversion' of innocent tribal people. At the beginning of 1986, Ramakant Deshpande wrote three letters to the President, prime minister and Pope John Paul II (on the eve of his first visit to India).[85] These letters provide an understanding of the VKA's opinion and the critique of the works and conversion of tribals through alleged 'force and allurement' by Christian missionaries. The letters also underline the VKA's views about non-Hindu religious groups, particularly Muslims and Christians.

In January 1986, on the eve of Pope John Paul II's visit to India, Deshpande wrote him a letter, similar to the one he sent to the President of India. The key points can be explained as follows: First, Christian missionaries have indulged in conversion since the colonial period by using wrong and unethical means.[86] Second, before secularism was coined, India developed a culture of respect for all beliefs and religions from time immemorial, and the Indian Constitution also reaffirms this idea. However, he underlines that Christian missionaries have created problems for communal harmony and peace due to their efforts to increase their numbers through converting innocent tribal peoples. He argues that the Christian missionaries are traders of human misery.[87] Third, the pope's visit will be misused as a catalytic agent for strengthening anti-national and anti-government activities. At the end of his letter, Deshpande urges the pope to tell the Catholic church to stop conversions and declare all religions equal. He writes, 'let selfless service to the people, and not the destruction of their native faith, culture, tradition, and way of life, be the Spirit of Christianity . . . advice your followers to give up religious conversion and creating conditions hostile to the solidarity of our nation'.[88]

In his letter to then prime minister Rajiv Gandhi, Deshpande praised him for his concern for neglected and deprived sections, including tribals. He also attached the letter he sent to Pope John Paul II. Interestingly, in his letter to Rajiv Gandhi, he introduces the VKA in the following words: 'we are a non-political voluntary organization dedicated to the service, welfare, and upliftment of our vanvasis brethren, who live in forest and hilly areas spread over several states of our country. We started our work in a humble way and now our work stands extended to almost all vanvasi areas of our country.'[89]

Deshpande glorifies Hinduism in his letter to the President by saying that Hindus have been known for their tolerance and beliefs. He expresses his sorrow and anger over the continuous 'aggressive behaviour' of the Muslim and Christian minorities. He claims that the Hindus are in a state of continuous siege by these aggressive minorities, resulting in the murder of Hindus, abduction and rape of Hindu women, demolition and desecration of Hindu temples, and burning and looting of Hindu houses.[90] He makes a strong charge against Christian churches and argues that they are working for the fragmentation of India with the support of foreign money and intelligentsia. He underlines a relationship between churches and insurgency in Nagaland, Mizoram, Manipur and Tripura and according to him, it is not an accident that all key rebellious leaders in these states are Christians (Phizo and Muiva in Nagaland; Laldenga in Mizoram; and Vijay Hrangkhal in Tripura). Deshpande also emphatically argues that due to conversions, there is an alarming upswing in the Christian population in several parts of Bihar (now Jharkhand), Madhya Pradesh (some areas are now parts of Chhattisgarh), Orissa (now Odisha) and the North-east. In his letter to the President and prime minister, he asserts unequivocally that churches indulge in proselytization and their humanitarian and welfare works are just a façade. He recognizes that the change of faith with conviction is a personal liberty given by the Indian Constitution, but conversion through inducement, force and fraud is wrong and creates social tension. Furthermore, he asserts that Christian missionaries convert poor and ignorant tribals to Christianity, primarily, if not wholly, by force, fraud and allurement. Deshpande argues that the Indian government should control Christian organizations, which are 'mainly engaged in forming the front of Dalits, Muslims, Harijans, Khalistanis and similar other disgruntled elements in the country'. He requests the President to ask the government to take 'effective and time-bound legislative and administrative to probe and curb the anti-national, anti-state and anti-Hindu activities of the Christian Churches and Missionaries . . .'[91]

The VKA passed a resolution on 17 November 2018 at its Yavatmal meeting, which demanded that the conversion of tribals in Andaman and Nicobar Islands by Christian missionaries be stopped, and demanded the enactment of stringent anti-conversion laws.[92] Though the VKA opposes the conversion of tribals by Christian missionaries and it has always demanded strict laws against conversion, its activists have adopted the method of reconversion or ghar wapsi.[93]

Expanding Contours of the VKA: Works in the North-east Region and the Idea of Sanatan Dharma as Indigenous Religion

At a meeting in August 1978, due to the threat of the increasing influence of Christian missionaries, the VKA decided to expand its organization across the country, including the North-east. In the beginning, it took the help of some Congress leaders to expand its work in these areas. For example, in Nagaland, N.C. Zeliang, who was the state Congress general secretary and a member of the Legislative Assembly, helped VKA leaders.[94] Also, since the RSS began its work in this region in 1940s, the VKA already had an ideological support base to expand its works. The RSS gave the responsibility for the expansion of the VKA in this region to Basantrao Bhatt, the *prant pracharak* (RSS worker in charge of a province) of Bengal. As mentioned earlier in the chapter, the VKA tried to appropriate different figures of this region for its expansion. The VKA expanded to Guwahati, Silchar, and Agartala. Ramakant Deshpande visited the North-east region many times after 1978. In one such visit, he met the leaders of the Khasi community who were suspicious about the work of the VKA. They argued that '(Christian) missionaries come to convert us to Christianity, have you come to convert us to Hinduism?' Deshpande replied 'we have not come here to convert you to Hinduism. We accept you as our own with your identity'.[95] Indeed, the VKA presented itself as an organization different from Christian missionaries, who used social service for proselytization. The VKA, on the other hand, claimed that it was working selflessly to protect tribal cultural values and had no agenda to convert them to Hinduism. Indeed, many tribal leaders of the North-east were significantly influenced by the approach of the VKA, and some even suggested that they should form a non-Christian front. This suggestion was given by N.C. Zeliang in 1981 at one of the conferences organized by the VKA. Zeliang was a member of the Nagaland legislative assembly and the leader of the Heraka Association.[96]

Indeed, due to the experience of Deshpande during his interactions with tribal community leaders in the North-east, the VKA stopped to claim in the North-east that all tribals are Hindus. Rather, it started to focus on the idea of Sanatan Dharma. The VKA has always used the idea of Sanatan Dharma as an umbrella for all 'indigenous religions', i.e. religions which began in this country and whose most sacred religious places are situated in India. As mentioned earlier in this chapter, the VKA has been vehemently opposing the idea of indigenous people, however, it uses the idea of indigenous religion to accommodate all sects followed by tribals, except Christianity and Islam. In this context, RSS activist B.B. Jamatia's views are important. He underlined the key elements of the 'religious philosophy of the janjatis of North-east Bharat', which includes the following elements: the importance of a 'Supreme Being', soul, karma, rebirth, food, nature, anti-conversion and Mother Earth'.[97] Scholars sympathetic to the VKA have argued that the 'real indigenous' people of India are those who still preserve their 'religion and culture' in contrast to those who have adopted the 'alien religion'.[98] Earlier in this chapter, it was mentioned that the VKA activists try to present Rani Gaidinliu as 'Hindu' (or like Hindu) in their literature.[99] Similarly, in many publications by the VKA, it has been argued that tribal people worship nature, which is intrinsic to Sanatan Dharma.[100] So, when the VKA talks to tribal communities, who are not ready to identify themselves as Hindus, they emphasize the idea of indigenous religion or Sanatan Dharma. Based on this understanding they have questioned the eligibility of converted tribals to claim reservations and other facilities given by the Constitution to STs.[101] For common workers of the VKA and its affiliated organizations, Hinduism and Sanatan Dharma are synonymous. They define a Hindu as a term that captures the idea of Sanatan Dharma, which carries values of eternal religion and culture. For them, followers of Sanatan Dharma are a distinctive kind of Hindu, where the names of their gods are different and they follow different modes of worship.[102]

In nearly four decades, the VKA has expanded its work in the interior parts of different states. As mentioned in chapter one, there are many state-specific organizations affiliated with the VKA. The medical/health facilities and *Ekal Vidayalas* (Single Teacher Schools) played crucial roles in expanding the work of the VKA-affiliated organizations. In the North-east, the VKA runs twenty-eight hostels—twenty for boys, eight for girls. In Arunachal Pradesh, it also runs a kindergarten school or *balwadi*.[103] The VKA also runs the Heritage Foundation, which works with the religion, culture, philosophy, etc., of the tribal communities of the North-east. The VKA and its affiliated organization publish many books and journals etc through the Heritage Foundation. It publishes the *Heritage Explorer*, a monthly magazine in English and *Adichya Varta* in

Assamese. It has also published more than 200 books/booklets in Hindi, English, Bengali, Assamese, and local dialects of the North-east region.[104]

In Mizoram, the VKA (and its affiliates) helps tribal communities, who follow their own religion (Swa-Dharam), by sending their children outside Mizoram for education. It also runs a few schools and medical centres. There are around 6,000 Mizos, who are not Hindus, but nature-worshipping Sanatanis. The VKA affiliates also work among Chakma people, who are followers of Buddhism. The VKA has always supported the cause of the Reyang community in Tripura and helped 36,000 people of this community settle legally. In the Peren district of Nagaland, a VKA affiliate runs a school with around 450 students. The VKA has established a hostel and runs Ekal Vidyalayas and medical centres in Dimapur district. In Meghalaya, the affiliates of the VKA, have established schools in non-Christian Khasi tribal areas and has a strong presence in the Khasi, Garo and Jaintiya Hills. Apart from running schools and medical centres, it also helps these communities to protect their language and culture. The Khasi people, for instance, invite the VKA office-bearers and affiliates to their functions as guests.[105] It is interesting to note that when VKA was formed, its leader Deshpande used force on some tribals to compel them to chant 'Bharat Mata ki Jai' (Long live Mother India) and Arkotong Longkumer suggests that it is still remains an important mission for the VKA (and other Sangh activists in the North-east). Those Christians who hesitate to chant this slogan are declared anti-national.[106]

Summing Up

The VKA's aim is the spread of Hindu values in tribal areas and opposing Christian missionaries. The VKA has not only focused on the spread of Hindu religious values through Hindu religious texts, festivals, rituals, etc., but it has simultaneously adopted a method of celebrating the culture and customs of tribal society. Most importantly, it has emphasized the diverse cultural milieu of tribal society and emphatically opposes any proposal for the implementation of the UCC on tribals. It has tried to accept and appropriate the tribal historical characters and freedom fighters like Birsa Munda and Rani Gaidinliu, depicting them as icons who resisted Christian missionaries and as followers of Hinduism or at least sympathetic to Hindu values. The VKA has criticized the use of indigenous people in the context of India because acceptance of the concept would imply the acceptance of the separation between tribals and Hindus. So, the VKA has termed that tribals are integral to Hinduism and its basic slogan is 'Tu Main Ek Rakt'. It always prefers to call tribals, vanvasis or janjatis, rather than adivasis. Since its inception, the VKA has always strongly criticized and opposed the works of Christian missionaries and demanded that the government of India should have strict laws against the proselytization of tribals through wrong means. To intensify its opposition to Christian missionaries, the VKA has been trying to mobilize non-Christian tribals by asserting that it has no intention to convert them. It uses the idea of Sanatan Dharma as an indigenous religion to differentiate them from Christianity and Islam. Though the idea of Sanatan Dharma accepts the customs, rituals, worship and autonomy of tribals of the North-east, in practice, VKA activists treat them as Hindus.

4

Politics of Service: Key Aspects of the Vanvasi Kalyan Ashram

The VKA was formed to resist the influence of Christian missionaries in tribal areas and to spread Hindu values among tribals and it has made a serious attempt to expand its works to tribal areas. Though it started with works like education and shradha jagran, it gradually moved on to health services, women empowerment, interest protection of tribals over forest land and its resources, urban works, etc., and strengthened its influence among them. It is interesting to probe how far these works have helped tribal communities and whether it created an environment for the extension of the VKA's footprints. It's also important to understand whether such initiatives, particularly education and women's empowerment works, created a consciousness in tribal youths and women to counter and defy exploitative structures imposed by the society or state. This chapter aims to present a systematic analysis of certain seva or service works of the

VKA in tribal areas. The VKA's concerns and works for tribal rights over forest resources have been dealt with separately in chapter five. This chapter presents an analytical study of the VKA's works in urban areas and its services in the fields of education, health services, and women's empowerment.

The VKA and the Mission of Education

Education is one of the most crucial components of the VKA's work and it runs schools at the primary, middle and higher education levels for tribals. Its hostels, for instance, have allowed tribals to connect with other parts of India in urban settings. This section of the chapter is divided into two sub-sections: the first analyses the school structure of the VKA; the second deals with its suggestions to make tribal education better and highlights its policy interventions to protect the interests of tribal people. From the beginning, the founder of the VKA, Ramakant Deshpande, tried to bond with young tribal boys and girls through schools, emphasizing that schools could be developed as a concentrated centre of physical power.[1]

Synergy of Formal and Informal Systems: Structure of the VKA's Education System

Indeed, the VKA has been constantly working to expand the number of schools and hostels. According to a report presented at the VKA's annual meeting in November 2023, this is the list of hostels and educational centres run by the VKA:

Table 3: Number of Hostels and Education Centres Run by the VKA

Hostels	
Boys	176
Girls	53
Number of Hostels: 229 Beneficiaries Boys: 6,018 + Girls: 2,216 = 8,234	
Formal Education Centres	
Middle and High (from 6 to 12)	77
Primary	126
Pre-primary	02
Total	205
Beneficiaries: 28,042	
Informal Education Centres	
Ekal Vidyalaya (Single Teacher School)	2,024
Balwadi/Vidya Mandir	29
Balsanskar Kendra	
Daily	996
Weekly	273
Night School	16
Free Coaching	121
Library and Reading Rooms	50
Any Other	84
Total	3653
Total Number of Beneficiaries	70,406

Source: ABVKA (2023b), Karyavrit, November, Bhagyanagar, Telangana, in *Van Bandhu* (November, 2023), p. 60.

It is clear from the above table that the VKA runs both formal and informal educational institutions for tribal boys and girls.

Its formal schools work in areas where there is no government school, while its informal initiatives include Ekal Vidyalayas, Balwadis, Night Schools, Free Coaching and Libraries. These informal methods are crucial because they create an alternative structure for education in tribal villages. For example, the VKA activists claim that their *Ekal Vidyalaya* (Single Teacher School) experiment has been very successful. It works in tribal villages, where a single teacher teaches primary school students. Generally, the teachers working at an Ekal Vidyalaya are members of the VKA, so they also work to expand the organization in the village where they are teaching. The Ekal Vidyalayas began in different tribal areas in the late 1970s, when the VKA decided to expand. The VKA faced economic problems and those who stepped in to help financially tried to establish control. The VKA leadership sternly opposed any such attempt and Bhaskar Rao, who was organization secretary, from 1984 to 1999, mentions that he faced such problems. But neither he nor Ramakant Deshpande accepted the idea of making the Ekal Vidyalaya a tool to earn profits and they shunned the role of private players. Indeed, the VKA collected money from different sources but never compromised its purpose behind these schools.[2]

Table 3 shows that the total number of Ekal Vidyalayas is not sufficient vis-à-vis the total number of villages in tribal areas. Even in many areas where these vidyalayas are working, the work pattern is unsatisfactory because one teacher is unable to handle all the students in a village, and the focus has been more on the other works of the VKA than imparting knowledge.[3] The Ekal Vidyalayas have therefore been successful in spreading the ideology of the VKA through one educated activist (the teacher), who villagers respected. The teacher also nudges the villagers and their children towards Hindu values. However, this experiment is limited and does not cover a majority of villages in tribal areas.

In many areas, it has also established preschool centres (*balwadis* and 'Baal Sanskar Kendras') where children learn reading and writing apart from 'values' and 'practices of life', primarily Hindu values. Tribal students are taught to say pranam or namaskar to greet elders, rather than the traditional tribal greeting of saying '*Johar*'. Teachers in these centres tell students to touch the elders' feet to greet them and raise slogans like '*Saraswati Mata ki Jai*' (Hail Mother Saraswati!), '*Mahapati Ram Ki Jai*' (Hail Lord Ram!) etc. The VKA has also established the 'Eklavya Khelkud Kendra' (Eklavya Sports Centres) to attract youth. They are instructed to say '*Bharat Mata ki Jai*' (Hail Mother India) at the beginning and end of a game. It organizes a sports competition every four years for tribal youth at the national level. The office-bearers of the VKA also try to encourage students of other schools except Christian students, to participate in different competitions.[4]

The hostels established by the VKA in different rural tribal areas and urban areas have provided tribal students with opportunities to get proper education. The VKA has been using these hostels as a site to inculcate Hindu values in tribal children and create future activists of the VKA. It is also a fact that when Deshpande started the first hostel in Jashpur, only a few students joined. However, VKA hostels gradually became attractive for boarders and many tribals started sending their children to these schools. Deshpande underlined that,

> We know that all students of our hostels will not become full-time workers, but all of them will get our values . . . and running hostels smoothly is the most important work for us. The values of our hostels are generally different from the purposes of their establishment. We want to make our hostels

> in such a way that people in the area would be attracted to them. Through them, we want to create consciousness in the whole region.[5]

The practice started in the Jashpur area and was later extended to all those tribal areas where the VKA began work, including the North-east. According to Atul Jog (the current organisisation secretary), the VKA runs 240 hostels in different tribal areas of the country.[6] The VKA office-bearers compare their own schools to those run by Christian missionaries, and say those schools not only propagate foreign values but also impede tribals from learning their own culture. The VKA says its own hostels and schools, in comparison, teach tribal students respect for Indian values, culture and ethos. But there is emphasis on Hindu values, which VKA activists normalise because they consider tribals to be part of Hinduism, or in the case of the North-east, very closely aligned to the idea of indigenous religion. There are pictures of different Hindu gods and goddesses within VKA hostel buildings and the purpose behind these pictures is to give all boarders information about Hinduism and its symbols. There is a fixed routine for all boys and girls living in the hostel: they must participate in the morning and evening prayers and daily shakhas. The students also recite some prayers or songs related to Hinduism. All these activities create a profound influence on the minds of tribal girls and boys.[7]

The VKA also tells students in its schools and hostels about tribal heroes who struggled against colonial rulers, engendering a sense of pride in them about their own icons. However, there is a flip side in the description of such warriors, social activists and freedom fighters—most are described as warriors who fought against foreign rule and opposed foreign religion, particularly Christian missionaries. Indeed, religion is the sole criterion to select a hero for the tribals. So, Jaipal Singh Munda who struggled for a separate state for adivasis and played a crucial role in securing many rights for them in the Constituent Assembly is not part of the VKA's list of heroes.

Sohini Chattopadhyay in her study on VKA hostels of Mollarpur, West Bengal, underlines that the VKA tries to teach Hindu values to tribal girls and boys (the Mollarpur hostel is only for boys). She writes,

> The day starts at 4.30 am and ends at 10 pm, except Sundays or holidays. Tuitions are organized in Maths, English, and Science for the students. However, the emphasis is on learning Sanskrit and the history of 'Hindustan', which is imparted through daily readings and discussions and special sessions such as Rashtra Chintan on Sundays—a 90-minute capsule of Sanskrit lessons, Indian history and nationalist ideology.[8]

She says that the boys recite the *Gayatri mantra* or read from the Gita or other religious texts in the morning, evening and during night prayers. In the RSS-style shakha in the morning and evening, students chant Sanskrit mantras. Chattopadhyay also underlines that the entire ambience of the (Mollarpur) hostel is distinctly oriented towards an upper-caste Sanskritized Hindu culture. Apart from the pictures of Birsa Munda, who revolted against the British in 1894, and Sidhu and Kanu, who led a rebellion against the British in 1855, there is little representation of tribal culture in the hostel.[9] Indeed, all education activities run by the VKA give primacy or central space to Hindu values.

It is noteworthy that earlier, only upper-caste male Hindus had the right to recite the Gayatri mantra which was extended to upper-caste women and other castes after the Hindu reform movements of the twentieth century. In this sense, the VKA hostels represent a liberal face of Hinduism, which has been systematically working to accommodate different groups within Hinduism along with the expansion of Hindu values.

The concept of nation underlines most hostel activities and discussions, and patriotic songs are part of the daily prayers. Both morning and evening shakha meetings are dedicated to the nation.[10] However, here the nation is related to Hindutva, which also emphasizes the exclusion of others within the Indian nation-state (primarily Muslims and Christians).[11] It is important to note that in non-tribal areas, Muslims are synonymous with Christians as the dangerous 'other' against whom all Hindus should be united.

It is also true that with the emergence of the BJP–RSS at the Centre and in different states, the recognition of the works of the VKA in the sphere of education has also increased. For instance, former president Ram Nath Kovind, along with Uttar Pradesh Governor Anandiben Patel and Uttar Pradesh Chief Minister Yogi Adityanath, went to Chapki Karidand village in the Sonbhadra district of Uttar Pradesh on 14 March 2021. The President went to inaugurate the new building of the Birsa Munda Vidyalaya and hostel, which is run by an affiliate of the VKA, the Seva Samarpan Sansthan. The President praised the VKA for its constructive work for the welfare of tribals and endorsed the description of vanvasis presented by the VKA by emphasizing that Bhagwan Ram won the battle against Ravana with the help of the vanvasi communities.[12]

There is a similarity between the system of education established by the Christian missionaries and the VKA. Christian missionary schools have indeed been trying directly and indirectly to attract tribal children and youth towards Christianity. On the other hand, the VKA's schools continuously spread Hindu values and rituals among vanvasi (adivasi) students. There is a fundamental difference between these two organizations: whereas in most cases, the Christian missionaries try to create opportunities for tribal students to get higher education, the VKA has been creating minimal opportunities for higher education. Abhay Xaxa has underlined that the Christian missionaries and the VKA work on two distinct models: the VKA model is related to the protection of tribal people, particularly from attempted conversion; the Christian missionaries focus on education, health and social services. Their educational institutions have created enormous awareness among educated tribals regarding their land rights.[13] Undoubtedly, the educational institutions established by Christian missionaries provide far better opportunities for higher education than the VKA. Xaxa's critique of the VKA is partially correct, and it is true that in comparison to Christian missionaries, the VKA provides less opportunity in higher education. Having said that, the VKA has, of course, established hostels in big cities like Delhi to provide better opportunities to tribal youths. Many former residents of the VKA hostels mentioned to the author that VKA hostels played a crucial role in their lives because it provided them with a stable and disciplined setting to complete their education. One former student asserted that all students living with him in the VKA hostel could not go for higher studies due to their family condition and academic orientation, but the VKA office bearers helped those students who wanted to pursue higher education.[14]

The middle/high schools run by the VKA follow the syllabus of the National Council of Educational Research and Training (NCERT). However, teachers accentuated the agenda of the VKA through their teaching style and many extracurricular activities. As mentioned, in the case of hostels, the residents are always trained to follow the Hindu way of life.

However, as far as schools are concerned, it is not necessary that the parents who send their children in the schools run by VKA (and other affiliates of the RSS) also share the RSS/VKA vision of the society. Indeed, for tribal parents, there are other more important factors to consider. As Nandini Sundar has underlined,

> In sum, while religion evidently plays a role, the ultimate criterion for parents in selecting schools appears to be exam results and cost of schooling. In the public perception, RSS schools fare well on results and are affordable for the lower middle class and thus manage to attract a range of children whose parents are not necessarily committed to the Sangh agenda. Children who graduate from these schools, however, seem to end up with a strong sympathy for the Sangh.[15]

It is also noteworthy that it emerged with the interaction of the students studying in the VKA's schools that they were conscious about their Hindu identity, and they did not find any contradiction between their Hindu and tribal identity. Indeed, some High school students of Jharkhand argued that Christian missionaries and Muslim infiltrators from Bangladesh had created problems for the tribals in Jharkhand.[16]

The VKA has always focused on the use of sports as a means to attract tribal youth into its fold. In hostels and schools, sports were an important component, but from 1985, it started a separate sports department, which focuses on organizing sports competitions in tribal areas. The VKA runs 559 daily centres and 1,519 weekly centres,[17] which are separate departments, formally started in 1985. These centres attract youths to participate in sports activities, and they create goodwill for the VKA. The VKA has been organizing the

National Sports Festival for tribal youth in different parts of the country. For example, in 1988, it organized a Rashtriya Vanvasi Krida Pratiyogita (National Vanvasi Sports Competition), a sports festival in Mumbai, and 392 players from fifteen states, participated. Festivals were organized in Indore (1991), Udaipur (1995), Ranchi (2000), Amravati (2005), Pune (2011) and Ranchi (2015), each seeing increasing participation of tribal youth. For instance, at the Amravati Sports Festival, 1,528 tribal players participated. It has also been organizing annual sports festivals focused on games like archery and Kho-Kho etc.[18] In 2024 it was held in Raipur, Chhattisgarh from December 27 to 31, 2024. The Vanvasi Vikas Samiti, an organization affiliated with the All India Vanvasi Kalyan Ashram, organizes the competition.[19] The VKA office-bearers claim that such activities have inculcated a sense of patriotism and community in the hearts of tribal youths. Through these programmes, the VKA not only attracts tribal youth but also tries to spread Hindu values.

The VKA and the Proposals to Make the Education System More Vibrant for Tribals

In 2015, the VKA released the Vision Document[20], which is based on its experiential understanding of various complex issues of tribal life, including education. It recommended numerous steps to improve education facilities in tribal areas and underlined that in the matter of literacy, tribals lag behind the rest of the country. According to Census 2011, the literacy rate for India is 73 per cent, while for STs, 59 per cent, 14 per cent lower. Similarly, the literacy rate of STs is 7 per cent below that of SCs.[21] The Vision Document of the VKA suggests different measures for primary, secondary, and higher levels of education.

The Document underlines that the government should try to establish *anganwadis* (rural childcare centres) in every hamlet for primary education. Anganwadi workers should get supplementary training to integrate child development, inculcating education in health, academics and samskaras. The local cultural values should be given primacy and local dialects should be the medium of education, supplemented by the standard regional language. The local tribal teachers should get primacy for this work, and they must encourage them to create glossaries, dictionaries and multilingual material at every primary school. The Vision Document suggests that at the upper-primary level, students should be given information about local as well as national issues, local traditions, natural resources and technology. It mentions that 'janjati children were proficient in their natural habitat, agriculture, food-gathering, fishing, house-building, etc. These may be incorporated in the curricula for upper primary and secondary stages'. In addition, tribal students should know tribal heroes and freedom fighters, which should be included in the curriculum.[22]

The VKA emphasizes that the social sciences curriculum at the secondary level should give students knowledge about the essential Constitutional provisions, laws and schemes related to STs. It praises the successful experiment of ashram schools in tribal areas and recommends efforts to upgrade them like the Eklavya and Kasturba Vidyalayas. It emphasizes the importance of residential schools and demands that such schools be established in all those blocks where 20 per cent of the population belongs to tribal communities. These schools should give primacy to tribal students and only 25 per cent of non-tribal students should be admitted to such schools. It is noteworthy that the VKA talks about imparting knowledge to tribal students about their traditions, but also focuses on encouraging scientific and technical education.[23]

The VKA also presents a clear framework for the secondary stage (high-school level) of education and underlines that the syllabi must include local traditional knowledge, skills and practice related to language dialects, history and sciences (such as zoology, botany, chemistry, environmental sciences, etc.). It mainly emphasizes the need to preserve and give students knowledge regarding local artefacts and traditional craftsmanship, as well as science and computer laboratories. In addition, the Vision Document focuses on three important matters: first, the student should be given practical knowledge regarding local trade; second, at least 5 per cent of students should be given merit-based scholarships for higher education; and third, there is need to establish a students' exchange programme between tribal and non-tribal students at this level.[24]

The VKA demands that engineering or polytechnic colleges should be opened at the block level in tribal areas, and every university in Scheduled Areas must have a department of tribal studies. A Janjati University should be established at the national level to encourage teaching and research in all disciplines from a tribal perspective. The Centre and state governments should provide tribal students facilities to prepare for all-India competitive exams like Joint Entrance Examination (JEE), Union Public Service Commission (UPSC), etc. The government should also encourage exchange programmes and fellowships for tribal students with foreign universities. Tribal students must be encouraged to be teachers in their areas or join the police or armed forces, and the government should help them in this goal.[25] It is noteworthy that the VKA welcomed the draft and the final National Education Policy (NEP), 2020 of the Government of India because it gives importance to primary education in the mother tongue, emphasizes on scholarships for tribal students to motivate them to become teachers and underlines the importance of vocational education. All these points are an integral part of the VKA's Vision Document. However, some senior VKA activists criticized NEP for not taking a clear stand on contract teaching, and for missing a critical chance to address the inequalities in the education system.[26]

The NEP incorporates many aspects of tribal education given in the Vision Document. It accepts that tribal children should be given education at an early stage in their dialects, and at the middle/higher level they must be taught about Constitutional rights. It also recommends that *ashram-shalas* (schools with hostels) should be established in tribal areas. Certainly, this idea is influenced by the VKA's recommendations in its Vision Document. Like the VKA, the NEP also emphasized that tribal students should be taught traditional knowledge along with scientific foundations and the use of technology to expand skill development. The NEP wishes to decolonize the whole education system and asserts that Indian values should be enhanced through education. However, like the Vision Document of the VKA, there is a danger that the NEP will enhance Hindu values in the name of 'Indian values'. Though many recommendations of the NEP are attractive, there is no clear provision for budget allotment. If the state becomes dependent on the private sector to implement these policy measures, it will lead to the exclusion of poor and marginalized communities, including tribals.[27]

The VKA has also taken a stand on the crucial issues related to the interest of STs in government jobs, including jobs in higher education institutions. For example, it took an unambiguous and sharp stand on the controversy related to the rejection of the 200-point roster system in favour of the thirteen-point roster system in jobs in higher education. In April 2017, the Allahabad High Court gave a negative verdict that had a far-reaching impact on the Constitutional scheme of reservation for scheduled castes and scheduled tribes in teaching posts and vacancies in the central higher educational institutions (universities and colleges affiliated to them).[28] In 2018, this judgment was approved by the Supreme Court of India. The Ministry of Human Resource Development (MHRD) and the University Grants Commission (UGC) submitted a Special Leave Petition against this judgment before the Supreme Court. On 22 January 2019, the Supreme Court dismissed these two petitions also. The Supreme Court also rejected review petitions filed by the MHRD and UGC on 27 February 2019.[29]

The VKA opposed the judgment for implementing a thirteen-point roster and instead supported a 200-point roster. The key difference between a 200-point roster and a thirteen-point roster was that while the former used an institution as a unit, the latter used a department within the institution as a unit. It was argued by many organizations, including the VKA, that since the thirteen-point roster would not treat the institution as one unit, the entry of ST candidates at teaching institutions of higher education would be closed. The VKA expressed its deep disappointment with this verdict and argued that introducing a thirteen-point reservation roster will completely block the recruitment of STs in faculty. It also underlined that between 5,000 to 6,000 vacancies were reported in the higher education institutions of which 350 to 400 places were assured for STs in the old reservation roster system. However, in the new system, they would not be able to get even thirty places!

The HRD minister stated in Parliament that the government would not let the Constitutional rights of the weaker sections of society suffer. Reminding the minister of this assurance, the VKA demanded that the Centre bring an ordinance fulfilling its Constitutional obligations and that there was no option but the ordinance. Considering the sensitivity and probable fallout of this issue that would cause grave injustice to janjatis, the Centre must bring an ordinance restoring the old reservation system of 200 points in higher education institutions. It underlined that the janjatis, SCs, OBCs, and differently abled persons cannot afford to wait for six months for a new government to form to address this burning issue.[30] The government restored the 200-point roster through an ordinance on 7 March 2019. The government introduced The Central Educational Institutions (Reservation in Teachers' Cadre) Bill, 2019 in the Lok Sabha on 27 June 2019. It was passed by both houses of the Parliament and after the President's assent, it became law on 9 July 2919.[31] Indeed, this issue underlined VKA's intent to take a stand for the interests and rights of marginalized sections, particularly tribals.

Medical Services and the VKA

Like Christian missionaries, the VKA has also focused on providing medical facilities to tribal people. According to Snehlata Vaid, the primary motive behind starting medical facilities was to counter the work of the missionaries because tribal people 'convert into Christianity after getting one tablet by the priest of the church'.[32] The VKA has established hospitals in Chhattisgarh, Jharkhand, and many other places. It tries to stem malnutrition among tribals and provides primary healthcare, organizes health camps and runs around 400 medical centres, including a few big hospitals.[33]

The VKA began medical services at the suggestion of sarsanghchalak M.S. Golwalkar, when he had come to Jashpur to inaugurate the VKA's new building. He suggested that 'our schools and hostels are good. We should start medical services'.[34] Due to his inspiration, an ayurvedic hospital was established in Jashpur in 1965. Radhika Ladha presents an anecdote that underlines the philosophy behind the medical services provided by the VKA. According to her, in 1967–68, Eknath Gore, a wealthy man from Mumbai, gave a proposal to Deshpande regarding foreign help to establish hospitals and other works of the VKA. However, Deshpande rejected it and focused on the opening of small dispensaries in tribal areas. He felt that small dispensaries were ideal for an organization dedicated to social service; would enhance the reach of the VKA; and mobilize tribal people for a larger cause. He felt critical patients could be sent to Ranchi.[35]

Table 4: Medical Services of the VKA

Daily Centre	19
Village Health Workers (Arogya Rakshak)	4,982
Hospitals	8
Any Other (Mobile Health Centres)	2
Total Beneficiaries	6,49,259

Source: ABVKA (2023b), Karyavrit, November, Bhagyanagar, Telangana, in *Van Bandhu* (November 2023), p. 60.

Table 4 mentions the permanent structure of the medical services of the VKA. With the help of around 2,000 doctors (most of them are not permanently with the VKA), it organizes approximately 1,500 health camps annually including regular and surgical health camps.[36] It also organizes special health camps and distributes medicines to eye patients or for illnesses-related to itching or stomach problems. The VKA organizes a cataract operation camp in the Birsa Seva Sadan of Lohardaga (Jharkhand) twice a month, attended by a doctor from Ranchi. Dr Pankaj Kumar Bhatia, the president of the All-India Medical Department (Akhil Bharatiya Chikitsa Ayam) of the

VKA, says that in Assam the *sangathan mantri* (organization secretary) of the VKA, gets patients from villages and facilitates their operations in Guwahati with the help of the Rotary Club and the Lions Club. The VKA also operates medical camps during emergencies. For example, after the tsunami of 2010 in the Andamans, the VKA established a medical camp there, which later became a hospital. Similarly, VKA medical activists worked during floods in Assam and Kerala.[37]

The VKA teaches first aid to at least one man and one woman in each village every year and provides them with a medical kit. These trained persons are called *argoya rakshaks* (Health Protectors) and they help fellow villagers in emergencies and make them aware of the primary health facilities in the village. The VKA has so far trained 4,982 villagers as health protectors (See Table 4). In Uttarakhand, 300 workers of the VKA run tuition centres in the mountainous villages in the interiors and also provide primary health facilities. Senior VKA activists argue that through these measures, the workers have largely prevented conversions. Bhatia claims that the government praised their tireless work during an earthquake in Sikkim. In Maharashtra, these health workers use an ayurvedic kit and Paracetamol tablets and help thousands of tribals. Over the years, many doctors also help out.[38]

The VKA also runs primary medical centres, where trained MBBS doctors come every day, and specialist doctors, weekly. At present, the VKA has thirty-one day-to-day primary medical centres and 131 weekly centres. In addition, it has established a weekly medical centre at Melghat (Maharashtra), where in 1997, many children died of hunger. It also has twenty-four ambulances which helps tribals in Andhra Pradesh and Telangana.[39]

The VKA runs fourteen hospitals with the help of other organizations. Kerala's Swami Vivekananda Medical Mission situated in Mutil was established by former sangathan mantri Bhaskar Rao. In 1965, a Dharmarth Chikitsalay was established in Jashpur, while in 1971, a Dr Shilendar from Nagpur established a hospital in Lohardaga (Jharkhand) called the Birsa Seva Kendra. Different doctors regularly visit these hospitals which ensure tribals get treatment since the primary health system in these areas is poor.[40] The VKA organizes conferences in tribal areas of Maharashtra and Chhattisgarh, among other states, and invites *van vaidyas* (forest doctors) to discuss the use and importance of herbs available in the forests. They have no formal MBBS degree, but they know about different herbs and their use for human health, and most of them have degrees in Bachelor of Ayurvedic Medicine and Surgery (BAMS). Due to the efforts of the VKA, the Chhattisgarh forest department has issued identity cards to such doctors. These conferences also discuss many diseases and their possible herbal cure. For example, two herbal remedies for malaria were cleared at a conference: two neem leaves every day for two years will keep the person immune from malaria forever; drinking the kadha (decoction) of Chirayata or Bhuin Neem for two months will ensure immunity to malaria.[41] There could be a debate between ayurvedic and allopathic experts regarding the scientific basis of such suggestions, but the use of such herbs has been immensely helpful for tribals to tackle many health-related problems in their day-to-day lives. It is also true that the use of such ayurvedic methods is now very popular, not only in India but world over.[42]

As mentioned in Table 4, in 2023, the total number of annual beneficiaries of the VKA's health resources was approximately 6,49,259. But Bhatia claims that with the help of other resources, the VKA provides medical services to between 12 and 15 lakh people every year.[43] Moreover, it is trying to expand its work to reach the interior areas, where people are deprived of basic medical facilities. The extent of the work of the VKA is less than Christian missionaries, but it does provide healthcare to many tribal communities.

The VKA's Suggestions for Better Health Facilities in Tribal Areas

Based on its vast experience in health-related works in tribal areas, the VKA has suggested many crucial steps to improve health services in these areas. In its Vision Document, the VKA accepts that a combination of diverse factors, like geographic isolation, poor economic conditions, absence of livelihood and nutritious food, and lack of adequate hospitals and health providers, have created a problem of quality healthcare in tribal areas. The mortality rate in all age groups of tribal communities is much higher than the rest of India's population.[44] The VKA praises programmes like midday meal schemes in tribal areas but suggests that the government should prepare a more focused programme for nutritious food in backward tribal regions also. It appreciates the Modi government's 'Swachh Bharat Abhiyan' for creating awareness about sanitation and suggests that since trained healthcare workers do not want to work in tribal areas, the government should think about establishing a separate cadre for the healthcare professionals in Scheduled Areas. It should establish special medical colleges and other institutions for this cadre. Until this kind of system exists, the government must focus on encouraging paramedical forces to work in tribal habitats. Based on its medical services, it also suggests creating mobile medical units and ensuring the availability of ambulances in every block to transfer patients from remote areas to better hospitals.[45] The VKA also underlines the need to do serious research on diseases of tribal areas.

The VKA argues that given the considerable prevalence of alcohol and tobacco addiction among the scheduled tribes, special awareness drives need to be undertaken. Besides healthcare professionals, community and religious leaders may also be involved in building a powerful movement against addiction. In addition, healthcare facilities in these areas must be equipped and professionals working there trained to undertake de-addiction activities.[46] This point is crucial because it shows that the VKA is not ready to abandon tribal communities to their habits in the name of 'tradition' and prefers intervention to 'reform' the 'negative' aspects of tribal culture. It is also true that while it does not support the idea of prohibition in tribal areas, alcohol is prohibited in VKA offices. It is noteworthy that Gandhi also talked about reforms in the context of alcohol consumption in tribal areas and the Constituent Assembly discussed the issue of alcohol prohibition in tribal areas. Jaipal Singh Munda opposed it and he argued that alcohol consumption is part of adivasi life and culture and a ban would be an unnecessary intervention in their lifestyle. Consequently, the Constitutional Assembly did not accept the proposal of a total ban on alcohol and put it into the chapter of the Directive Principle of state Policy.[47]

Attempt to Create Ideal 'Hindu' Women: The VKA and Its Women's Work

The VKA has encouraged tribal women to participate in collective life outside the family and has formed self-help groups for different types of work. It is essential to note that though it tries to make women capable of taking their own decisions and being self-dependent, it also foists many traditional Hindu rituals on their lives. The website of the VKA presents a description of its women's work and says,

> In our country, women are like epitome of power and they are creators. As far as tribal society is concerned, the women not only take care of their household but also help in the work related to agriculture, animal husbandry, etc. They also bring firewood from the forest. In all vanvasi areas, one can find women present in market spaces in larger numbers, not only just as buyers, but they also do business. There are many villages in the country where justice panchayats work and, in their meetings, the voice and opinions of women are given special importance. There are many tribal areas in the North-east, where women have a central position in the home and the larger society.
>
> Many women have been active in the VKA since its formation. However, when Lilabai Pardkar joined the VKA, a systematic programme of women's work developed. She joined as a full-timer in 1973 in Jashpur. Gradually, the women's work expanded. A national convention was organized in 1981, in which 250 women activists participated. Later on, such conventions were organized at different places, and now women work in different tribal areas, along with the other works of the VKA.[48]

Undoubtedly, the foremost aim of the VKA is to spawn faith in the minds of tribal women regarding the different rituals of Hinduism. Snehlata Vaid underlines that women activists of the VKA conduct many activities in tribal areas related to popularizing Hindu cultural practices among tribal women. For example, the practice of offering pure water to Lord Shiva has been integral part of the worshipping among the Hindu women of north India. The VKA has tried to establish this practice among tribal women too. The VKA has organized a 'Satsang Kendra' (centre for religious discussions) in the North Cachar (NC) Hills of Assam, it mobilized women to recite songs dedicated to Lord Shiva. The women activists of the VKA also run 'Bal Sanskar Kendras' (moral, spiritual, cultural educational programme for children) in different states.[49] Even though such activities are essentially cultural and/or religious in nature, tribal women are now going beyond their immediate families and connecting with the larger community which helps them diversify their activities which are based on traditional art or collecting forest produce.

It is noteworthy that women (both tribal and otherwise) are working in tribal areas in different departments of the VKA like education, medical services, and interest protection. The VKA has also established hostels for girls in different tribal and urban areas to provide better educational and career-related opportunities. Studies of the VKA's girls' hostels have revealed that there is a code of conduct for residents related to the values of Hinduism. For example, the Shabri Kanya Ashram is a women's hostel run by the VKA in Raipur, and one of their fourteen hostels in Chhattisgarh and houses thirty-seven school-going adolescents from the North-east. The girls have a packed day. They wake up before sunrise and assemble for *jagran prarthana* (daily prayers), followed by yoga, including the Surya Namaskar. Then there is a Ramayana reading and *svadhyay* (self-study) of the Vedas and other Sanskrit texts. Then they go to their school, the Saraswati Shishu Mandir, less than a minute away from the hostel; in the evening they line up in front of a saffron flag and chant Sanskrit shlokas. After that, they play Kabbadi, tug-of-war and some girls also learn archery. After one hour of play, they go to their rooms to freshen up and then they gather in a hall on the first floor and sit cross-legged in front of a small temple where there are images of gods like Ganesha, Shiva and Saraswati. They sing bhajans and then collectively chant, 'Jai Shree Ram', 'Hindu Dharm ki Jai', etc.[50] Interestingly, the warden of the hostel, Madhvi Joshi, who is a senior activist of the VKA since 1981, denies the claim that they are Hinduizing tribals; 'they are Hindus', she emphasizes.[51] Though there is a discipline in the VKA's girls' hostels based on Hindu values, it does not prohibit girls from participating in different activities conducted by the VKA, like sports festivals. They have actively contributed to papers and magazines published by the VKA in different state units. In a nutshell, women activists play an important role in the functioning of different departments of the VKA.[52]

The VKA tries to create a system in tribal areas so that women can use their traditional knowledge for career options. It has also started certain programmes for the formation of self-help groups and the development of small-scale collectives. In Karnataka, the VKA is working to empower the women of the 'Jenu Kurba' tribal community, primarily situated in Mysore, Chamrajanagar and Coorg districts. 'Jenu' is a word in Kannada, which means honey and collecting honey is the key source of their livelihood. With a population of around 40,000, the community is backward and isolated and the Indian government has included them in the category of the Particularly Vulnerable Tribal Group (PVTG). The VKA has started a sewing training centre in the Udpur Hadi village, where thirty Jenu Kuruba women regularly come for three hours to work on sewing machines. The training begins after the lightning of the lamp before a picture of Bharat Mata. They are also taught patriotic songs here.[53] Young women from thirty-two villages of this tribal community, teach school children at the 'Manepata Kendra' (coaching centre), which while providing employment, also creates an environment for education. The VKA also works to provide benefits of the government's programmes to the members of this community, particularly women. Its workers helped the Gram Samiti make Aadhar cards, ration cards and voter cards for 500 people and ensured the payment of pensions to around 300 tribal women.[54]

The VKA has also glorified those tribal women activists and fighters who struggled against foreign rulers (not only British, but also Mughals). Rani Gaidinliu and Rani Durgavati are two such tribal women characters, who have been adopted and popularized by the VKA. Rani Gaidinliu fought against British rule, but the VKA has also always presented her as a fighter who opposed the activities of Christian missionaries, and supported Hindu values.[55] Similarly, it praises many tribal women warriors who fought against Muslim rulers, particularly, Rani Durgavati, Sinagi Dai and Kaili Dai. Recently, a VKA delegation met with President Droupadi Murmu and informed her about their work.[56]

The VKA office-bearers claim that it has always supported more representation and an active role for women in public and political life. To validate this point they underline that the VKA has continously supported the reservation of seats for women in representative bodies, including panchayati raj institutions, legislative assemblies, and the Parliament.[57] It welcomed the enactment of 'Nari Shakti Vandan Adhiniyam' by the Parliament, which proposes 33 per cent reservations for women and separate reservations for janjati women within it.[58] In its press release, the VKA underlined that 'the voice of Nari Shakti will now echo in Parliament and the Vidhan Sabhas'.[59]

VKA activists claim that the leadership of their organization has always tried to include tribal women and it inculcates the values of service and dedication to the RSS ideology and takes care of them. Many prominent leaders of the VKA, including Ramakant Deshpande, Vasantrao Bhatt, Bhaskar Rao, etc., have particularly encouraged women to work in tribal areas, and its leaders have always given primacy to create a safe and familial atmosphere for women activists. However, the relationship between male and female activists and the division of work has been determined by following some traditional and patriarchal norms. A senior pracharak of the RSS, Jagdamba Mall, worked in the North-east and played a critical role in expanding the VKA in this area, particularly in Nagaland. He asserts that in the late 1970s and early 1980s, Vasantrao Bhatt was the organization secretary (sangathan mantri). He was very concerned about the safety of the women activists in the North-east and wanted an older woman to take care of women activists.[60] Of course, it was a valid concern, but it seems that he wanted to put certain restrictions on their activities.

> On one occasion, senior Pracharak, Rambhau Godbole, participated in a meeting of the VKA workers of Nagaland in Deemapur, and Vasantrao was also present in the meeting. Rambhau expressed a critical point regarding the behaviour of the workers with each other. He emphasized that male workers should have good relations with male workers in work areas, and female workers should maintain good relations with female workers. However, the male and female members should have close relations only within a limit. They should treat each other as brothers and sisters. The unnecessary closeness between male and female workers can create a possibility of disgrace. Indeed, both Rambhau and Vasantroo keep repeating this clear message to the young workers.[61]

The situation has not changed within the VKA and it controls the agency of its workers vis-à-vis their personal choices. Creating a fearless, cordial and safe work environment is crucial for making women comfortable in any organization. However, instructing them to treat all male members as 'brothers' is undue control.[62]

Though the VKA eulogizes Rani Gaidinliu and Rani Durgavati, it prefers to spread Hindu family values among tribal women. It tries to make women self-reliant while underlining the importance of family values. Since as an organization, it does not believe in any kind of confrontation with government agencies and any radical challenge to family values, its women activists are not reactionary enough to mobilize any movement against the excessive behaviour of forest department officials in their area or challenge the patriarchal mindset of male activists or their family members. During my fieldwork in Dudhwa National Park (DNP), I studied a women's organization, Tharu Adivasi Mahila Mazdoor Kisan Manch (TAMMKM).

The comparison between TAMMKM and VKA provides crucial insights regarding the limitations of the VKA. First, the TAMMKM's concern is to ensure the rights of local communities, particularly women, over forest resources. It has used the strategy of mobilization and litigation against forest department officials. The VKA is a much larger organization than the TAMMKM, and the struggle for forest rights of women is just one facet of its work. Both organizations claim to work to create more opportunities for women.

Second, the TKMMKM has made Tharu tribal women conscious of the value of education. They are informed about patriarchy and encouraged to oppose the misbehaviour of their husbands and other family members. The VKA, on the other hand, has never used the term patriarchy in its meetings or published literature, and it always emphasizes the family value system. Undoubtedly, the VKA underlines the importance of education of girls/women and making them self-dependent. It does not encourage foundational questions related to gender inequality.

Third, for the TKMMKM the religious identity of the tribals is not the key factor. It only emphasizes on the liberty of tribal men and women to follow their religious faith. For the VKA, however, religious identity of tribal men and women is the most crucial aspect and its aim is to spread Hindu values among them. So, unlike TKMMKM, the VKA's idea of empowerment of women is related to giving them certain rights and opportunities, but it does not allow them to question deep-rooted patriarchal structures within the society.[63]

Village Development, Skill Enhancement and Protection of Migrated Tribals

Village development is another important aspect of the VKA. This overlaps with different works earlier mentioned in this chapter like education, medical services and making rural women empowered. Senior activist, Kripa Prasad Singh, underlines that '[T]otal development of a village means you have to think about the empowerment of women, empowerment of traditions and cultures, value addition of village products and available material of village like river sand, water, forest wood, forest produce, etc'.[64] So, through village development, the VKA focuses on the holistic development of tribal villages.

The VKA has emphatically argued for conserving traditional knowledge, developing new skills in tribal communities and creating a bridge between them and the market. It argues that since janjatis are traditionally highly skilled communities, using forest resources and making beautiful and valuable items from bamboo and metal, they need to recognize their skills and create more opportunities. It also praises their skills in carrying out cultivation under challenging situations, and their traditional way of seed selection and preservation, preparation, and sowing of the fields, cleaning and weeding, using limited water resources, etc. The VKA demands that the government establish an institutional mechanism to perpetuate tribal skills from one generation to another and enrich them with requisite modern technologies. The spread of their traditional skills and the different objects they produce would enrich their livelihood and create more connectivity between them and other societies. The VKA also emphasizes protecting the environment of tribal villages.

To achieve these goals, the VKA suggests important measures: first, the schools in tribal areas should teach students their traditions, and engineering colleges in tribal areas should teach and document different local skills and teach students about modern technologies, which can promote traditional skills.[65] Second, medical colleges, especially the ayurvedic colleges in the janjati areas, should be mandated to collect and document herbal and therapeutic knowledge available in the communities within a defined geographical area. Students and faculty in these institutions should be encouraged to research their traditions and find ways to connect with new technologies. Third, while the National Skill Development Policy has given space to tribal communities to enhance their skills, the Ministry of Skill Development should focus on the needs of tribal communities and work to update traditional skills. In this context, the vision document makes particular reference to the Prime Minister Kaushal Vikas Yojna (PMKVY). It demands that different ministries of the Union government allocate finances for skill development of tribal communities.[66]

The VKA has raised issues that tribal organizations do not discuss readily, like the problem of bonded labour and human trafficking. Indeed, in many areas, both tribal men and women migrate to rural or urban areas (including metropolitan cities) of non-tribal regions to earn a livelihood. Tribal men face the trauma of forced and bonded labour, whereas women, apart from the same problems, can be forced into prostitution. The VKA emphasizes the need to update laws related to such problems and that state governments should implement these laws properly. The officers who implement laws against bonded labour and human trafficking must be trained and sensitized about the complexities of these issues. The VKA suggests that migrant workers be allowed to use their voting rights either in their home state or in the state they have migrated to. It also demands the formation of Special Courts to adjudicate matters related to bonded labour and human trafficking and create a special cell by the Ministry of Tribal Affairs (MoTA) to help tribals. It also suggests that Gram Sabhas maintain a register of persons who migrated for their livelihood.[67]

The Quest to Create a Feeling of Attachment: The VKA and Its Urban Work

Since the VKA is the tribal wing of the RSS, it has always had an urban connect and it desires that urban people feel a sense of belonging for tribals. Their slogan, '*Vanvasi, Nagarvasi, Ham Sab Bharatvasi*' (forest-dwellers, urban-dwellers, we are all Indians), encapsulates this ethos. It organizes programmes to create awareness among urban people regarding the handicrafts and the cultural values of tribal people, while the VKA's hostels in urban areas give tribal boys and girls the opportunity to study and live in cities or small towns. VKA founder Ramakant Deshpande always underlined the importance of creating a feeling of *ekatm bhav* (unity and oneness) within society. Snehlata Vaid also emphasized that 'the work of the Kalyan Ashram (the VKA) is to construct ekatm bhav. When we contact each other, we develop acquaintance, and gradually we become close and a feeling of sympathy emerges, which naturally makes relations deeper . . .'[68]

To ensure ekatm bhav, the VKA has consciously worked for social harmony between urban people and tribals and its activists have always been in a dialogue with other constituents of the RSS. However, from 1983 onwards more than 200 activists from urban areas like Ranchi, Kolkata, Sambalpur, Raigarh, Ambikapur, Bilaspur, etc., went to work in forest areas with the VKA to establish close contact with tribals. Gradually, the urban work the VKA did was accepted and the Urban Committees and Urban Women Committees were formed.[69] The Urban Committees work in around 300 towns and Urban Women Committees are active in around 119 towns. An Urban Committee can form other committees to enhance its work.

Through Urban Committees, the VKA tries to develop a sense of belonging among urban people regarding the life and cultural values in tribal areas. It tries to develop a connection both at the level of ideation and emotion and organizes annual functions centred around tribal culture. An example of such a programme is the Janjatiya Gaurav Divas on 15 November to celebrate the life and works of Birsa Munda. On this date in 2019, the Delhi unit of the VKA organized a programme, where speakers discussed the life of Birsa Munda, even as the entire programme was a reflection of the ideological outlook of the VKA and RSS. The poet Rajendra Solanki recited a poem on the Ram Mandir and the abolition of Article 370 of the Constitution.[70]

The VKA organizes visits of different tribal groups in urban areas to present their dances, songs, and other aspects of their lives. For example, in April 2019, the VKA, Haryana, organized a visit of fifty-five students from the North-east who live and study at the VKA Eklavya Hostel in Bhiwani, to Amritsar in Punjab.[71] The VKA organizes functions that publicize the uniqueness of tribal life through audio-visuals. Their monthly magazine and other publications attempt to make urban people aware of the complex issues of tribal areas and their press conferences draw public opinion to the problems of tribals. The VKA has begun expanding to towns and in 2018 it formally started work in Amritsar and the urban committee organized its first annual function in August 2019 inaugurated by the then VKA president Jagdev Ram Oraon. The students of Shahid Jadonang Hostel of VKA's Narela facility in Delhi, presented a cultural programme attended by 400 people. Here, Oraon requested help in the works of the VKA.[72]

The VKA also arranged visits to tribal areas to allow urban families understand the grave difficulties of tribal life and the challenges faced from an international and disruptive force (Christian missionaries). It also educates these urban people to the different facets of the VKA's works and motivates them to contribute to the development and welfare of tribal society through their professional expertise. For example, it requests doctors to visit tribal areas for health camps; veterinary doctors help with animal husbandry; a teacher's monthly visit or after a certain interval, can motivate tribal students living in the hostels of the VKA, etc. The VKA also urges different sections of society to help tribal people in towns. So, an advocate can help and guide tribals in legal matters; urban people can help ease the way for tribal students living in urban areas. It often arranges the visits of tribal students to urban areas and organizes community feasts or inter-dining where people from tribal communities and urban people eat together. It also uses *Raksha Bandhan* (the ceremony of a bond of protection between a brother and sister) to create social harmony between tribal and urban people.[73]

Urban activists are encouraged to provide tribals with better techniques and markets to sell their handicrafts or Minor Forest Produces (MFPs). New techniques help them to minimize cost of their production and increase efficiency. For example, providing a tractor to a village could increase agricultural production. This kind of intervention is crucial because most of the tribal villages are still using old methods to do agricultural work.

The VKA also helps tribals minimize the role of middlemen and ensures better prices for tribal people for handicrafts or MFPs. The VKA inspires urban people to contribute to the VKA, for example, in some shops, it put a *seva patra* (service box) where the shops contribute a certain amount every month. The VKA also organizes annual campaigns, different schemes, to get contributions from different sections of urban society. For instance, the 'Mangal Smriti Yojna', is a scheme where families donate money on any happy occasion within the family, while the 'Van Mitra Yojna' works in schools where urban students help tribal students.[74] Indeed, financial help from urban people is the key element of the urban works of the VKA. For example, at the annual function of the Delhi urban unit of the VKA, the keynote speaker was national executive council member and senior pracharak of the RSS, Indresh Kumar, who requested the people of Delhi to help the VKA.[75]

All these aspects of urban work make it an important department within the VKA. People do not always contribute selflessly; sometimes the purpose is to develop a close relationship with the VKA office-bearers and RSS pracharaks and derive benefits thereof. The VKA uses urban committees to give persons a sense of belonging to the RSS. In cities like Delhi, the VKA's urban unit organizes different programmes and creates a consciousness in the minds of urban people regarding tribal life, culture and their problems.

The VKA also has a 'Prachar Aayam' (publicity department) which focuses on the spread of information regarding the works and ideology of the VKA. On the one hand, it tries to provide information to the tribal people, and on the other hand, it creates awareness about the works of the VKA in non-tribal areas. It uses different methods for its works, which include the publication of pamphlets and magazines and social media platforms like YouTube and WhatsApp etc. It focuses on countering different kinds of narratives, that are against the basic ideology of the VKA, which includes a tendency to present tribals as adivasis or non-Hindus.[76]

Summing Up

Malini Bhattacharjee has underlined that 'a series of affiliates of RSS such as VKA, VHP, Vidya Bharati and Seva Bharti . . . adopted seva as an important strategy in furthering the agenda of Hindutva.'[77] Indeed all the above-mentioned seva works have created a positive image of the VKA in tribal areas. Through its available resources, the VKA has always tried to help people in challenging situations and extended its footprint in tribal areas by changing the lives of thousands of tribals through its programmes. The VKA has argued that its works have been overlooked by scholars and media and decades ago, its founder Ramakant Deshpande lamented that,

> Many persons have a soft corner for Christian missionaries' work in the form of establishing educational, and medical institutions and helping people in times of natural calamities. Mainly English media gives them significant space. However, the similar social service and humanitarian works carried out by Hindus and their organizations do not get due recognition. The Christian missionaries do relief works and services in times of natural calamity, but all their works are solely designed to convert the sufferers.[78]

The VKA has been trying to spread Hindu values in tribal areas through its works. Since the VKA considers tribals as vanvasis (forest-dwelling Hindus), it uses such activities to exert influence in the lives of tribals and embrace them within the fold of one religious group—Hinduism. In the North-east, the

VKA and its affiliates do not claim that all tribals are Hindus, but they use the idea of 'indigenous religion' to assert that all tribal groups are closer to Sanatan Dharma and Christian missionaries are representing foreign forces and they should be resisted. Interestingly, one can find that the VKA's seva works generally follows the model of the Christian missionaries and largely focuses on those areas (like education and medical services, etc.,) where missionaries have been working before them. However, unlike missionaries, the VKA's works have been used by a political party—the BJP—for its benefits and the party has utilized it to create a strong base in many tribal areas of the country.[79] They have also extended their works on the issues related to tribal rights over land and forest resources. This aspect will be explored in the next chapter.

5

Forest Resources, Tribal Rights and the Vanvasi Kalyan Ashram

The VKA's core agenda when it was formed was to resist the influence of Christian missionaries in tribal areas; the rights of tribals over forest resources were not a big consideration. It adopted many measures like shradha jagran, education, medical services, etc., and tribal rights came much later on the agenda. In the first four decades of its work, VKA activists helped many vanvasis on an individual basis to ensure concessions or better payment by contractors. However, this work was minimal and there was no systematic attempt to raise the issue of forest rights until the formation of the 'Hit Raksha Vibhag' (Interest Protection Department) in 1990.[1] That was when the VKA finally took a stand on issues of village autonomy, forest rights and extension of Constitutional provisions in new tribal areas. This chapter probes whether the VKA has successfully secured the rights of tribals on their forest land and its resources and its works on PESA [Panchayats (Extension to Scheduled Areas) Act of 1996 and FRA (Forest Rights Act)]. It also discusses many other issues related to the extension of the Fifth Schedule areas, displacement, etc. The chapter explores whether the VKA has been successful in influencing government policies at the Centre or in BJP-held states. It attempts to compare and contrast the VKA's differences with a Left-oriented tribal organization All India Union for Forest Working People (AIUFWP). In this context, it focuses primarily on their policies and strategies regarding the forest rights of the tribal communities.

The chapter has five sections: the first section evaluates the background of the formation of the 'Hit Raksha Vibhag' or HRV (Interest Protection Department) and its initial position on and the key elements of the PESA and the FRA, and its work in tribal areas on the issues related to forest rights. The second section evaluates the key points that emerged in the Vision Document released by the VKA in 2015. It is a crucial document because it encapsulates the basic premise of the VKA on different issues related to tribal forest rights. The third section evaluates the work and the stand of the VKA on forest rights in the last few years (after the formation of the Modi government). The fourth section focuses on the VKA's stand to make tribal areas more inclusive. The fifth section of the chapter compares the VKA's understanding and strategy on forest rights issues with the AIUFWP.

Formation of the 'Hit Raksha Vibhag' and Issues of Forest Rights

The struggle for forest rights in post-independence India began in the late 1970s. Before Independence, tribal people vehemently opposed the extraction of natural resources from tribal-dominated areas, which resulted in revolts. However, colonial rulers managed to establish a legal system to extract natural resources from the forest areas of India to fulfil their imperial interests. To control the tribal revolts, they also gave them certain rights through the creation of 'excluded' and 'partially excluded areas' and enacting laws like the Scheduled Districts Act of 1874 and the Chota Nagpur Tenancy Act of 1908. The Constitution of Independent India also makes some crucial provisions for the welfare of scheduled tribes with special provisions for Schedule V and Schedule VI areas. However, the extraction of forest resources continues under the name 'national development', which creates dispossession for tribal communities. There is also a tendency to centralize forest management through laws like the *Wildlife (Protection) Act* of 1972 and the *Forest Conservation Act* of 1980. A distinct process started after the Emergency, and various grassroots movements emerged in tribal areas, which raised the issue of dispossession and displacement of the tribal communities and thereby created some awareness. In many places, tribal people started to question and oppose the arbitrary behaviour of the FD officials.[2]

The 'Hit Raksha Vibhag'[3] was established in 1990 to formally extend the works of the VKA in areas related to the protection of the livelihood of tribals and their ownership over forest land and its resources. In conjunction with other organizations, the issue of the rights of tribals over forest resources became part of the discourse of tribal social and political life. The VKA realized that it could no longer ignore the livelihood issues of tribals and the formation of the HRV became a part of its fundamental goal of spreading Hindu values in tribal society and resisting the influence of Christian missionaries.[4] It could be treated as complementary to the key agenda of the VKA because the works of 'Hit Raksha Vibhag' have enhanced the credibility of the VKA in tribal areas.[5]

The PESA was enacted in 1996, and it extends Panchayati Raj institutions in the Fifth Schedule areas. Its enactment was a result of the demand for more powers by adivasis to manage local affairs based on their customs and to ensure their rights over local community lands and resources. The B.D. Sharma-led 'Bharat Jan Andolan' and other grassroots organizations participated in a movement for the enactment of the PESA between 1994–96,[6] but the VKA stayed away though it supported the idea of the PESA. The PESA is an important law, which extends the Panchayati Raj system in Fifth Schedule areas and recognizes that the gram sabha has the right to be consulted on matters of land acquisition. It has the power to act on many crucial issues related to tribal rights in Fifth Schedule areas, such as land alienation, minor forest products, and control of money lending to the STs, etc. It underlines that an organic self-governing community, that is, *tola/para* or hamlet, is the basic unit of self-governance and has the right to preserve their culture and resources. It presents a framework for the autonomous gram sabha in Fifth Schedule areas.[7]

Similarly, there was a systematic movement for enacting the FRA. The Campaign for Survival and Dignity (CSD) emerged as an umbrella organization to mobilize and coordinate many grassroots tribal organizations in favour of the FRA. It should be noted that in 2002 the FD demolished the houses/huts of tribals, based on an order of the Supreme Court to clear all 'encroached' forest land. This brutal activity of the FD (in Assam, FD officials used elephants to demolish houses of tribals) worked as an immediate reason for the demand for a law for recognizing land rights for the forest-dwelling communities.[8] The VKA was not part of the CSD, but it supported forest rights for forest-dwelling communities. In its 'Karyakari Mandal Meeting' on 26 September 2002, the VKA condemned the FD for demolishing houses of tribals by wrongly interpreting an order of the Supreme Court. The VKA resolution did not directly accuse the FD of wrongdoing, and it underlined that the Chairman of the Scheduled Areas and Scheduled Tribes Commission invited VKA workers to visit the demolished houses of the tribal people in the Golaghat, Kalakandi, and Cachar districts of Assam. The resolution mentioned that the Inspector General of Forests, Ministry of Environment and Forest (MoEF) had issued a letter dated 5 March to all state governments to clear all encroachments by 30 September 2002. However, 'the main target in the circular letter is forest mafia which has grown into a powerful lobby in spite of the stringent provisions of the Forest (Conservation) Act of 1980'.[9] It also accepted that instead of 'forest mafia the poor tribals are being chased allegedly without even following the due process'.[10] It emphasized that all problems related to the so-called 'encroachment' should be addressed according to the 1990 circular of the Ministry of Environment and Forest (MoEF). It underlined the following points from the 1990 circular vis-à-vis disputes related to the encroachment that should be followed: 1) clear identification of disputed claims according to category and also encroachment on forest land, both eligible and non-eligible for regularization in association with concerned gram sabha; 2) examination of each case individually based on all relevant evidence, including official documents by a committee comprising forest, revenue and tribal welfare officers. In its resolution, the VKA requested all concerned parties (the government, tribal organizations, etc.,) to implement these circulars and end the victimization of tribals and the confrontation with the state.[11]

Its inputs played a vital role in the inclusion of the promise of legal recognition of the rights of forest-dwelling communities in the 2004 election manifesto of the BJP.[12] It is also noteworthy that a Joint Parliamentary Committee

(JPC) was formed after introducing the FRA in Parliament. The members of all political parties from both Lok Sabha and Rajya Sabha were members of the JPC. The final and consensus report of the JPC changed the nature of the Forest Rights Bill introduced in Parliament in December 2005 and added many progressive and pro-forest dwelling provisions to it. The BJP parliamentarians within the JPC also supported the demands of tribal organizations. Indeed, the strategy of the BJP within the Parliament on the issue of the enactment of the FRA was influenced by the earlier stand of the VKA and its inputs.[13]

The FRA, enacted in 2006, was a result of an extensive movement by tribal organizations from different tribal areas to ensure the rights of forest-dwelling communities on forest land and its resources. It gives many Individual Forest Rights (IFRs) and Community Forest Rights (CFRs) to forest-dwelling STs and Other Traditional Forest Dwellers (OTFDs). As IFRs, it recognizes that every nuclear ST and OTFD family would get a *patta* (ownership document) of a maximum of four hectares of 'encroached' forest land[14] and makes a provision for the 'joint patta' for both husband and wife. The cut-off date for STs was demarcated as 13 December 2005, when the Forest Rights Bill was introduced in Parliament. However, according to the FRA, OTFDs must prove that they have been residing or dependent on forest land for the last three generations and at least seventy-five years before 13 December 2005. It gives rights to CFRs on Non-Timber Forest Produces (NTFPs) to manage forests. It accepts the right to habitat and habitation for Primitive Tribal Groups (PTGs), who are now known as Particularly Vulnerable Tribal Groups (PVTGs). Section 5 of the FRA is related to the duties of the holders of forest rights and empowers right holders to protect wildlife, forests and biodiversity.[15]

Understanding the Vision of the VKA on the PESA and FRA

As mentioned earlier, the VKA did not actively participate in the movements to enact the PESA or FRA. However, as mentioned in the previous section of the chapter, there is ample evidence to argue that it supported such laws (particularly the FRA) as an organization. It has therefore been demanding the proper implementation of both PESA and FRA in the last many years. This section of the chapter is divided into two sub-sections and evaluates the VKA's views on the PESA and FRA through its Vision Document. It is important because the VKA prepared this document after extensive internal consultation and discussion with many stakeholders.

The VKA and PESA: Support of Autonomous Village

Many studies have underlined the dismal implementation of the PESA.[16] The VKA has accepted the importance of the PESA because it not only formally recognized for the first time the right to self-governance of the janjati communities, but it also created a legal and administrative framework for the practice of such self-governance and autonomy.[17] Unfortunately, the Act has not been implemented in the spirit in which the Parliament enacted it. In its Vision Document, the VKA underlines that the gram sabhas cannot effectively exercise their vast powers under the PESA for various reasons. First, state authorities are not ready to give up the powers they enjoy in Fifth Schedule areas. In many states, the authorities have tried to bypass the provisions of the PESA in forest management. Second, different state governments have not shown the necessary political will to implement the PESA. Areas of ten states come under the Fifth Schedule, but only five states, namely Andhra Pradesh,

Telangana, Himachal Pradesh, Maharashtra and Rajasthan have notified rules under the PESA.[18] It is a clear violation of the provisions of the PESA because it makes it mandatory to implement it within one year of enactment. Third, though the PESA gives lots of power to the gram sabha, there is no structural support system for the gram sabha. Fourth, there is no separate law for urban areas of the Fifth Schedule and they are out of the purview of the PESA. Fifth, there is no coordination between the Centre and states regarding the implementation of the PESA. Sixth, tribal communities are not aware of the rights given in the PESA and their importance.[19]

The VKA has made some suggestions for states and tribal communities to better implement the PESA, arguing that there is a need for better coordination between the Ministry of Tribal Affairs (MoTA) and the Ministry of Panchayati Raj (MoPR). There is a need to notify rules of the Fifth Schedule to all states, but the rules of Maharashtra may be taken as a model for other states.[20] All ten states with Fifth Schedule areas should coordinate and develop a consensus to remove discrepancies in the central PESA, and they must learn from each other's experiences.[21] The Central Government should ensure that all concerned states declare that hamlets will be treated as the gram sabha unit rather than revenue villages. In its Vision Document, the VKA also demands that there must be clarity on gram sabha functionaries and funds, and the state must ensure that they get the actual power mentioned in the PESA. It also suggests the formation of a separate janjati cell in the governor's office in all the ten states with Fifth Schedule areas, and that all ministries should work according to the provisions of the PESA. It makes an important suggestion to incorporate knowledge about laws like the PESA into formal and informal education and urges the Tribal Research Institutions (TRIs) to promote research on effective implementation of the PESA and other policies. It has also emphasized a separate law for municipalities in Fifth Schedule areas as envisaged by Article 243-ZC (1) and (3) of the Constitution.[22] It is noteworthy that the Bhuria Commission had presented a separate report for the municipalities in the Fifth Schedule areas, but a separate law was not enacted.[23] The VKA also urges the Centre to reconsider the proposed Draft Panchayats (Extension to Scheduled Areas) Amendment Bill 2013 and make it a law as soon as possible.[24]

The VKA also urges all traditional and modern institutions of tribals to develop a better understanding of laws like PESA and their implementation. It underlines that community elders and other prominent personalities of the communities should focus on long-term interests and not on immediate personal gains.[25] Similarly, the Vision Document also requests social activists and organizations to educate, awaken, and organize tribal communities and develop effective leadership therein. It would help ordinary tribals to understand the complexities of the law and prepare them to participate in the functioning of the gram sabha. The VKA supports the idea of empowered local communities and the Vision Document mentions:

> We have a vision that the spirit of the PESA Act would be imbibed by all concerned. As a result, the janjati communities would soon begin to govern themselves according to their customs and traditions, dispute resolution mechanisms, and resource management systems. They would have control over their land, water and forest. They would enforce the prohibition, money-lending, social development, and similar other matters within their areas. All this has been envisaged in the PESA Act and we hope that this would become the reality of the janjati areas soon.[26]

Though the VKA wholeheartedly supported the PESA, it strongly condemned the Pathalgadi Movement of 2016 in Jharkhand. The movement focused on the rights of the Fifth Schedule areas and PESA. The supporters of the movement put a stone slab (*Pathalgadi*) outside the boundaries of the village and inscribed important Constitutional provisions and PESA-related tribal rights on it and declared their villages as village republics (*gaon ganarajya*). The VKA opposed it because it was claimed the movement was instigated by Christian missionaries and Naxals. It underlines two things about the VKA's stand on the PESA and the powers of the gram sabha: first, the VKA is not ready to support aggressive mobilization for the PESA (and other Constitutional rights); second, for the VKA, opposition to Christian missionaries, the Church and Naxalism are more important than the rights of tribals.[27]

The VKA and FRA: Support for the Rights of STs and OTFDs

Many studies have accepted that the FRA's implementation is not satisfactory.[28] In its Vision Document, the VKA expresses dismay over the slow and partial implementation of the FRA. It underlines that though the FRA was notified on 2 January 2007, the actual implementation started in 2008 due to opposition from conservationists. So, there was almost a year's gap between its notification and actual implementation.[29] The Ministry of Environment and Forest (MoEF) used this period to notify and establish thirty-six tiger reserves across the country.[30] The VKA has expressed its displeasure regarding the implementation status of both IFR and CFR given in the FRA. It notes that half of the IFR claims have been rejected, and less than 10 per cent of CFR claims are approved. It underlines that forest-dwelling communities are not aware of the provisions of the FRA, particularly the CFR, and neither do many district-level officers and ground-level officials.

The forest officers are usually uninterested in implementing the FRA and also create hurdles through different mechanisms, including the Joint Forest Management Committees (JFMC). The state Forest Trade Corporations have no direct role in the implementation of the PESA or FRA, but since these laws are against their interests, they stymie their implementation. The VKA regrets the fact that many states are settling the CFRs through doubtful and hasty means, defeating the very purpose of the FRA.[31] It also argues that the conflict between the provisions of IFA 1927 and FRA 2006 has created many problems in the implementation of the FRA. It expresses concern that FD officials have carried out the evacuation of forest land under the possession of forest-dwelling communities for generations, resulting in many suicides.[32]

The VKA also gives some critical suggestions to state and policymakers, local communities and tribal organizations for the better implementation of the FRA. First, the officers and other persons participating in the FRA implementation should be sensitized. The MoTA should also take the help of experts and forest officials. The Tribal Research Institutes in the states should also help in this process, and the role of the JFMC should be redefined in the light of the FRA. Second, the concerned officials should start a mass campaign among forest-dwelling communities to generate awareness regarding the FRA. Third, it demands that the Indian Forest Act of 1927 be replaced by a new and suitable law, which must conform to the FRA, Forest Conservation Act (FCA) of 1980 and the Wildlife (Protection) Act (WLPA) of 1972. Fourth, it underlines the need to create a new authority similar to District Consumer Courts at the lower level, and at the central level, the National Green Tribunal

(NGT) should be assigned appellate work. Fifth, it advocates the conversion of Forest Villages into Revenue Villages.[33]

The VKA also suggests that tribal communities and concerned organizations should give special attention to the CFRs, and local communities must be trained regarding the processes of claiming rights under the FRA. It urges tribal communities and organizations to resist any dilution in the FRA by using democratic means. It may be recalled that the VKA has been desisting politics based on mass mobilization, but indirectly, it urges other organizations to use this method. However, the VKA also accepts the significance of the idea of development, which works against the proper implementation of the PESA and the FRA. The Vision Document underlines:

> Since the law's passing (FRA), 'development' has loomed much more prominent in the national polity. As a result, an opinion is building up that we need to do everything necessary to facilitate 'development projects'. In this atmosphere, laws like the FRA and the PESA and the laws relating to environmental protection have come to be seen as unnecessary obstacles in the path of progress. Furthermore, there are attempts to devise bureaucratic ways of bypassing and going around these laws. This atmosphere of distrust of FRA and similar other laws is perhaps a matter of the most serious concern for the forest-dwelling and other janjatis.[34]

Indeed, the concerns of the VKA are valid and it urges local communities to resist dilution in the FRA by using democratic means. But it has never mobilized local communities against any such dilution and followed a policy of persuasion through statements, memorandum, etc. In the next section, we will consider how far such strategies have been successful.[35]

The VKA, the Politics of Persuasion and Interests of Forest-Dwelling Communities

This section will consider the VKA's stand on issues related to the forest rights of tribals, and its politics of persuasion for the protection of the interests of tribals. This politics is entirely non-violent, but it also deliberately desists the use of any kind of mobilization of the masses. Rather, it heavily depends on methods like press releases, submitting a memorandum, writing articles, etc. This section will focus on two case studies, where the VKA took a stand in favour of tribal rights, and put pressure on the government to ensure the protection of the interests of tribals.

Danger of Eviction and the VKA

It is noteworthy that after the enactment of the FRA, many conservationists and former forest officers filed petitions against this law in high courts in many states to stall its implementation. The basic claim was that this law is detrimental to the forests and wildlife and violates the existing legal structure to manage and protect forests. These petitions were clubbed together and the SC started hearing them in 2015. On 13 February 2019, a three-judge bench of the Supreme Court comprising Justice Arun Mishra, Navin Sinha and Indira Banerjee passed an order. It told the FD to evict those STs and OTFDs, who could not provide appropriate documents or proof according to the provisions of the FRA to prove their claim on forest land. This order could evict 11 lakh ST and OTFD households from forest lands in sixteen states.[36] Although the same bench kept the order in abeyance on 28 February 2019,[37] it created a state of perpetual danger and fear that the court, could in fact, uphold the order. The VKA strongly criticized the order of the Supreme Court and questioned the functioning of the concerned ministries of the central government.

The Central Executive Board of the VKA met on 24 February 2019 in Satna, Madhya Pradesh, and passed a resolution against the Supreme Court's order, criticizing the government for not stopping the order. The resolution emphasized that available sources suggest that 40.54 lakh personal and 1.44 lakh community claims totaling 41.98 lakh claims were registered. Out of these 18.89 lakh individuals and 46,649 community-based claims that total to 19.36 lakh claims, which means nearly half of the claims, were wrongly rejected. Out of the approved sanctions, 17.97 lakh personal claims and 70,164 community-based claims totaling 18.67 pattas/leases were allocated. According to the provisions of the FRA and as per the guidelines issued by the MoTA, the task of analysis, review or appeal concerning the rejected claims was necessary.[38] The VKA therefore claimed that the order of eviction of forest-dwelling communities was unjust without completing this process. It also criticized the role of public prosecutors in the last three hearings of the case, who did nothing to protect the interests of the forest-dwelling communities. It demanded that the Government of India ensure a stay on the SC order by bringing an ordinance and by filing a review petition on this issue. The VKA said that the process related to the rejected claims should be settled first. Then the government should deliberate regarding the problems of those people whose claims would be rejected even after the completion of review processes.[39]

S.K. Kaul, the then editor of the VKA's monthly magazine, *Van Bandhu*, wrote an essay on the order of the SC, which was published in three parts in its May, June and July issues of 2019.[40] In his essay, Kaul criticizes both the National Democratic Alliance (NDA) and United Progressive Alliance

(UPA) governments for diluting the FRA. He underlines that the NDA government diluted the FRA to the extent that all crucial safeguards provided for the welfare of STs are no longer in operation. In 2013, the UPA government said that a gram sabha's consent for linear projects (like construction of roads etc.) is not needed. However, in the last few years, a new trend has emerged related to the absolute lack of actual consultation and consent of gram sabhas, even for non-linear projects, such as mining and hydropower. Kaul emphasizes that compliance with the provisions of the FRA only allowed in-principle approval of projects, often leading to controversies and fait accompli situations.[41]

Kaul also questions the MoTA and MoEFCC in the ongoing cases in the SC and describes the role of Left leaders in a positive manner. He writes,

> The signs were ominous. In the three hearings that the apex court held in 2018, MoTA and the Ministry of Environment, Forest, and Climate Change were either absent in the Court or did not speak up. Organizations working on FRA such as Campaign for Survival and Dignity, All India Forum of Forest Movements, political leaders viz., Brinda Karat and D. Raja, and former chairperson of the Adivasi Congress, V. Kishore Chandra, protested the ministries acts and sent letters to Union Tribal Affairs Minister Jual Oram on February 4, 2019.[42]

Kaul also emphasizes that the FRA mentions a specific process for reviewing the claims of STs and OTFDs regarding Individual Forest Rights (IFRs), and in most states, these processes have not been completed. Indeed, he argues, even in Sundargarh, Odisha's second-largest district in terms of forest cover and the constituency of the Union Tribal Affairs

Minister Jual Oram, the land titles that have been accepted are the lowest in number. Similar situations exist in many other areas represented by the leaders of other parties. In most areas, concerned authorities argued that they rejected the claims due to a lack of necessary and adequate proof. However, Kaul asserts that the real reason for the rejection of claims in Sundargarh is that the district is highly industrialized and has iron ore, coal, manganese, limestone and dolomite reserves. One of the country's largest steel plants is at Rourkela in Sundargarh district, and there are many other big industrial units of steel, cement, sponge iron, etc. Apart from these big industries, many small-scale industries are also working in this district, and all of them depend on forest resources. There are many ongoing mining projects to extract these resources, and many others are in the process of finalization. Kaul cites activist Litu Minz, to argue that due to these reasons, 'the government deliberately rejects individual forest rights claims to divest the land for such expansion . . . '[43] Similarly, he argues that the FDs in different states are not ready to give CFRs because it reduces their hold on the forest. Indeed, the recognition of the CFR's rights is the most empowering provision of the FRA because it restores the gram sabhas' control over the governance of forests.[44]

It is noteworthy that on 29 February 2019, during the hearing of the cases mentioned earlier in the SC, the Centre, through its solicitor general Tushar Mehta supported by all states and many NGOs, pleaded with the court, to withhold its February 13 order. The Centre stated in the SC that the claims of the forest-dwellers were rejected summarily and affected illiterate persons could not get a chance to defend or review their claims. The SC agreed to study the issue in detail but also underlined that an unauthorized person could not use its order to grab forest land. After the SC's 29 February order, the imminent danger of eviction of lakhs of forest dwellers was averted. However, Kaul underlines that there is a need to continuously pressurize the MoTA to protect the interests of forest-dwelling communities and represent their interests in the SC vocally and adequately.[45]

This incident highlights some crucial aspects of the VKA's work: first, though, it is the tribal wing of the RSS, it is not averse to criticizing the policies and actions of the BJP led Central Government on issues related to tribal interests. Second, though in day-to-day politics, RSS and VKA strongly condemn the politics of the Left parties (usually many RSS-BJP activists use the term 'anti-national' for them), the article written by *Van Bandhu's* editor mentioned the works of Left leaders like Brinda Karat and D. Raja positively. Third, it is also evident from the above description that for the VKA, the FRA is a crucial tool to protect the interests of the tribals and other forest-dwelling communities. As S.K. Kaul underlines '. . . whatever its small flaws, the Forest Rights Act 2006 is a reminder that people are sovereign, not the state and its agencies'.[46]

Proposed Amendments in the Indian Forest Act 1927 and the VKA

On 7 March 2019, the Central Government sent a 123–page first draft of the comprehensive amendments to the Indian Forest Act, 1927, to state-level FDs. India's Inspector General of Forests (IGF) (Forest Policy), Noyal Thomas, was sent the 'secret' document, which contained the proposal to replace IFA 1927. Indeed, the Central Government formed a committee headed by former cabinet secretary T.S.R. Subramanian in 2015 to consider the issues related to the amendments in the IFA 1927. Before the Subramanian Committee, the M.B. Shah Commission also suggested amendments to IFA 1927 in 2010.[47]

Again, another committee was formed in 2016 to consider the issues and controversies related to the amendment of the same law. In both committees, there was no representation of the MoTA or any members/activists from STs or OTFDs.[48]

The draft sent by the IGF had many problematic and questionable proposals because they were against the rights of local communities sanctioned by laws like the PESA and FRA. Many sections of the draft were indeed against the idea of rights and empowerment of local communities. For example, Clause 22 of the proposed draft had a provision that even in a village forest, where tribal communities use timber and other forest produce, pasture rights and its protection and management, would be in consultation with the FD. This clause was against the spirit of the PESA and FRA. It also gave power to the forest bureaucracy to record forest rights and gave it extraordinary power to create a 'reserve forest' and cancel IFRs and CFRs given according to the FRA, by giving affected parties compensation. Clause 26 of the draft had a provision that in case of fire in a reserved forest or theft of forest produce or grazing by cattle, all rights of forest produce or cattle grazing would be suspended. It also inserted a new provision (Clause 66), to check forest offenses, which proposed to allow FD officials to use firearms and search any premises after informing the gram sabha.[49]

Like the Armed Forces (Special Powers) Act (AFSPA) of 1958, it also gave immunity from prosecution for excesses or wrongdoings. No prosecution could have been started against forest officials without prior sanction of the state. Clause 66 was related to shifting the burden of innocence to the accused, which was a deviation from the existing jurisprudence, except for terror laws. It thereby made forest offenses equivalent to terror laws. It also sought to criminalize an entire community for the mistakes of one individual or some individuals because it defined a person to include 'a forest-dwelling community and any organization registered under the prevailing laws'. It also proposed to make a wide range of offenses unbailable and that state governments should not have the power to withdraw registered cases. It also ensured more power to the Central Government in the management of forests. Clause 11 (3) of the Draft empowered the Forest Settlement Officer to acquire land according to public needs.[50]

The Kendriya Karyakari Mandal (Central Executive Board) of the VKA met on 19 September 2019 at Haridwar and passed a firm resolution against the proposed draft of the Central Government. Its deliberation also raised the issue of sending the 'secret' draft in one language—English—which went against the norm of sending government proposals in at least two languages—Hindi and English. According to the VKA leadership, it was an attempt to thwart discussion by common tribals and OTFDs.[51] It demanded the following things from the Central Government: first, it should direct concerned authorities to withdraw the proposed amendment; second, a new draft should be prepared with the consultation of the MoTA, and the elected representative of the tribals and NGOs working in tribal areas should be included in the discussion processes; third, before starting the process of change in the IFA 1927, a new forest policy should be announced and all amendments must follow the larger framework of the new forest policy; fourth, the new forest policy or amendments of the IFA must respect the critical provisions of the FRA, PESA and Biodiversity Act; fifth, the traditional knowledge of the tribals should be used in forest development and environment protection. In this context, the Resolution of the VKA mentioned places like Mendhalekha and Baripada (Maharashtra), Jhabua (Madhya Pradesh) and Jardhargaon (Uttarakhand), where local communities have worked for the conservation and development of forests. It also underlined that in different parts of the country, many communities, like the Bishnois in Rajasthan and Khonoma in Nagaland, etc., are working to protect wildlife and natural resources.[52]

The VKA called upon tribal society, particularly its elected representatives, chiefs of their traditional institutions, youths, and all nationalist organizations working in tribal society and its workers to influence public opinion so that the government can positively consider the issue. It also cautioned the Central Government that the tribal communities have huge expectations and the proposed amendments would dampen their expectations and make the image of the Central Government anti-tribal.[53] It is also crucial to note that other tribal organizations, intellectuals and activists also opposed the proposed amendments in the IFA, 1927.[54]

The VKA also contacted many retired forest officers, tribal ministers, the NCST, BJP MPs, and many other eminent persons in society and informed them regarding the negative aspects of the proposed amendments in IFA 1927. It submitted a memorandum to the MoEFCC and attempted to pressure the government with the help of tribal MPs and other organizations. At its meeting on 14 November 2019, the VKA warned the government that if it did not withdraw the draft of the amendment, tribal society would lose faith in the government. Due to constant pressure and protests, the government ultimately withdrew the amendment draft. The VKA welcomed this decision and mentioned that it was taken on the birth anniversary of Birsa Munda, but clarified that the tribal community has still not received the rights given by the FRA and hoped that the government would ensure and prioritize the proper implementation of the FRA.[55]

Apart from taking a stand on emerging issues against tribal forest rights, the VKA has constantly tried to persuade the government to take measures for the better implementation of the PESA and FRA. Constant pressure played a crucial role in the formal agreement between the MoTA and MoEFCC which gave the right to manage forest resources, their protection and consumption to gram sabhas. Since MoEFCC is the party to this agreement, FD officials cannot deny the existence of the CFRs of the FRA. The ABVKA welcomed this initiative and demanded that state-level FDs recognize it and ensure the actual transfer of power to the gram sabhas, to manage, protect and use the forest according to the provisions of the FRA. The FD should determine the boundary of the CFRs of the gram sabhas. Currently, in most of the areas, the FD does not deny CFRs in totality and the VKA has underlined that the agreement between the MoTA and MoEFCC on this issue is a positive development.[56]

The VKA has severely criticized the BJP-led government at the Centre and while the VKA avoids street politics or mobilization, it is not because the BJP is the ruling party at the Centre or in several states. Indeed, it had never adopted this method even during the Congress rule and it emphasizes the need to resolve issues through dialogue with the government. The VKA has done its bit by organizing seminars and workshops to create awareness about the PESA and FRA. Undoubtedly, to some extent, its pressurizing tactics have been successful, but it can not be denied the mass mobilization or fear of movement by the grassroots tribal organizations also compelled the government to reconsider its stand on thses issues.

The VKA and the Quest for a More Inclusive System for Tribals

Apart from the demand to implement the PESA and FRA properly, the VKA has evolved a set of demands and suggestions to govern tribal areas better. The VKA's views on several aspects of the governance of tribal areas underline that it has accepted a radical agenda for the tribal areas. It has demanded that it should be clearly stated that governors are not bound by the recommendations of the state cabinet in performing his/her duties related to the Fifth Schedule provisions. Every state with the Fifth Schedule area must establish a 'Janjati Cell' to help governors effectively understand and make decisions regarding Fifth Schedule areas. Laws and policies enacted by the Parliament and state legislatures should be deliberated in the Tribal Advisory Council (TAC), and the governor should make a considered decision in the light of its recommendation. The VKA also demands the inclusion of new areas in the Fifth Schedule.[57]

The VKA supports the provisions of the Sixth Schedule of the Indian Constitution because it gives many rights, including the right of Autonomous District Councils (ADC), to the tribal-dominated areas of North-east India. The VKA demands that one-third of the ADC seats be allotted to women and the ADC should directly get funds related to their activities. The VKA accepts the need for fair distribution of resources between the state and ADC and demands the formation of a state finance commission for this purpose. The VKA suggests that to make ADCs more accommodative, one-tenth of seats should be reserved for the non-ST representatives, and the smaller janjatis should be nominated in the ADCs. It also underlines the importance of documenting the customary laws of janjatis to protect their identity. It is also important to note that the VKA proposes extending some of the crucial provisions of autonomous functioning in the Fifth Schedule areas.[58]

The VKA has also raised a grave issue related to the governance of non-schedule areas—those with a substantial tribal population—which are not part of the Fifth or Sixth

Schedule of the Constitution. The VKA had underscored that all those villages and blocks must be declared as part of Scheduled Areas (i.e. Fifth Schedule) where the population of tribals is 40 per cent or more. This will provide these areas the benefit of the Fifth Schedule and PESA.[59]

The VKA has expressed its concern and plan for the Particularly Vulnerable Tribal Groups (PVTGs), earlier known as Primitive Tribal Groups. A total of seventy-five tribal groups from eighteen states and the union territory of Andaman and Nicobar are included in this category. However, all PVTGs are not part of the ST category, which makes their situation more complicated.[60] The VKA emphasizes the need to give due importance to the livelihood, education and health of the PVTGs and underlines that the 'right to natural resources is a necessary pre-condition for their development'.[61] Therefore, they must be given rights over important NTFP and the state administration should help them channel procurement, processing and marketing remuneratively. Indeed, the VKA wishes to make tribals aware and capable of using markets and underscores that the government should give importance and promote the tribals' traditional knowledge about forest conservation and herbal medicine. It also accepts the need to spread education in these areas and suggest the recruitment and training of para-teachers from PVTGs for tribal villages.[62]

The VKA accepts the negative impact of mining on the life and livelihood of tribal communities and emphasizes that most of the mining activities are related to Fifth Schedule areas. The VKA reiterates that it is not against mining and supports it as a tool for regional development, but opposes the exploitation of minerals for export and profit. It demands that all illegal mining be quashed and the government desist irrational exploitation of resources for short-term gains. It supports mining that is strictly compliant with environmental, social and labour laws, and strategic mining of those minerals which are crucial for development. However, it emphasizes on the anlaysis of long term environmental impact of such mining. It underlines that if there is a possibility of long term environmental crisis due to mining then it should be desisted. It also desires that Indian demands get primacy over exports and that mining should also ensure new opportunities for local tribal communities. The VKA points out that there is a need to invest in the exploration of new resources. Primarily, the VKA stresses giving local communities the benefits of mining and imparting skills to janjatis in mining areas.[63]

The VKA has questioned the approach to wildlife conservation in India, which is governed by the Wildlife (Protection) Act, 1972, (hereafter WLPA) and largely follows the policy of 'fence and fine'. The VKA criticizes the mechanism of the WLPA because its provisions result in conflicts between PAs (Protected Areas) administrators and local communities (primarily tribals). It is noteworthy that the Vision Document of the VKA accepts that in some instances, it may be true that tribal communities give shelter to poachers and provide them information to help snare animals; however, many tribal communities are indeed working to protect wildlife. It also criticizes forest officers for harassing innocent forest-dwelling people and underlines the importance of creating mutual trust among them, and suggests that PAs administrators should in fact, tap the knowledge of local communities to protect wildlife. It suggests that any developmental activity in forest areas must give primacy to both the welfare of janjatis and wildlife; second, community institutions must be consulted regarding the plans for sustained utilization of forests and natural habitats; third, PAs should be declared after evolving consensus, and this process should be participatory and transparent. The fourth point would be developing an alternate source of livelihood for tribal communities in the interests of wildlife (however, the VKA supports community-based wildlife tourism) and the fifth point is that the FD should develop mutual trust with local communities and use their traditional knowledge for wildlife protection.[64] The VKA has asserted that the forest-dwelling communities shall have an unfettered right to collect NTFP and the contradictions between different laws should be worked out to give more power to local communities. It urges policymakers, governments, NGOs and local communities to work together to achieve the above target.[65]

The VKA emerges as an organization that remains concerned for all important issues related to tribals. On the one hand, it has continuously tried to push the government for the betterment of tribal communities, and on the other hand, it has attempted to train and educate tribal people regarding the legal provisions of various Acts through workshops and seminars.[66] Indeed, there are examples where VKA activists, like Harsh Chouhan, for instance, did not hesitate to sacrifice their posts to protect the interests of tribals. Chouhan is a senior activist of the VKA and was appointed as the chairman of the NCST in February 2021 for three years. However, in October 2022, he took a strong stand against the MoEFCC's new Forest (Conservations) Rule, 2022 and wrote a letter to the MoEFCC and asserted that the rules would violate FRA by giving primacy to project clearance. It created an impasse, which ultimately resulted in his resignation as the chairman of the NCST in the last week of June 2023. Interestingly, the Congress general secretary (Communication), Jairam Ramesh praised him for his stand and stated that he was forced to resign. He underlined that 'he has been taking—like many activists and I have done—very strong objections to the way forest laws have been diluted in the last two years that hurt the interests of adivasis. He has confronted the Environment and Forest Ministry boldly.'[67]

The VKA and the All India Union for Forest Working People (AIUFWP): Possibility of Common Ground?

The VKA represents right-wing thinking and works to counter the influence of 'anti-Hindu' values in different sections of tribal society. Since it is affiliated to the RSS organization, it gets complete support not only from other affiliates of the RSS but also from the BJP-led governments at the Centre and states. This section of the chapter attempts to evaluate whether the VKA's understanding of forest issues is similar to other tribal organizations, mainly left-wing ones and compares it to another tribal organization, the All India Union of Forest Working People (AIUFWP), which claims to follow the Left ideology.

The AIUFWP tries to mobilize forest-dwelling communities based on Leftist ideas and works in many forest areas of the country. Earlier, it was called the National Forum of Forest People and Forest Workers (NFFPFW) and became a union or AIUFWP in 2012 to give an ideological basis to various local organizations. It has tried to encourage tribal communities to form local organizations and co-ordinates activities of such organizations. Though it has clearly expressed its leaning toward Leftist ideology, it has also declared Ambedkar, Jyotiba Phule, Savitribai Phule, Birsa Munda and Bhagat Singh as its icons. It tries to create opportunities for union workers to train and learn from the experiences of workers in other areas. To enable this, it organizes meetings in different areas, so that adivasis and other forest-dwelling communities interact with each other.[68]

The AIUFWP is not a pan-Indian organization and is primarily active in the Sonbhadra district of Uttar Pradesh, Dudhwa National Park in the Lakhimpur Kheri district of Uttar Pradesh; the Rajaji National Park in Uttarakhand, and in the Kaimur and Rohtas districts of Bihar. It has also expanded its work in some districts of Jharkhand and West Bengal. In its earlier form as NFFPFW, it participated in the movement for the enactment of the FRA. It was a founding and key member of the umbrella organization of many grassroots tribal communities, the Campaign for Survival and Dignity (CSD). It played a crucial role in mobilizing forest-dwelling communities for the enactment of the FRA and has created awareness among STs and other forest-dwelling communities about their rights in the areas of its influence. The initial draft of the FRA had provisions only for the rights of STs, but later due to the pressure of grassroots organizations, the Other Traditional Forest Dwellers (OTFDs) was included in the FRA.

The AIUFWP supports the rights of local communities over forest resources,[69] and it emphasizes that these communities are better equipped to protect these resources. It has continuously supported the forest rights of local communities in PAs (Protected Areas) and has termed PESA and the FRA as significant laws to ensure the rights of forest-dwelling communities over forest land and its resources, especially since it has been working for the better implementation of the FRA at the grassroots level.[70] The AIUFWP has demanded the inclusion of many tribal areas in the Fifth Schedule of the Constitution.[71] It has given autonomy to different constituent organizations at the grassroots[72]and has been earnestly trying to ensure that women should be given prominent and active roles in its local constituent-level organizations. It has firm faith in the politics of movements and mass mobilization, but gives due importance to dialogue with government officials and the members of other organizations. It takes the help of prominent advocates in high courts and the Supreme Court to fight against the arbitrary behaviour of FD officials. As an organization, it has continuously condemned the use of violence, especially the activities of Maoists. It also protests state violence and state-sponsored movements like Salwa Judum or Operation Green Hunt and the arbitrary arrest of adivasis on the pretext of curbing Maoist violence. The AIUFWP emphasizes the cultural and religious autonomy of adivasis and believes that only they can decide, based on their Constitutional rights, whether they are Hindus or want to convert to Christianity or any other religion or as 'adivasis'. It primarily emphasizes and struggles for the autonomous life of adivasis and other forest-dwelling communities and wants to ensure their rights over forest land and its resources.

One can easily find an excellent common ground between the VKA and the AIUFWP, though they follow different ideologies. In their policy documents, statements, pamphlets, etc., both organizations have been emphasizing the proper implementation of the PESA and FRA, an extension of Fifth Schedule areas, inclusion of many forest-dwelling communities in the category of scheduled tribes and opposition of land acquisition by violating the rights of tribals and other forest-dwelling communities. It is also true that there are fundamental differences between right wing and left wing organizations. The VKA termed leftist organizations as 'Naxals' and their enemy, because it assumes such organizations support violence and are 'anti-Hindu'. Indeed, it tars all leftist organizations with the same brush and terms them as Maoist supporters. The VKA and other affiliates of the RSS supported the Salwa Judum campaign in the Bastar area of Chhattisgarh.[73] On many occasions, they have criticized left organizations by claiming that they have been supporting the activities of Christian missionaries. Left organizations like AIUFWP view the VKA as the representative of the communal politics of the RSS, which imposes Hindu values on adivasis and creates division and hatred between them on the issue of religion.[74]

However, in their vision and work for the rights of tribals over forest resources, two key distinctions can be underlined: first, for the VKA, the most important agenda is to save vanvasis from the influence of Christian missionaries and enhance the values related to Hinduism through educational, cultural and social means. The issue of forest rights or implementation of progressive laws like PESA and FRA is only one aspect of its work. The AIUFWP, on the other hand, is fully dedicated to fighting for the rights of adivasis and other forest-dwelling communities over forest land and its resources. Second, as discussed in the previous section, the VKA has also adopted a radical agenda for the rights of tribal people, by pressurizing the Centre and state governments for its demands. But apart from some exceptions, it has never tried to mobilize tribals for forest rights and resources. In an important article, Mahesh Kale, a senior activist of the VKA, has compared Surgana Tehsil (Maharashtra), a CPI(M) stronghold with Baripada (Odisha), a VKA bastion. He sympathetically discusses the struggle for mobilization and protest marches in Surgana and argues that there are two ways to do it: struggle and coordination/cooperation. The CPI(M) fomented struggle but could not achieve much. While the VKA changed much in Baripada with the cooperation of the people and state officials.[75] The AIUFWP, on the other hand, has always focussed on creating political awareness among tribals and other forest-dependent communities and emphasized the strategy of mobilizing them through dharnas, demonstrations and sometimes road blockades, to meet their demands.

These two different strategies make a huge difference in the political consciousness of the communities living in the areas where these organizations work. In the areas of influence of AIUFWP, both activists and tribals are aware of the PESA and the FRA. Of course, most of them do not know all sections of these laws, but they do know their crucial provisions and claim that these laws give rights over forest land and its resources. There are many examples where AIUFWP activists and other grassroots tribal organizations challenged local FD officials based on their understanding of the FRA.[76] In the VKA itself, very few people (mostly senior office-bearers) are aware of the rights given by the PESA and FRA, and it tries to dissuade vanvasis from mobilizational politics against the FD.

Summing Up

It is clear from the above discussion that though VKA systematically formed a 'Hit Raksha Vibhag' after four decades of its formation, in the last two decades, it has started to intervene in crucial policy decisions related to the rights of tribals over forest land and its resources. It is pertinent to claim that the works of many grassroots tribal organizations (many influenced by left-wing ideas) led to a political consciousness among tribals about their forest rights. It motivated the VKA to work on the issues of hit raksha and it has taken a radical stand on issues related to forest rights of tribal communities. It has vehemently opposed any negative changes in the provisions of the FRA and also denounced policies that create displacement of tribal people. Like most tribal organizations, it also supports the extension of the Fifth Schedule, inclusion of new communities in the category of the STs, and better implementation of laws like PESA and FRA. Undoubtedly, the VKA has presented a broader vision to include almost all crucial aspects of tribal life and adopted a radical agenda on these issues. On some occasions, it has criticized certain ministers of the Modi government for misconduct towards tribal people, but always desisted from any direct criticism of Prime Minister Narendra Modi. Politics of persuasion has its limitations and most of the demands supported by the VKA are still not fulfilled. Though the VKA is doing some serious work for the forest rights of tribals, it is not the primary goal. The primary goal is the spread of Hindu values in tribal society and issues of forest rights are only complementary to that higher goal.

6

The Vanvasi Kalyan Ashram and Hindutva: Ruptures in the Vision of a Hinduized Tribal Society

The VKA has emerged as one of the most influential organizations in tribal areas and has done substantial work for tribals and raised several issues related to their lives and interests. It has taken a strong stand on the Hindu identity of tribals and simultaneously and ceaselessly worked to make Hindutva politics more deep-rooted and effective in tribal areas. This chapter evaluates the role of the VKA on important issues in tribal areas. The demand for the Sarna Code (a resolution passed by the Jharkhand government in 2020 to include Sarna as a separate religion in the 2021 census) by certain groups in tribal areas has been a contested issue. This demand denounces the VKA's basic claim that all tribals are Hindus. This chapter shows that for aggressive mobilization on certain important and contested issues, the VKA has been dependent on some 'other' organizations. The demand for delisting is one such issue on which the VKA has tried to mobilize tribals for the last many years. The VKA has always opposed and resisted Maoist violence, and like other affiliated organizations of the RSS, it has supported many initiatives by the Indian state to curb Maoist politics. In many tribal areas it has also espoused the strategy of ghar wapsi of Christian or Muslim tribals to Hinduism. Indeed, in many areas, such a strategy, combined with the threat of violence or actual violence against minorities, has been used to mobilize tribals who follow Hinduism, and other sections of Hindu populations, against Christian tribals. This strategy helps the Sangh Parivar create majoritarianism in tribal areas. Though the VKA presents itself as a non-political organization, it plays a crucial role in Hindu right-wing politics in tribal areas. However, the confusion and duality in such contested issues underline the ruptures in the VKA's ideological position.

This chapter is divided into five sections, which evaluate different shades of the VKA's views and activities on the above-mentioned issues. The first section deals with the debates surrounding the issue of the Sarna Code and the VKA's attempt to denounce it. The second section analyses the demand for 'delisting' by Hindu right-wing organizations, including the VKA. The third section of the chapter discusses the RSS and the VKA's view on Maoist violence and the politics of tribal organizations with left/Gandhian leanings. The fourth section focuses on the politics of reconversion ghar wapsi and aggressive mobilization against Christian missionaries in tribal areas. The fifth and last section of the chapter evaluates the different shades of VKA's involvement in electoral politics.

The VKA and the Sarna Code

The Sarna Code is both a contested and an old issue. The followers of the Sarna faith present themselves as the worshippers of trees, hills, and other elements of nature. They do not consider themselves Hindus and have been fighting for a separate religious identity for decades. Within the groups who claim to follow Sarna, there are different categories. Certain groups have converted to Christianity and they have been strongly opposing attempts by the RSS and VKA to declare all tribals as Hindus. However, some of the supporters of the Sarna Code have also demanded that the benefits given to STs should be passed on to them, and not to those tribals who have converted to Christianity. Indeed, scholars have argued that both Hindutva groups and Christian missionaries converted tribals to their respective religions and one should see the demand for the Sarna Code as a serious attempt to resist such conversations. The core of this demand is related to the institutionalization of the indigenous faith of the respective tribal communities to maintain their unique identity.[1] For example, consider the case of Jharkhand, where there are thirty-two tribal groups of which eight groups are also included in Particularly Vulnerable Tribal Groups (PVTGs). It is noteworthy that in these tribal communities, many follow the Hindu religion, while some have converted to Christianity. The supporters of the Sarna Code have termed this situation as a threat to their traditional identity and have raised the demand for a separate code to save 'religious identity'.

The demand for the Sarna Code is old and was even supported by politician and member of the Constituent Assembly, Jaipal Singh Munda. Between 1871 and 1951, tribals could register themselves for the census under different codes, but it changed during the 1961 census, which supporters of the Code called 'historical injustice'.[2] The Sarna Code is related to recognizing the separate religion of adivasis and accepting them as nature worshipers. Adivasi leaders across the state have been demanding the implementation of the Sarna Code in census surveys, which would allow tribals to be identified as followers of the Sarna faith during census 2021. (This census had not begun at the time of writing this book). Until now, the census surveys have included them as 'others' in the religion column. Earlier, the National Commission for Scheduled Tribes recommended the addition of the Sarna Code in 2011 but the recommendation was not accepted by the then United Progressive Alliance (UPA) government. Due to the initiative of the Hemant Soren-led Jharkhand Mukti Morcha (JMM) and the Indian National Congress government, the Jharkhand Legislative Assembly passed a resolution on 11 November 2020 to include the Sarna Code in the 2021 census. Currently, citizens can choose from only six religions—Hinduism, Islam, Christianity, Sikhism, Buddhism and Jainism. There has been a column of 'other religion and persuasions' and 'religion not stated'. If the Central government accepts the resolution of the Jharkhand Legislative Assembly, the Sarna code would be added as the seventh religion in the census.[3]

VKA activists have opposed the idea of the Sarna Code and the common description against this demand is that it is a conspiracy to divide Hindus and reduce their overall population. The VKA has intensified its campaign in the areas, where the demand for the Sarna Code emerged, holding meetings with such groups/communities and emphasizing how they are an integral part of the Hindu religion. It also decided to intensify campaigns in other states where tribals are sizeable, like Chhattisgarh, West Bengal, Rajasthan, Odisha, Maharashtra, Gujarat, Telangana and Andhra Pradesh. The local-level activists of the VKA narrate stories from epics like Ramayana and Mahabharata which contain characters who are tribals. The VKA activists use such stories as proof of tribals being an integral part of Hindu society. Many VKA functionaries have argued that in the 2011 census, 79 lakh individuals identified themselves as ORP (Other Religion Peoples), in which at least 44 lakh were from Jharkhand, and it was observed that later they converted to Christianity. They underline that the idea of the Sarna Code is against Bharat and Bharatiyata (India and Indianness). It is a political move to break Hindu *samaj* (society) and Christian and Muslim groups are responsible for it.[4] Some activists have also underlined that the demand for the Sarna Code is a conspiracy to exclude tribals (who accept this Code) from the category of ST and turn them into a minority. Such tribals will lose the benefit of reservation and protection under Sanatan Dharma.[5] Interestingly, one can find a duality in the VKA's stand about Sanatan Dharma in the North-east and other parts of the country. As discussed in Chapter 3, the VKA activists have been using the idea of 'Sanatan Dharma' as an umbrella concept to include all indigenous religions.

The VKA Karyakari Mandal passed a resolution on 29 April 2018 against the demand for a separate code for tribals in the census. The resolution termed the demand of the Sarna Code as a conspiracy against Sanatan Hindu Dharma. According to the resolution:

> Forces indulged in the religious conversions of janjatis are creating confusion not only by conspiring to reduce the number of those who follow Sanatan Hindu Dharam but also by separating the STs by attempting to increase the number of ORP (Other Religion People) to weaken them so that they can be an easy target for conversions in future, as these agencies have been doing in the provinces of North-east in the last fifty years.[6]

The VKA delegation, led by the then president of the VKA, Jagdev Ram Oraon met the then home minister Rajnath Singh on 31 October 2018 and urged that the government should ignore the demand by misguided persons for an illogical and misleading separate religion code in the census.[7] *Van Bandhu* (the monthly magazine of the VKA) published many articles that questioned the demand for the Sarna Code and termed it as a challenge for Hindu society. Dr Manmohan Vaidya, the *sah sarkaryavahs* (joint general secretary) of the RSS, also emphasizes the internal diversity of Hinduism and underlines that tribal communities are also part of Hinduism. He says that leaders supporting the Sarna Code are complicit in the attempt to disintegrate India.[8]

Though the Central Government did not accept the demand of the Sarna Code, there are groups and political parties that want it implemented. On 15 November 2023, the then Jharkhand CM Hemant Soren, reiterated the demand for the Sarna Code at the time of Prime Minister Narendra Modi's visit to Ranchi.[9] During their election campaign, both Congress President Mallikarjun Kharge and senior party leader Rahul Gandhi promised that if their alliance won the election, they would fulfill the demand of the Sarna Code.[10] It is interesting to note that in February 2019 before the Lok Sabha elections, the then chief minister and BJP leader Raghubar Das, announced in the state assembly that he would recommend the Sarna Code for tribals.[11] However, the BJP lost the 2020 legislative assembly election and after the assembly election, the BJP never brought up the implementation of the Code. Indeed, it underlines that the BJP has been ignoring the stand of the VKA on certain issues related to tribals for electoral benefits.

The demand for the Sarna Code lays bare the internal ideological contradiction within the VKA and the larger Sangh Parivar. The VKA has used the idea of Sanatan Dharma to incorporate tribal sects who have emphatically argued that they are different from Hindus. The VKA leaders, including Ramakant Deshpande, have made it clear to the tribal community leaders of the North-east that they would never support the conversion of the non-Christian tribal communities into Hinduism. The VKA has consistently emphasized that all such communities are part of 'Sanatan Dharma' and there is no need to declare them 'Hindus'. However, the VKA is not ready to accept the Sarna Code as an expression of indigenous religion. Though it has also demanded that tribals should not be included in the UCC because it would be detrimental to their diversity, it is not ready to accept the demand for diversity in the form of the Sarna Code, because it fears that its recognition would divide Hindus, and would be beneficial for Christians. The VKA is certainly prepared to accept the diversity of tribal society but if it feels that it would benefit 'foreign' religion, or create a conducive situation for the conversion to Christianity, it opposes such diversity vehemently.

The VKA and the Demand of Delisting

The core argument behind the demand of 'delisting' is that if individuals from the tribal communities converted to a faith other than their original faith (for the VKA it is Hinduism), they have then given up tribal traditions and practices. After conversion, such individuals should be prevented from reaping the benefits of the Constitutional protections and provisions assigned for STs. They should be excluded from the category of STs so that they could not take such benefits. 'Delisting' is a core demand of the VKA, and it has been raising this issue since the late 1970s. However, the VKA never focused on systematic mobilization but raised the issue on many occasions. For example, in December 2003 the VKA organized a rally in Bhubaneswar attended by approximately 15,000 people. The then VKA president Jagdev Ram Oraon insisted that tribals converting to Christianity should not be allowed to access the benefit of 'reservation'.[12] More systematic mobilization on this issue started with the formation of the Janjati Suraksha Manch (JSM).

The JSM was formed on 30 April 2006, and it is fully dedicated to the issue of delisting. Many senior members of the VKA played a crucial role in its formation and held important positions in the organization. A senior tribal leader of Jharkhand and former MP, Moren Singh Poorti, became its first national convenor. He retired from active politics in 1981 and became a full-time activist of the VKA and later its national vice-president.[13] Interestingly, one can find many articles regarding the works of Moren Singh Poorti in the monthly magazine of the VKA, *Van Bandhu*, but they do not mention his role as convenor of the JSM or his relationship with this organization.[14] Many senior activists of the JSM have been involved in the works of the VKA; for instance, Harsh Chouhan, was the national convenor of the JSM in 2010.[15] While he bore responsibilities in the VKA, he was later appointed as the chairman of the National Commission for Scheduled Tribes (NCST) in February 2021. Interestingly, while VKA activists proudly discussed his relationship with the VKA, they never mentioned his role as national convenor of the JSM.[16] In 2023, Ganesh Ram Bhagat, a former minister in the Raman Singh-led Chhattisgarh Cabinet, was the national convenor of JSM. The co-convenor Raj Kishore Handsa was a full-time worker of the VKA.[17] The VKA supports the issue of delisting, publishes articles in favour of delisting and celebrates the life of Kartik Oraon, who first raised this issue. However, the formation of a separate organization to work on this systematically, indicates that the VKA does not wish to involve itself in the aggressive mobilization of a controversial issue.

Kartik Oraon was a leader of the Indian National Congress from south Bihar (now Jharkhand) and was the first leader who raised the issue of delisting in Parliament. He belonged to the Oraon community, graduated as an engineer in India and went to England for his post-graduation in the field of engineering. He had good career opportunities both abroad as well as in India, but he wanted to work for the progress of tribal people, and so joined politics. In 1967, he was elected to the Lok Sabha from the Lohardaga constituency of Bihar (now part of Jharkhand) and is remembered for raising issues concerning the lives of tribals in Parliament.[18]

The Scheduled Castes and Scheduled Tribes (Orders) Amendment Bill, 1967 introduced in the Lok Sabha in 1967[19] and a Joint Parliamentary Committee (JPC) of both Lok Sabha and Rajya Sabha was constituted to study it. There were thirty-three members in this committee, of which twenty-two members were from Lok Sabha and eleven were from the Rajya Sabha. Kartik Oraon was a member of this JPC. The JPC submitted its report on 17 November 1969 and 2A of Clause 2 of the report said, 'Notwithstanding anything contained in paragraph 2, no person, who has given up tribal faith or faiths and has embraced either Christianity or Islam, shall be deemed to be a member of any Scheduled Tribe'.[20]

However, since this recommendation was controversial, the government did not act on it. On 10 November 1970, Kartik Oraon submitted a memorandum signed by 348 MPs (322 from Lok Sabha and twenty-two from Rajya Sabha) and demanded that the government must accept the report of the JPC. On 17 November 1970, the government tabled a proposal in the Lok Sabha to reject the recommendation of the JPC regarding the exclusion of tribals who converted to Islam and Christianity from the ST list. Kartik Oraon gave a speech on 24 November 1970 and underlined that converted individuals from the tribal communities were taking a large share in the reservation benefits and demanded that Constitutional benefits like reservation should not be given to those tribals who left their original faith. Clearly, Indira Gandhi did not want rumbles in her government on this issue and the recommendation of the JPC on delisting was not accepted. However, the JSM has argued that it was international forces and Christian missionaries which successfully pressurized the government for such a decision.[21]

The JSM underlines that tribals have unique cultures, which is apparent in the worship of their own gods and goddesses, social systems and structures, value systems, etc. Therefore, no tribal can discard faith in their gods and goddesses and claim to follow tribal culture. The JSM also asserts that converted tribals should not be eligible to enjoy the rights prescribed for the STs in the PESA and FRA, because such individuals or groups of individuals have adopted a different culture.[22] The JSM has constantly demanded that Parliament should pass a law on this issue and exclude converted tribals from the list of STs. The JSM has been conducting various seminars and reaching out to socially aware citizens, students, bureaucrats and politicians from tribal communities, labourers, farmers, etc., to spread awareness about delisting. It has been doing this on a mass scale by organizing several meetings and seminars on the issue.[23]

The JSM also organizes mass mobilizations in the form of demonstrations and rallies etc. to press its demands of delisting. In such mobilizations, it uses placards with slogans which express the essence of its work: 'converted tribals are outcasts', '*Kul devi tum jaag jao, dharmantarit tum bhag jaao*' (family deity awaken, the converts get out), '*Jo Bholenath ka nahin, woh hamari jaat ka nahin*' (one who is not with Bholenath [Lord Shiva] is not from our community), etc. These slogans also underline the carefully constructed Hindutva iconography of Lord Shiva being the tribal god.[24]

Indeed, the VKA and other RSS-affiliated organizations present their demands as the interests of 'actual' (non-converted) tribals. They assert that the government must conduct surveys across India's tribal belt to understand the actual impact of the implementation of reservation for STs. Only such a study can clarify whether converted tribals have snatched away the rights of 'actual' non-converted tribals.[25] 29 November is celebrated as the birth anniversary of Kartik Oraon, and on this day, the VKA submits memorandums to district magistrates of 288 tribal-dominated districts and the governors and chief ministers of states with a substantive tribal populations. The memorandum demands the exclusion of converted tribals from the list of STs. The VKA also published articles in *Van Bandhu* in support of delisting, though it maintains a distance from the mobilization works organized under the banner of the JSM. Yet, *Van Bandhu*, does publish reports of the JSM's mobilizational works.[26]

Virginius Xaxa has argued that the advocates of Hindutva conveniently overlook the fact that tribes have distinct religions of their own and that tribals have been converted not only to Christianity (or Islam) but also to Hinduism.[27] He underscores that individuals are identified as tribes because they belong to a group or community that has been enumerated as STs through the provisions of the Indian Constitution. So, following a particular religion is not the basis of the inclusion of a group in the category of STs. Different groups are included in this category because they constitute a particular community, which is distinct from the dominant regional community. Denying the Constitutional provision to certain members of the community just because they choose to practice another religion goes against the very spirit of the Indian Constitution.[28]

The issue of delisting has been used to create a communal divide in tribal areas, particularly in states like Jharkhand, Chhattisgarh, Madhya Pradesh, etc. For example, before the

Chhattisgarh assembly elections of 2023, the JSM ran a campaign against tickets being given to converted tribals in ST-reserved seats.[29] Likewise, a rally was organized on 24 December 2023 in Ranchi to support the demand for the delisting of converted tribals. The speakers argued that converted tribals were availing of the benefit of being both tribals and religious minorities. A senior BJP leader, Kariya Munda, also participated in the rally and underscored that,

> converted tribals are getting triple benefits: minorities get funds from India and abroad for the socio-economic upliftment of their community; they get the benefit of schemes meant for religious minorities; and they also get the benefits meant for adivasis. At the same time, the non-converted tribals get miniscule benefits.[30]

Interestingly, this demand has been echoed by almost all leaders of different organizations of the RSS, who have been working in tribal areas, for example, Vishnu Deo Sai, who became CM of Chhattisgarh in December 2023. He was earlier active in the VKA and has been demanding that those tribals who converted to Christianity or Islam should be excluded from the list of the STs.[31]

The BJP has not accepted the JSM and VKA's demands for delisting because it is fraught with many contradictions. The key contradiction is that those demanding the delisting of converted tribals have simply assumed them to be Hindus. As discussed in the first parts of the chapter, this is an incorrect understanding of tribal society. Some groups are also demanding the recognition of a tribal religion—Sarna. Another crucial problem is related to the BJP's ambition of expansion. The party has found a strong base in the North-east states and any move towards delisting of converted tribes could antagonize the Christian voters in this region. So, the issue of delisting is a sharp political arm in the hands of VKA and JSM to create majoritarian mobilization (Hinduized tribals and other Hindus) against the minority Christian tribal groups in states like Chhattisgarh, Jharkhand, etc.

The VKA, Maoism and the Pathalgadi Movement

Many tribal areas of India are affected by the left extremism where the Communist Party of India (Maoist) has a strong hold. Indeed, many districts of Chhattisgarh, Jharkhand, Andhra Pradesh and Telangana have been facing continuous violent activities by Maoists.[32] There is a clear distinction between Maoist politics and the works and agenda of the VKA. For the Maoists, the cultural autonomy of the tribals and their rights to forest land and its resources is the central theme. However, since they understand the nature of the present Indian state as a tool in the hands of the corporate-capitalist class, they focus on overthrowing this state by waging guerrilla warfare. Due to this reason, the Maoist Party—the Communist Party of India (Maoist)—is a banned organization. The VKA, as discussed in the previous chapters, claims that tribals are Hindus, and it opposes proselytization to any other faith. It also does different kinds of *seva* (service) works. It staunchly opposes the Maoists due to their rejection of religious values and violent activities. It is also noteworthy that the VKA has supported forest rights of local communities, but it is not against corporate capital or developmental activities. It focuses on securing tribals' rights through proper implementation of laws like the PESA and FRA. Though the VKA has been ferociously critical of the violent activities of the Maoists, it has never questioned the violence by the state. For the Maoists, organizations like the VKA represent reactionary forces, which are not only working to change the identity of tribal people but also creating a path for the implementation of the neo-liberal agenda of the state. For the VKA, the Maoists are anti-national, violent forces, which must be curbed by the use of state machinery.

In 1978, the VKA decided to extend its works in the different tribal areas of the country. Interestingly, one of the key reasons mentioned by the then RSS sarsanghchalak Balasaheb Deoras, and VKA's president, Ramakant Deshpande, was to control the menace of Naxalism.[33] Vasantrao Bhatt, who was the *sangathan mantri* (organization secretary) of the VKA in the early 1980s, emphasized the need to make tribals aware of the negative aspects of Naxalism.[34] He argued that 'society is full of diversity and the idea of making all classes equal is fundamentally wrong. The diversity of flowers in the garden made it beautiful. This is the law of nature'.[35] Pramod Petkar, a senior activist of the VKA and managing editor of *Van Bandhu*, argues that all former presidents, organization secretaries and senior activists have been unanimous regarding their analyses of the Naxal movement. All of them termed it a serious menace for the country and society and underlined the need to crush it. According to him,

> this notion is entirely wrong that tribals are supporting the Naxals. It seems that some tribals are supporting them, but the fact of the matter is that they are doing so only due to the fear of violence by the Naxals. They are against communication, roads, and education because if these things reach tribal areas, it would be difficult for them to hide themselves The Naxals claim to be sympathetic to tribals, but actually, they do not want development in tribal society. They are exploiting them. Even they want their share in Tendu leaves and they take money from contractors too. It is a wrong perception that tribal society is with them.[36]

He also emphatically criticized the 'Urban Naxals' (supporters of Naxals living in urban areas) who have been raising the issue of human rights of those who kill innocent people. For him, they are also dangerous and governments should try to control them.[37]

The RSS has always seen the Maoists as its primary enemy and always supported the measures adopted by the state to control Maoists. When Salwa Judum was started in 2005, the RSS and its other affiliates, including the VKA, lent full support to it. Salwa Judum was started by Mahendra Karma, a senior Congress leader and Leader of Opposition in the Chhattisgarh legislative assembly. The Raman Singh-led BJP government in Chhattisgarh provided full support to this campaign where arms were given to young tribals, who were called Special Police Officers (SPOs) to drive out the Maoists. Those villages that owed allegiance to Maoists were vacated and residents were put in camps. Many tribals were murdered and tribal girls were raped in this campaign.[38] An RSS think-tank underlined the continuous history of conflict and struggle between sangh organizations like the VKA, Vidya Bharati, etc., and the Maoists and confirms the role of the RSS in Salwa Judum:

> The participation of Gayatri Parivar, Sangha Parivar and the Divya Seva Sangh [sic] situated in Gumaragunda village of Dantewara is incredible . . . This movement [Salwa Judum] started fifteen years ago through the peaceful People Awakening Programme. The overall objective of the movement is to form a village security committee. This movement stays away completely from any publicity or propaganda. This is their main strength.[39]

Nandini Sundar says that many tribal students displaced due to Salwa Judum were taken away to hostels run by the VKA. She underlines that the administration had more faith in schools run by the VKA, because it feared students would be influenced by Maoist propaganda in interior school.[40] In other words, the VKA not only supported the Salwa Judum but also helped state authorities to fulfil their agendas. On 5 July 2011, the Supreme Court declared in the case *Nandini Sundar & Others vs. state of Chhattisgarh* that the appointment of untrained villagers as Special Police Officers (SPOs) in frontline counter-insurgency operations were illegal and unconstitutional. In a sense, the SC declared the foundation of Salwa Judum, i.e. giving arms to local tribals to fight against the Maoists, as 'unconstitutional'. [41] Interestingly, *Organizer*, the weekly magazine of the RSS, termed the SC judgment as the rationalization of the Maoist ideology.[42]

In this context, the discussion of the Pathalgadi Movement is important. Pathalgadi is a term used for the stone slabs erected by tribals to mark important events in a village, such as birth and death. After the enactment of the PESA, B.D. Sharma and the Bharat Jan Andolan began the Pathalgadi Movement to teach tribals about PESA by inscribing key provisions of both PESA and FRA on a stone pillar in tribal areas. Many studies have underlined that it enhanced the knowledge of local communities about these laws.[43]

The Pathalgadi Movement emerged due to certain decisions by the BJP-led Jharkhand government in 2016, which had brought an ordinance seeking to amend the Chota Nagpur Tenancy Act, 1908 and the Santhal Pargana Tenancy Act, 1949. The purpose of the amendments was to empower the government to acquire tribal people's land for commercial purposes. It also made possible the transfer of their land to non-tribal people. This was met with stiff resistance by the tribals in the form of a movement during 2017–18, which came to be known as the Pathalgadi Movement. The stone slabs were put up at key points in the village and key Constitutional provisions related to the rights of tribals were inscribed on them. They also declared their villages as republics (Gaon Ganarajya). Violent street protests took place and the state government slapped sedition cases against thousands of tribals. It was reported that in Khunti district alone, which is the birthplace of tribal icon, Birsa Munda, 10,000 such cases were registered. The then governor of the state, Droupadi Murmu, did not give her consent to the amendments and sent the ordinances back to the government in May 2017, which were later withdrawn.[44]

The then VKA president Jagdev Ram Oraon criticized the movement and argued that 'the rights of the Gram Sabha and the 5th Schedule are being misinterpreted. Objectionable, provocative, unparliamentary, and unconstitutional language has been used to criticize the government. It is a clear attempt to destabilize the harmony of the society and misguide the STs'.[45] The *Organizer* termed the Pathalgadi Movement as a misuse of traditional practices by the Church-Naxal-led extremism in scheduled areas, and that the objective of this movement was to incite people against the state and destabilize the state ahead of the 2019 Jharkhand Assembly elections.[46]

During the 2019 state assembly elections, the fear of Raghubar Das returning to power and enforcing the amendments to land acquisition played a crucial role in the victory of the JMM–Congress candidates in most of the tribal-dominated areas. After the election, the alliance of the JMM–Congress–RJD and CPI (ML) Liberation formed a government. Immediately after assuming office, Chief Minister Hemant Soren announced that all Pathalgadi cases would be withdrawn. After the 2019 Jharkhand Legislative Assembly elections, the Pathalgadi Movement gradually faded away due to the fear of state harassment and many tribal youths active in the movement withdrew. This movement underlined that tribal communities are politically conscious and can voice their views on issues affecting them. It also became clear that the VKA was not ready to accept any radical mobilization against the state machinery.

VKA activists have respect for other grassroots organizations, particularly those that have been following Gandhian principles, like the Bharat Jan Andolan (BJA) and its founder B.D. Sharma. Similarly, many senior activists praised the role of those grassroots tribal organizations, which were left-aligned but worked for the enactment and implementation of the FRA. It is discussed in the previous chapter that *Van Bandhu* not only criticized the BJP government for overlooking the interest of tribals but also praised the Congress and left leaders for raising the issues of tribals. Though the VKA supported state oppression to curb Maoists, on many occasions, it also supported speedy trial or bail for poor tribals incarcerated as undertrials since they cannot afford good lawyers.[47]

Violence, Mission of Ghar Wapsi and the VKA

Senior activists of the VKA always emphasize that the VKA never endorses any kind of violence, and while hugely critical of the works of Christian missionaries, it always uses creative and legal ways to oppose their proselytization efforts. Like many other RSS members, VKA activists do not condemn violence by other activists in the Sangh Parivar. And even in some exceptional conditions they criticize violent acts, their criticism is always conditional. For example, on 23 January 1998, Graham Stuart Staines was burnt to death along with his two sons by members of the Bajrang Dal. Though the activists of the VKA condemn such violent activity, they question the role of Christian missionaries and demand stringent laws against their activities.[48]

However, there are ample examples to underline that on many occasions the VKA activists have also indulged in violent activities. The ghar wapsi ceremonies have also been a source of tension and fear among Christian tribal minorities. Perhaps, the most large-scale incident of anti-Christian violence in the recent past took place in Kandhamal, Odisha, in 2008 after the murder of Lakshmanananda Saraswati by Maoists. But a year before in December, violence had erupted in Kandhamal, on the issue of conversion/reconversion.[49]

Lakshmanananda Saraswati was a leader of the Vishwa Hindu Parishad (VHP) and had done good work for the education of tribal boys and girls in different parts of Kandhamal district. He was also active against the Christian missionaries, which led to a violent clash in December 2007. Angana P. Chatterji presents the views of Vanvasi Kalyan Ashram's activists and close associates of Lakshmanananda regarding the work he did:

> Christian missionaries oppose nature worship so are opposed to our culture. We are promoting Hindu rituals amongst vanvasis who are all Hindus. Lakshmanananda Saraswati has been a restraining force on the Christians who were doing the conversion works. We have adopted the Hindu rituals and oppose those who are following Christian mode of worship.[50]

Indeed, in the description of the activists of the VKA, Lakshmanananda Saraswati emerges as a saint, who was working to protect Hindus and Indian culture in Kandhamal. However, Chatterji argues that the Lakshmanananda Saraswati incited violence against Dalit and adivasi Christians.[51] In her description of the violence during the Kandhamal riots, she notes that various organizations of the Sangh Parivar led the violence. She writes,

> On the morning of 24 December, at approximately 11.00 am activists from various Hindutva groups, including Bajrang Dal, VHP, RSS, Vanvasi Kalyan Ashram reportedly organized vandalism of Christmas symbols erected on the occasion of Christmas and unleashed turmoil in Brahmanigaon/Bamunigaon village in central Kandhamal.[52]

The violence and reconversion of Christian tribals to Hinduism by Lakshmanananda Saraswati led to his murder by Maoists on 23 August 2008, which caused even more violence in the area. Lakshmanananda Saraswati had a large numbers of followers, who were angry after his murder. According to one report, in the violence that erupted after his murder, ninety-three people were killed; over 350 churches belonging to the adivasi Christians were destroyed; and more than 56,000 people displaced.[53] Usually, the VKA does not condemn violence against Christian tribals, and on many occasions as apparent from the description of Kandhamal, its activists are complicit with other right wing organizations in violence. In fact, Christian tribals were frightened over the issue of ghar wapsi.

As mentioned earlier, when the VKA was formed, the Maharaja of Jashpur provided land and other help to the VKA. His son Dilip Singh Judeo has also played a pivotal role in the activities of the VKA. Indeed, from 1984 onwards he travelled to the hinterland to 'reconvert' Christian tribals to Hinduism.[54] His efforts towards ghar wapsi made him a politically influential figure within the BJP. Angana Chatterji says that in June 2002, the VHP pressured 143 adivasi Christians from forty-six families of the Oram, Munda and Khadia tribes into converting to Hinduism at Tainser village in Sundargarh district of Odisha.

In early March 2004, 212 Christians from fifty-three tribal families were converted to Hinduism in the Jharsuguda district in Odisha. The ritual was jointly convened by the VHP and the Vanvasi Kalyan Ashram and attended by BJP leader and former Union Minister, Dilip Singh Judeo. It was a controversial event because the Global Council of Indian Christians asked the President of India, A.P.J. Abdul Kalam to take action against the non-consensual conversion of Christians to Hinduism.[55] Interestingly, *Van Bandhu* republished the obituary of Dilip Singh Judeo published in the *Panchjanya*, the mouthpiece of the RSS. This obituary not only praised the work of Judeo but also called him as 'Hindu Hriday Samrat' (Emperor of Hindu Hearts). In 2003, Judeo was caught taking bribes on camera and had to resign from the Vajpayee government. However, his supporters termed this episode as an attempt of character assassination by Christians.[56]

But due to Dilip Singh Judeo's campaign, the BJP government in Chhattisgarh enacted a legislation—the *Chhattisgarh Freedom of Religion (Amendment) Act, 2006*. According to this legislation, anyone who converts a person to his faith must seek permission from the local District Magistrate at least thirty days in ahead. However, this law does not apply to a person who is returning to his original religion, which means it is not effective if a Christian tribal decides to convert to Hinduism. Violation of this law attracts a jail term of up to three years and a fine of up to Rs 20,000. Interestingly, the BJP's government in Chhattisgarh has proposed a bill in February 2024 to make conversion law more stringent. Christian organizations have opposed such a law, terming it unconstitutional because it does not propose any kind of restriction on reconversion from Christianity, or any other religion, to Hinduism. [57]

After the death of Dilip Singh Judeo, his son Prabal Pratap Singh Judeo continued the work of ghar wapsi.[58] In appreciation of the work of the Judeo family towards ghar wapsi, the RSS chief unveiled a statue of Dilip Singh Judeo on 14 November 2022,[59] ahead of the 2023 Chhattisgarh election. Ghar wapsi has been a way to polarize Hindus in general, and Hinduized tribals in particular, against Christian missionaries. For example, on 21 February 2023, in Jashpur, thirty-six Catholic tribal families took part in a series of rituals, starting with a *shuddhikaran* (purification), after which they reconverted to Hinduism. The ceremony of ghar wapsi was organized by the Dharma Jagaran Samiti (DJS) which is affiliated to the RSS. Many senior RSS functionaries and members of the Judeo family were also present at the function.[60] Women priests performed all the rituals and the representative of the erstwhile royal Judeo family, Prabal Pratap Judeo, washed the feet of converted tribals. Indeed, Judeo increased this ghar wapsi campaign before the 2014 general elections. He started the Akhil Bharatiya Ghar Wapsi Abhiyan and along with Christian tribals, he also converted Muslims to Hinduism.[61] Other BJP politicians also participated in the drive. After the 2023 state assembly election in Chhattisgarh, Vishnu Deo Sai was selected as the new chief minister of the state. Closely associated with the VKA and the Gayatri Parivar,[62] Sai had prioritized ghar wapsi over the last few decades. He backed another affiliate of the RSS, the 'Dharma Jagran Manch' (DJM) which organizes ghar wapsi ceremonies in the tribal belts of Chhattisgarh.[63]

It is clear from the above discussion that those activists or leaders who have been part of the VKA, use other organizations for the ghar wapsi campaign. Prabal Pratap Judeo's grandfather played a crucial role in the formation of the VKA, while his father was also active in the organization. However, for his reconversion drive, he used the banner of other organizations. Similarly, Vishnu Deo Sai, a member of the VKA, campaigned under the banner of the DJM during the ghar wapsi drives. Angana Chatterji says the ghar wapsi drive was jointly organized by the VHP and VKA[64], but it is an exception because there is no other example where the VKA organized such a campaign under its banner. Of course, many of its activists have participated in such acts earlier, but under the banner of some other organization. Though the activists are the same, they change the banner of the organization, for different works. For social welfare and constructive work, the VKA's banner is useful, but for other controversial works, the names of other organizations have been used. It is also clear that the ghar wapsi is a useful tool for the BJP to create a division in tribal areas and enhance its majoritarian politics. Such a campaign mobilizes a large section of society (Hinduized tribals and non-tribal Hindus) against minority groups.

It could be argued that if Christian missionaries are converting tribal people by using inducement and wrong means, is ghar wapsi conducted by the Hindu right-wing activists wrong? Undoubtedly, conversion by using illegal means is not only unethical but a crime. Our Constitution gives rights to individuals to accept any religion or change their faith. If someone is leaving or accepting a particular religion as his/her individual choice, legally it is not problematic. However, the problem with the ghar wapsi ceremonies is that they have been used as a political tool to show the power or dominance of Hindu majoritarian politics in tribal areas. It makes reconversion a public performance to mobilize and Hinduize tribals and other Hindus against a perceived enemy—converted Christian or Muslim tribals. Nandini Sundar has underlined that ghar wapsi campaigns do not give tribals a respectful social status in the Hindu community and they have remained at the lowest strata of Hindu society.[65]

The VKA, Hindutva and Electoral Politics

In the recent past, the BJP has had electoral successes in tribal areas. Out of a total of 543 seats in the Lok Sabha, forty-seven are reserved for STs. If one considers the party-wise performance of these seats since the 2014 election, it is clear that the BJP has outperformed all other parties. In the 2014 Lok Sabha elections, the BJP won twenty-seven seats out of the forty-seven ST seats, while the INC (or Congress) won only five seats. In 2019, the BJP increased its tally by winning thirty-one seats and the INC won four seats. In the 2024 Lok Sabha elections the BJP faced a setback but it still won twenty-five of the reserved ST seats, while the INC increased its tally in the election and won twelve seats. Other seats were won by the Jharkhand Mukti Morcha (JMM), Trinamool Congress and other regional parties.[66] Similarly, the BJP's electoral performance in tribal-dominated assembly constituencies has improved, which played a crucial role in its electoral success in Chhattisgarh, Madhya Pradesh, and Rajasthan etc. in recent years. Though it has faced debacles in many constituencies over the last decade, it has still established itself as one of the key players in electoral politics in almost all ST constituencies of these states. Since 2014, it has impressively expanded its footprint in the states of North-east region of India. Is there any relationship between the better electoral performance of the BJP and the VKA's work in tribal areas? Would it be correct to assert that the VKA has been doing the groundwork to provide electoral benefits to the political wing of the RSS, which is the BJP?

As mentioned earlier in this book, the VKA was formed to counter Christian missionaries and spread Hindu values in tribal areas, which was supported by senior Congress leaders, particularly Ravishankar Shukla, the former CM of Central Provinces (later Madhya Pradesh). Gradually, the

VKA established its foothold in tribal areas of Chhattisgarh, Jharkhand and Odisha. The political wing of the RSS, earlier the Jan Sangh which morphed into the BJP in 1980, has been active in electoral politics. It has been assumed that like other affiliates of the RSS, the works of the VKA have created a conducive environment for the BJP. It is discussed in earlier chapters that the VKA has been working on various areas including education, medical services, women empowerment, village development, etc. In the last few decades, it has also been working on the issue of forest rights of tribal people and it has adopted the agenda raised by grassroots tribal organizations, which follow the left or Gandhian ideologies. Through its long-term works on all such issues, it has created strong goodwill at the local level, which is of course helpful to the BJP.

The VKA and its activists claim that it is an 'apolitical' organization which works for the welfare of tribal people and resists the illegal conversion attempts of the Christian missionaries. It implies that the VKA has nothing to do with electoral politics, in which candidates compete with each other to get the support of the electorates. A senior activist of the VKA, Girish Kuber argued that,

> The purpose behind the formation of the VKA was not to provide an electoral base to one or another party. Ramakant Deshpande formed this organization, after consultation with and under the guidance of Guru Golwalkar (the then Sarsanghchalak of the RSS) to serve Vanvasis and to protect Hinduism and our motherland Bharat. The purpose of the VKA is much greater than the electoral victories or the formation of the governments. The VKA wishes to end the influence of anti-national forces, particularly Christian missionaries from the tribal areas. Changes through politics are not permanent, but changes through service work and

> continuous dialogue always make a lasting impact on tribals' lives.[67]

Such sentiments were also expressed by other senior members of the VKA. For example, Madhvi, a senior activist of the VKA, who started to work for the organization in the early 1980s is now a warden of Shabari Kanya Ashram in Raipur (Chhattisgarh). She also expressed the same sentiments and argued that 'politics is not permanent. What we do (in the VKA) is permanent—it changes a person from within'.[68]

VKA activists downplay the argument that the work of their organization helps the BJP in elections. A senior leader of the VKA, Suresh Kulkarni, underscores that,

> We have our specific agenda for vanvasi samaj, we oppose conversion by Christian missionaries and we want to fill the gap between vanvasis and other Hindu communities. Since the BJP adopts and follows our agenda, of course, it gets electoral benefits in tribal areas. Some other organizations could also support our agenda and they will reap the benefit of goodwill created by our work.[69]

Though the VKA office-bearers and senior activists deny any role in electoral politics, it is in fact, not true. Many BJP tribal leaders started their political careers from the VKA and then moved to the BJP. Many activists of the VKA also actively support many BJP candidates in their elections. The voice of local VKA leadership plays an important role in the distribution of tickets in the BJP, particularly in constituencies reserved for STs. It does not imply that all tickets are distributed according to the VKA's wishes, but if it opposes a particular aspirant of candidature, it would be difficult for him/her to get a ticket.[70] Indeed, the VKA has been providing help to BJP candidates in elections, for example, in the 2023 assembly election in Chhattisgarh. Some of its members also argued that it played a vital role in the defeat of the BJP in the 2018 assembly elections because the then government did not give any importance to the agenda of the VKA.[71]

In his study, Tariq Thachil argues that the works of the VKA played a crucial role in garnering votes in favour of BJP candidates. Thachil underscores that the VKA creates a depoliticized discourse surrounding its service works like education. Indeed, VKA activists have been trying to influence voters who interact with them even in the space of their seva or service works. Thachil quotes a VKA activist's account of the influence of their seva works on voters:

> See when the students come to our schools, their parents also start getting affected . . . Now if someone who we support enters politics then because [the parents] thoughts toward our school . . . they are opening to listen to our views. We will not campaign for any party, but from an individual point of view, we will say who we think would do well.[72]

However, there are few examples when VKA activists worked more closely with the BJP. Angana Chatterji notes that in the 2004 election campaign in Odisha, the VKA along with the BJP Scheduled Tribes Morcha was the key strategist and organizer for the BJP in the tribal belt.[73] VKA activists also play a different kind of role during elections like spreading rumours about leaders of non-BJP parties. The Congress leader Ajit Jogi was the best-known victim of this efficient rumour mill. In 2001, the National Scheduled Castes and Scheduled Tribes Commission (NSCSTC) was headed by BJP leader, Dilip Singh Bhuria.[74] It passed an order to declare that Ajit Jogi's ST category certificate was forged, and in reality, he was a member of the Satnami caste (SC category). The VKA leaders worked hard to plant seeds of doubt against the Congress leader among the adivasi communities. For ordinary adivasis, these accusations became more credible because they were also supported by the VKA activists, who were not an active part of politics. However, the Bilaspur High Court overturned the decision of NSCSTC in 2006, which again enabled Jogi to contest from the constituencies reserved for the STs.[75] Most importantly there has been a pattern in certain areas to create polarization through aggressive mobilization against tribal Christians on the issue of ghar wapsi. As mentioned, many VKA activists have been participating in such activities, but under the banner of some other organizations.

It has been argued by many scholars that the RSS and its affiliates, including the VKA played a crucial role in the electoral success of the BJP in many North-east states.[76] As mentioned in previous chapters (see chapters two and three), the VKA began work in the North-east region in the late 1970s and largely tried to mobilize tribal communities through its seva works and by creating a differentiation between non-Christian and Christian tribal communities. Undoubtedly, the continuous works of the RSS and its affiliates, including VKA created a base in these states. However, the BJP started to get electoral success only after the emergence of Narendra Modi as a strong pan-India leader. The BJP also focused on defection from other political parties, which provided it with some popular faces in different states (for example, Himanta Biswa Sarma in Assam, N. Biren Singh in Manipur, Manik Saha in Tripura, Pema Khandu in Arunachal Pradesh). These leaders helped the BJP emerge as a strong force in different states, which led to its electoral victories.

The BJP also tweaked its politics according to the needs of different states. For example, it presented itself as a 'secular' party in Meghalaya to get Christian votes.[77] Meghalaya BJP state president Ernest Mawire,[78] Pema Khandu and Kiren Rijiju have supported eating beef.[79] Apart from ideological flexibility, the BJP's promise of efficient governance also attracted voters. There has been a tendency at the local level for smaller groups to maintain a cordial relationship with the party that is in power at the state and central levels. This factor also attracted smaller political groups to the BJP. So, though the RSS and its affiliates like the VKA provided a base for the BJP in the North-east, its electoral success cannot be attributed to them alone.

Nandini Sundar underscores the works of VKA and other affiliates of the RSS as one among many reasons of the victory of the Raman Singh-led BJP government in the Chhattisgarh assembly elections. She writes that the reason behind the consecutive victory of Raman Singh (till 2018) can be attributed to his government's welfare measures like the Rs 2 rice scheme and the health (village-level auxiliary health worker) programme. Along with these programmes she also acknowledges the role of the Sangh Parivar and the VKA's welfare works.[80]

The VKA and its affiliate organizations have tried to push their agenda in politics of the BJP. For example, in 2015, the VKA released a Vision Document, that recommended many important measures to ensure the rights of tribal communities over forest resources and provide better education and health facilities. Though the VKA wanted to push forward this document, the BJP only accepted some suggestions because accepting all suggestions would have been detrimental to the interest of corporate houses. There are ample examples where the VKA criticizes the stand of the BJP government on the issue of weakening the FRA. Similarly, the VKA and its affiliates have been demanding the 'delisting' of those tribals from the list of the STs, who converted to Christianity and Islam, which has not been accepted by the BJP. It is likely that the BJP fears that acceptance of such a demand would negatively impact its prospects in North-east states.

The formation of the BJP government at the Centre and states with substantial tribal populations has only increased the influence of the VKA as an organization. Since it tried to project an 'apolitical' character in the early decades of its formation, it also received help from many state governments led by the INC. However, non-Congress or the BJP governments have been more helpful for the VKA. Ramakant Deshpande admitted that in 1968, the Samyukt Vidhayak Dal (SVD) had voted to extend credits to the VKA, which Congress rescinded after its return to power. Similarly, Larang Sai became minister of state in the Morarji Desai government and he visited Jashpur and expressed interest in and respect for the VKA.[81] The growing influence of the Jan Sangh in the seventies, which later morphed into the BJP in 1980, had helped the VKA expand its work in new areas.

Many activists of the VKA have become part of the government at both the central and state levels. The governments have provided the VKA and its office-bearers with help and special treatment both at the local level and at the upper strata of the power structure. For example, in the recent past, Harsh Chouhan, an activist of the VKA became the chairman of NCST (National Commission of Scheduled Tribes). As a president of the NCST, he tried to implement the agenda of VKA by organizing many functions to celebrate tribal freedom fighters, which presented all of them as Hindus.[82] Many state and central ministers or Members of Parliament have visited the VKA's offices or have attended programmes organized by it.[83] Even the President of India Ram Nath Kovind had inaugurated a hostel building constructed by one of the affiliates of the VKA in Sonbhadra.[84] This relationship with the BJP has not only provided posts, resources and respect to the VKA at all levels of governance, but has also provided legitimacy due to, for instance, visits by the President and several ministers to its functions.

It is also important to note that in tribal areas there are many other political parties, who denounce the vision of the VKA (particularly regarding the identity of the tribals). Parties like the Indian National Congress, Jharkhand Mukti Morcha (active in Jharkhand and Odisha), Bharat Adivasi Party (BAP)—primarily a Rajasthan-centric party, Bharatiya Tribal Party (BTP)—mainly a Gujarat-centric party, etc., do not accept the proposition that tribals are Hindus and that they should not be treated as 'adivasis'. So, though in tribal areas the RSS and the VKA version of Hindutva politics have been consolidated in the last few decades, it is not the only voice present in these areas. Apart from many civil society organizations, the left parties and state-level above-mentioned parties have also seriously questioned the RSS and VKA's politics of Hindutva in tribal areas. As discussed in chapter three, Rahul Gandhi's continuous objections to the use of the term 'vanvasi' compelled the Modi government to use the term 'adivasi' in its ambitious PM-JANMAN project.

Summing Up

The VKA has approached various contested issues according to its dedication to the larger Hindutva-based ideological framework of the RSS. It has strongly opposed the demand for the Sarna Code as it feels it would divide Hindu tribal society. Delisting and ghar wapsi have become prominent issues for the VKA and other affiliates of the RSS, because other things apart, they provide opportunities to mobilize the majority (Hinduized tribals and non-tribal Hindus) against the 'other' in tribal societies. Interestingly, the VKA has been conscious of trying to maintain its image as an organization that is primarily dedicated to constructive and service works. So, as an organization, it has maintained a distance from aggressive mobilization against minorities (Christians and Muslims). It has also declared itself as an organization, which has no role in electoral politics. But after some scrutiny, it is obvious that the senior activists of the VKA have formed different organizations for aggressive mobilization on issues like delisting and ghar wapsi. The VKA has also been playing an important role in the electoral politics of the BJP and must be credited with creating a strong base for Hindutva politics in tribal areas. It is one of several factors that led to the electoral victories of the BJP in these areas. It is observed that the BJP has changed its position on many issues according to the electoral needs of a particular space and its Hindutva agenda has faced many challenges from different tribal groups. Some of them are active in electoral politics (emergence of new tribal political formations) and some of them are challenging it through cultural discourses (demand for Sarna Code and use of other cultural means).

7

Conclusion: Is the Vanvasi Kalyan Ashram a Robust Ambassador of Hindutva Politics?

The RSS is the vanguard of Hindutva ideology, and works in different parts of society through various organizations, collectively called the Sangh Parivar. The VKA is an organization related to the Sangh Parivar, which has been active in tribal areas since 1952. It has gradually enhanced its work, extended it to new areas and incorporated the different concerns of tribals. The primary reason behind the formation of the VKA was a fear of the increasing number of Christians in tribal areas and VKA began to strengthen the ties between tribal communities and 'mainstream' Hindu society. It calls tribals vanvasis (forest-dwelling communities) or janjatis (tribes) rather than adivasis (original inhabitants) to underline that they are not the original inhabitants of India. Indeed, its basic understanding is that janjatis/vanvasis and Hindus are inseparable, and all janjatis are part of Sanatan Dharma. Its primary slogan is, 'Tu Main Ek Rakt' (You and I have the same blood).

Shradha Jagran and Creation of the 'Other'

The VKA focuses on bringing together different tribal communities under the banner of Hindu identity which is based on the idea of creating the 'other'. In tribal areas, both Christianity and Islam (but primarily Christianity) are the 'other' communities due to their foreign origin. Hindutva considers both Christianity and Islam as foreign religions and underlines that their *Pitra-Bhu* (fatherland) and *Punya-Bhu* (holy land) are not in India. It always censured Christian missionaries for converting innocent tribal people to Christianity by pressuring them or making false promises. When the VKA started to extend its works in the country's North-east region, it used the same argument. It also underlined that Christian missionaries were instigating anti-India feelings in the North-east region and therefore it used the more extensive idea of Sanatan Dharma as an umbrella category to include all Indian-origin faiths, to counter and exclude Christians (and in some instances Muslims). It underlines that Christians and Muslims are not part of Sanatan Dharma because they are foreign religions.

The VKA has focused on shradha jagran in tribal areas, which is the Hinduization of tribal communities and enlightening them about Hindu scriptures, pilgrimages and rituals. Indeed, as mentioned in chapter one, tribal communities in different areas have developed a close relationship with the Hindu population due to civilizational interactions, and also adopted many cultural aspects of Hinduism which has created a conducive environment for shradha jagran. The VKA has been using diverse methods to increase the Hinduization of tribal communities. However, to establish a strong bond with tribal communities, the VKA has also begun to celebrate many tribal festivals. It promotes folk music and dance, handicrafts and tribal art to different parts of the country, particularly in urban areas. Interestingly, though RSS has been a staunch supporter of the Uniform Civil Code and the BJP has made it a core political agenda, the VKA has strongly opposed the imposition of the UCC in tribal areas. It indicates that the VKA is not trying to unilaterally impose Hindu cultural values on tribals. This feeling is only for those communities, who have already accepted Hindu identity or are sympathetic towards it. As discussed in chapter six, the VKA has strongly opposed the demand for the Sarna Code because it feels that it is a ploy by the Christian missionaries to divide Hindus in tribal areas.

Seva and Hit Raksha: Creation of a Solid Base

The VKA conducts different kinds of social service work in tribal areas which have played a vital role in the lives of tribal people and helped the VKA to consolidate its support base. VKA founder, Ramakant Deshpande, started his work by establishing schools in tribal areas. Through its schools and hostels, it has created a considerable impact on different tribal areas. However, as discussed in chapter four, the VKA schools focus on establishing Hindu rituals and values as 'normal'. In this process, they deliberately overlook most of the cultural values of tribals. VKA hostels promote Hindu religious figures or deities among tribal youths, which, in most cases, weakens the tribal identity of the tribal students. There is no doubt that the VKA has also adopted/accepted specific cultural values of tribal people. It has permitted non-vegetarian food for students,[1] and as mentioned in chapter three, it also celebrates many tribal festivals. The VKA has been organizing different tournaments at the local level or the national tribal sports festivals at the national level.

The VKA has established some excellent hospitals in tribal areas, particularly the hospital of Jashpur. Its idea of a 'mobile hospital' (working out of ambulances in interior tribal areas) has also proved very helpful for tribals in interior areas. Certainly, the VKA hospitals do not discriminate against tribals on the basis of their religion, but it is also true that most Christian tribals prefer either government hospitals or hospitals run by Christian missionaries. The other crucial aspect of VKA's work is that it continuously promotes Ayurveda, tribal local medicines and the traditional knowledge of tribals to address different diseases.

The VKA has also done important work for the education and development of tribal women. In many areas, it has helped and inspired women to establish self-help groups and make themselves self-reliant through traditional handicrafts. However, it has always emphasized the importance of family values and has taught tribal women to respect family values and care for the welfare of family members.

The VKA has been doing many other works which include village development and works in urban areas. Through village development works it tries to enhance community works in tribal villages. It gives tribal villages information regarding various government projects and ensures their proper implementation. Through urban works the VKA collects funds from urban people for its projects. It makes urban people aware of tribal life, culture and the problems they face.

The VKA created a separate 'Hit Raksha Vibhag' (Interest Protection Department) in 1990 and systematically began work on the forest rights of tribal communities. However, many senior activists have argued that before its formation, the VKA had been raising issues related to tribal rights. Still, it would be correct to say that it started systematic work only after 1990. The formation of the 'Hit Raksha Vibhag' and its works, underline the capacity of the VKA to intervene in those issues which can extend its influence and legitimacy within the tribal communities.[2]

The VKA has emphatically expressed its displeasure regarding the half-hearted implementation of the PESA and FRA and argues that there is a need to do systematic work to ensure that all sections of STs and OTFDs benefit from the provisions of the FRA. It is also noteworthy that the VKA does not present any romanticized view regarding the relationship between tribals and wildlife. Many tribal organizations emphasize that tribals have always protected forests and wildlife. In such a narrative, the FD officials emerge as key villains because of poaching. The VKA, on the other hand, accepts the possibility that in specific situations, some tribals may indulge in poaching or even help poachers. Therefore, it focuses on creating a good relationship between the forest-dwelling communities and the FD. Thus, though it unequivocally supports the implementation of the FRA, it does not accept the view that the FD always plays a negative role. It has also supported the demand for the inclusion of new areas in the category of Scheduled Areas and new communities in the category of Scheduled Tribes. However, it emphasizes that such inclusion should be done after due deliberation, and not based on political or electoral pressure.

The VKA's Hindutva and Some Inherent Contradictions

The VKA has been opposing all those demands which could create a division in its vision of a 'Hinduized' tribal society and in its quest for just such a society, it has adopted many contradictory positions. For example, on the one hand, it has opposed the imposition of the UCC on tribal communities to protect the diversity in their customs and traditions, but on the other hand, it is not ready to accept the demand of the Sarna Code, that is related to the recognition of a separate adivasi religion. Its claim to be an organization dedicated to tribal welfare also carries many contradictions. The VKA has staunchly criticized the activities of the Naxal/Maoist groups because they have been responsible for the deaths of innocent people, including many activists of the RSS. However, the RSS and the VKA have supported the state machinery to suppress Naxals/Maoists, which in many instances resulted in violence against innocent tribals.

The contradiction of the VKA's claim becomes more evident if we consider its stand on certain issues, particularly the issue of 'delisting' and 'ghar wapsi'. Undoubtedly, the VKA has supported the demand of the delisting, i.e. exclusion of converted tribals from the list of STs, but never actively participated in aggressive mobilization on the issue. Similarly, it opposed proselytization by Christian missionaries by claiming that they had been using wrong and illegal means but supports the ghar wapsi of tribals from Christianity to Hinduism. Again, the VKA does not directly participate in such activities; other right-wing organizations do, and as discussed before, the irony is that senior activists of the VKA have formed and run such 'other' organizations.

Though VKA activists have always emphasized their 'apolitical' character, its works have created a base for the politics of the BJP in different tribal areas. Its constructive and seva works have created goodwill in tribal areas and the candidates who claim to follow the ideas of the VKA (BJP's candidate) benefit from its works. The VKA and RSS-affiliated organizations work to create a divide in the tribal society to make an electorally conducive environment in these areas. For example, in Odisha, Jharkhand, Madhya Pradesh and Chhattisgarh, these organizations use the issue of delisting or ghar wapsi as tools to mobilize Hinduized tribals and non-tribal Hindus against 'other' and 'enemy' Christian tribals. However, a grave contradiction in the VKA's stand is that it became indifferent to the changing attitude of the BJP in the North-east region. For example, as a pragmatic political party, the BJP has not opposed beef-eating in many states of the North-east, but the VKA (or the RSS) has never condemned such a stand.

As discussed in the chapter one of this study, the VKA carries the feature of two kinds of intellectuals classified by Antonio Gramsci, which means that one can find within the VKA the characteristics of the Traditional intellectuals and Organic intellectuals. However, one can find that in the last instance, the characteristics of Traditional intellectuals are dominant in the VKA. It implies that it wishes to establish a system based on Hinduism in tribal society, where these groups would live as vanvasis and follow Hindu rituals. It tries to establish the validity of the present system in the minds of tribals. While emphasizing the extreme version of nationalism, militarism and Hindu supremacy, it has reinforced that the legal and constitutional rights of tribals must be respected. In this sense, it emerges as an Organic intellectual because it moves beyond the existing model of development and underlines that tribal communities must have rights over forest land and its resources, and any development or mining project should not be imposed on them. Supporting the PESA also implies that the VKA wishes to create a situation where tribals can live their life according to their traditions and customs. But at this point, its role as a traditional intellectual gets prominence because on the one hand, it has unshakable belief on the present capitalist system and it never creates any problem for the working of Indian state, on the other hand, it emphasizes the vanvasi identity of tribal people based on the description of Hindu religious texts. It works with the belief that with all kinds of diversities, tribals are an integral part of Sanatan Dharma and there is a need to establish this situation strongly. It wishes to exclude Christian missionaries and followers of Islam from tribal areas and 'reconvert' converted tribals into Hinduism.

It is interesting to note that Christian missionaries have become an 'intimate enemy'[3] of the VKA, and to counter them, it has followed most of the strategies adopted by missionaries. Like Christian missionaries, the VKA has also established educational institutions and hospitals, among other developmental works. The VKA has been accusing Christian missionaries of converting tribals to Christianity through these seva works and by using other illegal means, but the VKA and other Hindu right-wing organizations have also followed the method of reconversion. The VKA has also focused on the issue of tribal forest and land rights but Christian missionaries have steered clear. As discussed in this study, the VKA started to work on these issues after the works of Gandhian or left-oriented tribal organizations, which became an integral part of adivasi consciousness.[4]

The VKA has played the role of a 'non-political' organization, which has been working for the betterment of the lives of the tribals. Since it is related to the RSS, its works and the goodwill created thereof gives benefits to the political organ of the RSS—the BJP. Its vision for tribal people creates internal contradictions within tribal society because it always tries to enhance Hindu rituals in tribal areas. However, no other political party has the support of an organization, which is not active in politics, and does continuous social welfare work. In this context, it is noteworthy that when India's first

President, Rajendra Prasad (then a senior leader of Bihar Congress) was concerned with the growing influence of the Adivasi Mahasabha and Jaipal Singh Munda in south Bihar (Jharkhand), he wrote a letter to Thakkar Bapa on 20 March 1939 for his suggestions.[5] In his reply on 27 March 1939, Thakkar Bapa suggested that the Congress should form a non-political organization that would work independently on social issues of tribals.[6] Perhaps those who feel that the RSS and VKA's politics are detrimental to unity with diversity inherent in tribal society, should focus on the suggestion given by Thakkar Bapa!

The VKA and the Challenge of Inclusivity

The VKA has a unique organizational structure. From the year of its formation till the death of its founder, Ramakant Deshpande, both the organization secretary (sangathan mantri) and the president were non-tribals. However, after Deshpande, a tribal activist, Jagdev Ram Oraon became the president of the VKA, and after he died in 2020, another tribal activist, Ramchandra Kharadi took over. Now, the president of the VKA is a tribal, but the organization secretary has always been a non-tribal. The work of the organization secretary is to ensure that the VKA is largely working according to the principles of the RSS. So, a tribal president cannot work independently and therefore there is a need to give actual power to the president and other activists of the VKA.

Another noteworthy thing about the VKA is that the women's representation, particularly the representation of tribal women, has been inadequate. Within the VKA, no woman activist ever received a prominent position. The VKA has been promoting the vision of an 'ideal Hindu woman' in tribal areas—educated, self-reliant, but must follow traditional family values. This implies that she should always live and work according to the wishes of the elders of the family, particularly her husband. Indeed, there is a need to discuss this issue openly and to give more leadership opportunities to tribal women within the VKA. In this context, it can learn a lot from the left or other tribal organizations.[7]

On the surface, it seems that VKA's Hindutva ideology is nothing but spreading Hindu values in the tribal areas. It has been trying to enhance the Hindu element in the tribal society through its schools and other activities. However, only constructive works are not sufficient for its survival and progress. Without hate and mobilization, it cannot achieve its aim of creating a majoritarian state, where minorities whose Punya Bhu are outside India, would be treated as constant enemies. The VKA lives with the idea of Hindutva, which emphasizes majoritarianism and extreme nationalism. However, this nationalism is not able to resolve the question of treatment towards minority groups. In most of the areas, Christian missionaries and Christian tribals are their perennial enemies, which cannot be a basis of Constitutional nationalism.[8]

In the last few decades, the VKA has started to focus on those issues that have been part of the agenda of left or Gandhian, or other non-RSS tribal organizations. The VKA has raised issues related to tribal rights, it has opposed the dilution of laws like PESA and FRA and it has presented a comprehensive agenda for giving more rights to tribal communities over resources. However, the VKA has always been in a dilemma about how far it should focus on such issues because they are not part of its core agenda. At best, it can be argued that they are complementary to its core agenda of the Hinduization of tribal communities and opposition of Christian missionaries. The VKA should make the protection of the rights of tribal people its core agenda and focus on allying with those left-oriented, socialist or Gandhian organizations, which have been mobilizing tribal communities at the local level against displacement and forced 'developmental' projects.

Indeed, there is a need for VKA to focus more on constructive programmes. It must try to assert its autonomy from the larger agenda of Sangh Parivar, or try to shape the agenda according to the needs of tribals. If it emerges as true protectors of the interests of tribal communities, there would be no need to spread divisive tactics in tribal society. Due to its works and dedication, most tribals would prefer the path advocated by the VKA. However, to do this, it needs to overcome the shackles of the ideology of the RSS, which was the primary reason for its formation. So, the rebirth of the VKA as an indomitable organization fighting for the protection of tribal interests, rather than the creator of animosity between communities, is the most desirable. Though many of its activists wish to enhance their work for tribal rights, they are a minority. The organization does not permit vocal criticism of the government, particularly prime minister Narendra Modi. Many activists feel that due to political power, they can do certain works, so opposing a government backed by the RSS is not a good idea. Due to this, they are not able to take a strong stand against the BJP-led government. Having said that, senior activists of the VKA enjoy the proximity to power which has helped them enhance their Hindutva-based ideological agenda in tribal areas.

Acknowledgements

When I started to work on tribal issues as a PhD research scholar, I found that most of the resources either overlooked Vanvasi Kalyan Ashram (VKA) or discussed it as an organization that is resisting the 'conversion' of tribals into Christianity, and simultaneously converting them to Hinduism. The mainstream academic world focused on ideological moorings, organizational structure and politics of the Rashtriya Swayamsevak Sangh (RSS), but there has been an absence of a systematic study of the VKA. Only a few papers were available, which could not do justice to its evolving nature as an organization. After my PhD and particularly after the general elections of 2014, the discussion regarding the role of VKA became more prominent in the media. Particularly when the BJP won elections in some North-east states, it was argued that the RSS and the VKA played a crucial role in the BJP's victory. It increased my curiosity regarding the organizational structure, ideological background and the role of the VKA. I received a project from the Indian Council for Social Science Research (ICSSR) to study the role of the VKA in the implementation of the PESA and FRA in January 2018. After the submission of the project report, I continued to pursue my work on the VKA. Later, I extended my research to understand the VKA as an organization and its impact on tribal areas. This book is the result of that research. It is an attempt to overcome that academic deficiency regarding the academic and comprehensive analysis of the VKA and aims to present the analytical study of the various aspects of the VKA. This book situates the VKA in the larger ideological and historical context of the RSS and discusses the various aspects of its works, including faith awakening, education, medical services, women empowerment and village development. It also evaluates the VKA's works on new kinds of issues, particularly issues related to the rights of tribals over forest land and its resources.

Initially, I went to the VKA office in Malka Ganj, Delhi to find useful literature on the VKA. After many emails, I met a senior activist of the VKA, who was furious that a researcher from a non-RSS background was researching the organization. After deliberations with his colleagues, he wrote a letter to the ICSSR for clarification in this regard and informed me that the VKA would not give me any information. However, many other VKA activists and office-bearers helped me during the research work. The long discussion with these activists provided me with an opportunity to understand the history, organizational structure and internal dynamics of the VKA's relationship with other members of the Sangh Parivar. I wish to express my gratitude to many senior members and officer bearers of the VKA, particularly Suresh Kulkarni, Girish Kuber and Pramod Petkar for their help and guidance. The experience also clarified that in all organizations there are some activists and office-bearers, who are hardliners and not ready for any kind of dialogue. On the other hand, some activists are more open-minded in their approach and ready to share not only ideas but also different documents and study materials. I am fortunate that I met with both kinds during my work on the

VKA. I am thankful to many other persons related to the VKA, who helped me to understand the complexities of the work of the VKA. In this study, I have also done a comparative study between the VKA and the All India Union for Forest Working People (AIUFWP). Many activists of the AIUFWP helped during my fieldwork in Dudwa National Park and other places. I am grateful to Ashok Choudhury, Roma and Rajneesh who helped to understand the complexities of tribal life.

I am thankful to *Pratiman* (journal published by the Indian language programme of CSDS) and *Studies in Humanities and Social Science* (SSHS) (journal of IIAS, Shimla) for the publication of peer-reviewed papers based on my research on this topic. I presented different parts of this research in the following institutions: the Indian Institute of Advance Study, Shimla; Indira Gandhi Tribal University, Amarkantak; Centre for the Studies of Developing Societies (CSDS), Delhi; Madhya Pradesh Institute of Social Science Research (MPISSR), Ujjain; Creative Theory Colloquium, Delhi; Azim Premji University, Bengaluru; Rajdhani College, Delhi. I am grateful to all these institutions and many esteemed scholars who gave crucial suggestions on my work.

Mohammad Naushad worked as a research assistant in the project on the VKA's role in the implementation of the PESA and FRA. He has always helped in this research. Pawan, Bhavana and Ashvin also helped me in field research for this project. I wish to express my gratitude to my teachers who provided me with all kinds of help and guidance during my research work. I am indebted to Ujjwal Kumar Singh, Nandini Sundar, Nivedita Menon, M.P. Singh, Aditya Nigam, Abhay Kumar Dubey, Mahesh Rangarajan, Manindra Nath Thakur, Ravi Kant, Ashok Acharya and Hilal Ahmad. I am grateful to Dhananjay who read some chapters of the book and gave critical comments on them, which helped me improve those chapters. Many thanks to Indrajeet, Rityusha, Gaurav, Vikas, Mithilesh, Naresh Goswami, Ramashankar, Vivek, Nikhil Jain, Prabhat Kumar, Vijay Jha, Praveen Kumar, Abhay, Nirmal, Nikhil Jain, Sujit Thakur and Rajesh Rao for helping in my study. Discussions with these friends and many others always inspire me to understand issues critically. I wish to express my thanks to Premanka Goswami, the editor in charge of Penguin for his help and constructive suggestions. Many thanks to Aparna Abhijit for her copy-editing and comments which helped me to improve the quality of my text and arguments. I also express my gratitude to Areeb Ahmad and other members of the Penguin team who helped during the production of this book.

My family members have always encouraged me in my research work. I am grateful to them, particularly my elder brother, Ashok Kumar, for his help and guidance. I am thankful from the core of my heart to my partner, Jyotsana, who helped me immensely in the completion of this work. Her critical comments and engaging discussions helped me immeasurably. I wish to express my gratitude towards my father for his continuous commendation of my work. This book is dedicated to him.

Notes

Chapter 1: Introduction: The Uniqueness of Vanvasi Kalyan Ashram

1 Roy (2018); Sundar (2019).
2 Mathew (2022).
3 Express News Service (2023).
4 Ghurye (1963).
5 Bose (1941).
6 Kosambi (1975).
7 Xaxa (2009), pp. 33-34.
8 This aspect is discussed in more detail in Chapter 3 and Chapter 6. Chapter 3 discusses it in the context of the extension of the VKA in the Northeast region, and Chapter 6 explores this in the context of the opposition to the Sarna Code by the VKA.
9 The VKA runs hostels in urban areas and gives opportunities to tribal students to study in urban centers. It also took a strong stand against policies that could hamper the interests of the educated tribal youths. The opposition of the thirteen-point roster system by the VKA is a solid example of its stand on such issues. For a detailed discussion see, Chapter 4.
10 In this context the work and functioning of the Janjati Suraksha Manch (JSM) and the issue of delisting are discussed in Chapter 6. Though the VKA also supports the issue of delisting

of converted tribals from the list of the ST, the primary work of mobilization has been done by the JSM.

11 Seshadri (1998).
12 Ambedkar (2019), pp. 26.
13 Sharda (2018).
14 Anderson and Damle (1987).
15 Anderson and Damle (2018).
16 Trivedi (2020).
17 Mukhopadhyay (2019).
18 For example, see Deshpande and Ramaswami (1981); Sharma (2014); Chauthaiwale (2014). There are some critical biographies of the RSS leaders too. For example, see Jha (2024).
19 Jaffrelot (2005), pp. 7–8.
20 Kanungo (2003).
21 Joshy and Seethi (2015). However, P. M. Joshy in his paper, state, Civil Society and the Process of Democratisation: A Study of Vanvasi Kalyan Ashram, discusses in some detail the works of the VKA, particularly shradha jagran (faith awakening) work. However, this paper gives a limited understanding or information about a few aspects of the VKA. See, Joshy (2011).
22 Vanaik (2017). Many other scholars have severely criticized the RSS ideology and its works for example, see, Goyal (1979); Narayanan (2025); Noorani (2020).
23 Dubey is focussing on larger ideological changes within RSS and its manifestation in the organization. See Dubey (2019).
24 Narayan (2021), p. 81.
25 During my PhD on tribal forest land rights and after that when I worked on the book *Jungle Ki Haqdari* (2015), I completely overlooked the aspect of the VKA's role in such issues. The primary reason for this was unintentional and was due to the structure of 'mainstream' academics, which were not ready to accept the relevance of the interventions made by the VKA.
26 From some recent examples see, Ambagudia and Xaxa (2021); Xaxa and Devy (2021).
27 Bhagat-Ganguly and Kumar (2019).

28 See Nilsen (2018); Ranjan (2022); Choubey (2923b). The VAK uses Birsa Munda as a figure who not only struggled against colonial rulers but also fought against the work of the Christian missionaries. For a detailed discussion see Chapter 3; Even my book *Jungle ki Haqdari* entirely overlooks the VKA. See Choubey.
29 See Baviskar (2005); Xaxa (1999) (2009); Sundar (2019).
30 Sundar (2004) (2006) (2019). It is interesting to note that Sundar (2006) is the only paper that has discussed the formation and work of the VKA in some detail. The paper is included in many other edited volumes, including Kumar and Sunny (2009) and Sundar (2016a).
31 Froerer (2008).
32 Chatterji (2009).
33 Thachil (2014) (2015a).
34 Longkumer (2019) (2022).
35 Saxena (1993) (1994) (2004); Vaid (2011); Ladha (2013).
36 ABVKA (2015).
37 These aspects are discussed more systematically in Chapter 5.
38 For detailed discussion see Chapter 3.
39 See. Chandwani (2023). For detailed discussion see Chapter 4.
40 Sundar (2006), pp. 83–85; Chatterji (2009) pp. 263–64; Citizen's Inquiry Committee (2006); Das and Thirumalai (2023), Jaffrelot (1996), p. 322.
41 The aspect has been discussed in detail in Chapter 6. *Van Bandhu* regularly publishes articles that severely criticizes works of Christian missionaries. See, Van Bandhu (August 2019) (December 2021). Also see Sundar (2019).
42 *The Collected Works of Mahatma Gandhi*, Volume 75, p. 146, quoted in Parel (2022), p. 35; To understand the idea of 'Purna Swaraj' in more detail, see Rai (2023).
43 Ibid., pp. 35–36.
44 Ibid., p. 36.
45 Thachil (2014); Bhattacharjee (2019).
46 These aspects are discussed in Chapter 6. The VKA has always supported the movement of 'delisting' of those tribals from the

list of the STs, who have converted to either Christianity or Islam. See *Van Bandhu*, (January 2021: 13); Chauhan (2022); Pratinidhi (2023), p. 21.

47 Joshy and Seethi (2015), p. 204.

48 Gramsci (1971).

49 Ibid.

50 To understand the life and ideas of Gramsci, see Hoare and Sperber (2015); Mouffe (1979); and Hoare and Smith (1971).

51 Interestingly, Deirdre O'Neil and Mike Wayne have argued that organic intellectuals can be divided into two parts: i) Hegemonic organic intellectuals who work to protect the interest of the capitalist class. Their primary function is to help the capitalist class shape the broader political, moral and cultural agenda. ii) Counter-hegemonic organic intellectuals who question the dominant frame of reference, the dominant assumption and dominant policy trends. Such intellectuals work to create awareness in the minds of the working class. They are organically tied to the classes and groups for whom stability is a state of emergency. See O'Neill and Wayne (2017).

52 Sundar (2016b), p. 34.

53 Ibid., Choubey (2018).

54 Sundar (2006), pp. 371–372.

55 For detailed discussion of this aspect, see Chapter 3.

Chapter 2: Footprints of RSS in Tribal Areas: Formation and Expansion of Vanvasi Kalyan Ashram

1 Sapre (1999); Sundar (2006); Saxena (2004); Ladha (2013).

2 Anderson and Damle (1987); Graham (1990); Hansen (1999); Jaffrelot (1996).

3 Chatterjee (1993); Lal (1995); Nandy (1983); Roychaudhuri (1995).

4 Sharma (2003).

5 Raghuramraju (2006).

6 However, Savarkar, who systematically presented Hindutva as a political ideology, never supported the idea of giving cows more importance than human life. For him, the value of a cow depended

on her role or utility in fulfilling human needs. Sampath (2019), pp. 429–32.

7 Joshy and Seethi (2015), pp. 84–85.

8 Sharma (2003), p. 59.

9 Tanika Sarkar has divided Bankim's literary career into two phases. Until the end of 1870, he had emphasized on caste, class and gender-based oppression in pre-colonial India. But in the last five years of his literary career, he focussed on the theme of Hindu–Muslim antagonism through his novels and essays. See, Sarkar (2005), pp. 162–3.

10 Savarkar (1989), p. 113.

11 Jyotirmaya Sharma notes that '[D]esecration of Hindu temples, conversions by force or fraud, corrupting of Hindu girls and the overall destruction of Hinduism—these themes were to forever remain Savarkar's short-hand symbols of characterizing Islam. Sharma (2003), pp. 126–139.

12 Savarkar (1940), p. 17, 23. See, Joshy and Seethi (2015), p. 94.

13 Mahatma Gandhi started the non-cooperation movement in 1920, and he urged people to boycott everything related to British rule, including clothes, educational institutions etc. The movement also challenged oppressive laws like the Rowlatt Act, with its ultimate goal to attain Swaraj. The Cahuri-Chaura incident took place during this movement on 4th February 1922 at Chauri Cahura in the Gorakhpur district of the United Provinces (now Uttar Pradesh). The incident took place when three protesters participating in the non-cooperation movement were killed in police firing. In retaliation the protesting mob set fire to the police station, killing 22 policemen. Gandhi condemned the violence and also stopped the movement on 12 February 1922. See Chandra et al (1989); Amin (1995).

14 Anderson and Damle (1987), pp. 24–36.

15 D.V. Kelkar, 'The RSS', *Economic Weekly*, (4 February 1950), p. 132, quoted in J.A. Curran Jr., 'Militant Hinduism in Indian Politics: A Study of the R.S.S.' (New York: Institute of Pacific Relations, 1951, pp. 12–13: Also see Anderson and Damle (1987), p. 34.

16 Golwalkar (1939), pp. 55–6.
17 Mukhopadhyay (2019), pp. 111–112.
18 Anderson and Damle (2018).
19 Wingate (1997), p. 35.
20 Xaxa (2009), p. 19.
21 Mehta (2002), p. 9.
22 For an understanding of the life and views of Golwalkar see, Mukhopadhyay (2019), pp. 98–163; Jha (2024). To understand the concern related to the issue of conversion in the work of RSS, see Anderson and Damle (1987), p. 13; pp. 20–21.
23 We will discuss the issue of proselytization and the VKA's stand and works against it in the next chapter. Here the main purpose is to underline that how the role of Christian missionaries worked as background for the formation of VKA.
24 It is noteworthy that in some of the letters written by Rajendra Prasad or Thakkar Bapa the Chota Nagpur has been mentioned as Chhotanagpur, but I have kept the 'Chota Nagpur' to avoid any kind of confusion for the readers.
25 At many places, Jaipal Singh Munda or Rajnedra Prasad used the term 'adibasi' rather than 'adivasi'. However, to maintain uniformity, I have used the term 'adivasi' throughout the book.
26 Choubey (2021c).
27 Choudhary (1984), p. 4.
28 Ibid., pp. 9–10.
29 Ibid., p. 128.
30 Ibid., p. 142.
31 Pankaj (2015), p. 63; Choubey (2021c), pp. 12–13; Rajendra Prasad in his letter to B.S. Jillani mentioned about the incident of writing a letter to the Catholic bishop of Ranchi. See, Kiro (2018), pp. 154–56.
32 Choudhary (1984), p. 36.
33 Ibid., p. 42.
34 Choubey (2021c), p. 12.
35 To know about the work of Thakkar Bapa, see, Tiwari (2017).
36 This is a description presented by the authors who have been closely attached with the VKA (like Radhka Ladha). The description related to Ramakant Deshpande is based on the

2 Chapter 4 discusses the education-related works of the VKA in detail.

3 Ladha (2013), p. 24.

4 However, he also emphasized the need to provide medical facilities to the tribal people. This aspect is discussed in chapter 4.

5 Ladha (2013), pp. 24–25.

6 Discussion with a senior activist of the VKA, Suresh Kulkarni, on 20 October 2019 at the central office of the Vanvasi Kalyan Ashram in Delhi.

7 Sundar (2006).

8 Babu (2020), p. 5.

9 This aspect is discussed in the last section of this chapter.

10 *Van Bandhu* (2019a, February), p. 10; this report by *Van Bandhu* underlines the VKA's plans for the Prayagraj Ardh-Kumbh; for the reporting of Janjati Samagam (Tribal Communion) in the Prayagraj, see Awasthi (2019), p. 7.

11 Babu (2023a); (2023b).

12 *Van Bandhu* (2019a, February), p. 9.

13 See, *Van Bandhu,* (November 2023c), pp. 67–68.

14 Sundar (2006), pp. 387–388.

15 Sundar (2006).

16 Markam (2021a), pp 10-11.

17 Markam (2021a), pp. 10-11; (2021b), p. 19.

18 Tripathi (2021), pp. 12–13.

19 For example, see, Ladha (2020), pp. 10–14.

20 Badri Narayan also underlines that through the VKA, the RSS has succeeded in Hinduizing tribals, Narayan (2021); however, he does not present any extensive description of this process.

21 *Van Bandhu*, (November 2021), p. 18.

22 To comprehend the different arguments of the UCC debate see, Menon (2012); Roy (2013).

23 Pandey (2023).

24 To understand the key features of the Uttakrahand Uniform Civil Code Act, see Mishra (2024).

25 For detailed discussion, see chapter 6.

26 For the VKA's description of some of the key tribal figures, see Kharwar (2020); Dr. Sonkar (2020); Sharma (2020); and *Van Bandhu* (November, 2023).

27 Longkumer (2022), p. 215.

28 Interestingly, whereas in other sources the name is mentioned as Andna Panre, in Mandal's article published in *Van Bandhu*, the name is mentioned as Anand Pande. See, Ranjan (2022), p. 11; Mandal (2019), pp. 6–7.

29 Singh (1983); Ranjan (2022), p. 13.

30 *Van Bandhu*, (November 2020), pp. 6–7. The VKA's activists always present Birsa as a follower of rituals close to Hinduism. See Mandal (2019), pp. 6–7: Vijay (2023), pp. 12–13.

31 Mahashweta Devi's book *Jangal Ke Dawedar* was inspired by K.S. Singh's book. See Singh (1983); Devi (1998).

32 English translation of the message and poster released by the VKA on 9 June 2020.

33 Mandal (2019), pp. 6–7.

34 Mall (2014) quoted in Longkumer (2022), p. 196.

35 Longkumer (2022), pp. 193–194.

36 Ibid., p. 196.

37 Ibid., pp. 198–199.

38 Ibid., p. 199.

39 Ibid., pp. 200–201.

40 Ibid., pp. 203–204.

41 Mall (2014) quoted from Longkumer (2022), p. 208.

42 Ibid. Though the RSS and the VKA present her as a tribal icon of the North-east, she is not popular in Nagaland, primarily due to her opposition to Phizo and NNC and her birth in Manipur. See, Longkumer (2022), p. 213.

43 For understanding this controversy, see Mahaprashasta (2023).

44 To understand the life and politics of Jaipal Singh Munda see, Choubey (2021); Kiro (2018).

45 This issue is discussed in detail in chapter 6.

46 Pandey (2019).

47 Vijay (2019).

48 Xaxa (1999), p. 3590.

49 UNDRIP (2007): Article 10, 26 and 20.
50 Ibid., Article 3.
51 Mahatma Gandhi and other leaders of INC were using this term. There was an organization in pre-colonial India named Adivasi Mahasabha, which was active primarily in the tribal areas of Jharkhand (then Bihar) and Odisha. Jaipal Singh Munda became president of this organization in 1939. Indeed, Munda unequivocally raised the issues of Adivasi rights in the Constituent Assembly. See Choubey (2021).
52 See ABVKA (1999); the memorandum is included in Saxena (2004). However, the exact date of the submission of the memorandum is not mentioned in the book.
53 Swartz (2019).
54 ABVKA (1999) in Saxena (2004), p. 148.
55 Ibid., p. 158.
56 Ibid.
57 Ibid., p. 152.
58 Ibid., p. 153.
59 Ibid., p. 163.
60 It is also important to note that the Government of India also raised a similar objection to the idea of indigenous people. See Ibid., p. 155.
61 Ibid., p. 166.
62 Lakshya (2019), p. 11.
63 Ghurye (1963). The ABVKA 1999 memorandum also uses the argument presented by Ghurye. See, ABVKA (1999) in Saxena (2004), p. 154.
64 Choubey (2015a).
65 Xaxa (1999).
66 In the course of my fieldwork I met many persons, who claimed that they were adivasis but their caste was not part of the ST category. See Choubey (2015a), Chapter 3.
67 However, she underlines that it has excluded many equally, or poorer, non-adivasi communities from the struggle. She underlines the need to create a coalition of adivasis with other marginalized communities (Baviskar 2005).

68 Niezen (2003), pp. 20–21.
69 For information about PM JANMAN, see Government of India (2024); one can find the use of the term adivasi in all speeches and interviews of the PM. For example, see Chaturvedi (2024); For other examples, one can watch and listen to the speeches of the PM in tribal areas on his YouTube channel, https://www.youtube.com/@NarendraModi
70 Xaxa (2009), pp. 20–21.
71 Sundar (2009) (2019); Xaxa (2009).
72 Sundar (2006).
73 Xaxa (2009), p. 27.
74 Xaxa (2009), pp. 22–23.
75 Furer-Haimendorf (1982), pp. 33–38.
76 Kosambi (1975).
77 Bose (1941).
78 Nandi (1973); Eschmann (1986); Sundar (2019), p. 251.
79 Sundar (1999).
80 Sundar (2019), pp. 251–52.
81 Dubey (2019), pp. 83–87.
82 Ghurye (1963), pp. 1–22; Xaxa says that he made this argument because there was so much similarity between the Hindu religion and the animistic tribal religion that the two could not possibly be distinguished from one another. He made this point based not on fieldwork data collection but on observations of the Census Commissioners between the period 1891 and 1931, where they had expressed their dissatisfaction over the fact that tribes were described as animists (Xaxa 2009).
83 Government of Madhya Pradesh (1956a) (1956b).
84 Sapre (1999).
85 All three letters were written in January 1886. The exact date of the letter to the President and Pope John Paul II is not available. However, he wrote a letter to the then Prime Minister Rajiv Gandhi on 3 January 1986. These letters are compiled in Saxena (2004), pp. 213–223.
86 Deshpande (1986c) in Saxena (2004), pp. 217–20.
87 Ibid., p. 219.

on her role or utility in fulfilling human needs. Sampath (2019), pp. 429–32.

7 Joshy and Seethi (2015), pp. 84–85.

8 Sharma (2003), p. 59.

9 Tanika Sarkar has divided Bankim's literary career into two phases. Until the end of 1870, he had emphasized on caste, class and gender-based oppression in pre-colonial India. But in the last five years of his literary career, he focussed on the theme of Hindu–Muslim antagonism through his novels and essays. See, Sarkar (2005), pp. 162–3.

10 Savarkar (1989), p. 113.

11 Jyotirmaya Sharma notes that '[D]esecration of Hindu temples, conversions by force or fraud, corrupting of Hindu girls and the overall destruction of Hinduism—these themes were to forever remain Savarkar's short-hand symbols of characterizing Islam. Sharma (2003), pp. 126–139.

12 Savarkar (1940), p. 17, 23. See, Joshy and Seethi (2015), p. 94.

13 Mahatma Gandhi started the non-cooperation movement in 1920, and he urged people to boycott everything related to British rule, including clothes, educational institutions etc. The movement also challenged oppressive laws like the Rowlatt Act, with its ultimate goal to attain Swaraj. The Cahuri-Chaura incident took place during this movement on 4th February 1922 at Chauri Cahura in the Gorakhpur district of the United Provinces (now Uttar Pradesh). The incident took place when three protesters participating in the non-cooperation movement were killed in police firing. In retaliation the protesting mob set fire to the police station, killing 22 policemen. Gandhi condemned the violence and also stopped the movement on 12 February 1922. See Chandra et al (1989); Amin (1995).

14 Anderson and Damle (1987), pp. 24–36.

15 D.V. Kelkar, 'The RSS', *Economic Weekly*, (4 February 1950), p. 132, quoted in J.A. Curran Jr., 'Militant Hinduism in Indian Politics: A Study of the R.S.S.' (New York: Institute of Pacific Relations, 1951, pp. 12–13: Also see Anderson and Damle (1987), p. 34.

16 Golwalkar (1939), pp. 55–6.
17 Mukhopadhyay (2019), pp. 111–112.
18 Anderson and Damle (2018).
19 Wingate (1997), p. 35.
20 Xaxa (2009), p. 19.
21 Mehta (2002), p. 9.
22 For an understanding of the life and views of Golwalkar see, Mukhopadhyay (2019), pp. 98–163; Jha (2024). To understand the concern related to the issue of conversion in the work of RSS, see Anderson and Damle (1987), p. 13; pp. 20–21.
23 We will discuss the issue of proselytization and the VKA's stand and works against it in the next chapter. Here the main purpose is to underline that how the role of Christian missionaries worked as background for the formation of VKA.
24 It is noteworthy that in some of the letters written by Rajendra Prasad or Thakkar Bapa the Chota Nagpur has been mentioned as Chhotanagpur, but I have kept the 'Chota Nagpur' to avoid any kind of confusion for the readers.
25 At many places, Jaipal Singh Munda or Rajnedra Prasad used the term 'adibasi' rather than 'adivasi'. However, to maintain uniformity, I have used the term 'adivasi' throughout the book.
26 Choubey (2021c).
27 Choudhary (1984), p. 4.
28 Ibid., pp. 9–10.
29 Ibid., p. 128.
30 Ibid., p. 142.
31 Pankaj (2015), p. 63; Choubey (2021c), pp. 12–13; Rajendra Prasad in his letter to B.S. Jillani mentioned about the incident of writing a letter to the Catholic bishop of Ranchi. See, Kiro (2018), pp. 154–56.
32 Choudhary (1984), p. 36.
33 Ibid., p. 42.
34 Choubey (2021c), p. 12.
35 To know about the work of Thakkar Bapa, see, Tiwari (2017).
36 This is a description presented by the authors who have been closely attached with the VKA (like Radhka Ladha). The description related to Ramakant Deshpande is based on the

writings and descriptions of many senior activists of the VKA. All of them are not clear about the dates. So, I have mentioned only the year in relation to the crucial events of his life.

37 Saxena (2004), p. 61.

38 Ladha (2013), p. 4.

39 The RSS was not in favour of the participation of its members in any political movement. In the 1942 Quit India Movement, the RSS chief, M.S. Golwalkar decided to stay away from the movement but did not prevent his swayamsevaks from participating in their personal capacities. See, Mukhopadhyay (2019), p. 126.

40 Radhika Ladha's book is based on the discussion of various activists of the VKA. It is interesting to note that in her description she mentions that a Muslim police officer, Sanawar Ali Khan, hatched a conspiracy against Deshpande and arrested him, while a constable, Bithoba, refused to give testimony against him, which ensured his release. See, Ladha (2013), pp. 5–9; Another biographer K.D. Spare presents him as a dedicated freedom fighter, who patrolled the street during the Quit India movement with his RSS friends to maintain law and order. He was arrested by the Muslim police officer of Ramtek and sent to jail on a false charge of looting and arson. He was acquitted because Ramtek Tashildar, Harkare, refused to testify against him (Sapre 1999). Nandini Sundar expresses suspicion over such accounts and argues that there is a strong likelihood that Deshpande was in fact engaged in communal and disruptive activities. See, Sundar (2006).

41 As it is obvious from the correspondence between Rajendra Prasad and Thakkar Bapa, both were concerned about the increasing influence of 'non-Congress' forces in the tribal areas. However, except the writings of the RSS and VKA activists (like Sapre and Ladha), no other source mentions the recommendation of Thakkar Bapa to appoint Ramakant Deshpande on an important government post to counter Christian missionaries. See, Sapre (1999); Ladha (2013), pp. 9–10.

42 Ladha (2013), p. 12.

43 Sundar (2006), pp. 370–372.

44 Ibid., pp. 14–15.

45 Sundar (2006).

46 Ladha (2013), p. 14.
47 Ibid., p. 14.
48 Ibid., p. 25.
49 Sapre (1999), pp. 11–25; Ladha (2013), pp. 18–19.
50 Dhingra (2023).
51 Deshpande 1990, p. 17.
52 Such description is prevalent in the writing and discussion of VKA activists. For example, they describe the relationship between its first president, Deshpande, and second president, Jagdev Ram, as the relationship between Ramakrishna Paramahamsa and Swami Vivekananda. See, Singh (2021), pp. 15–17; Nartam (2021), p. 28.
53 Chapter 4 has a detailed discussion on the education-related work of the VKA.
54 In chapter 3, there is a systematic and detailed discussion of the 'faith awakening' (shradha jagran) works of the VKA.
55 The old building fell in 1962 and then the process of making a new building started. The many sympathizers of the RSS and VKA in urban areas, contributed money for this work, particularly, Bhimsen Chopra. The owner of the Gita Press of Gorakhpur, Hanuman Prasad Poddar, also helped in the collection of money. This is an important instance of one key aspect of the VKA's work, which is creating consciousness in urban areas regarding vanvasis and taking help from urban people for the work of the VKA. See Ladha (2013), p. 26; Chapter 4 discusses the aspect of urban work in more detail.
56 On this occasion, Deshpande gave his speech in the local language Sadri, which underlines his commitment to the tribals of this area because he learnt it after coming to Jashpur. See Ladha (2013), pp. 25–26.
57 Ladha (2013), pp. 26–28; Choubey (2019).
58 Choubey (2019).
59 Ladha (2013), p. 28.
60 Madhavrao Sadashivrao Golwalkar (1904–1973) became sarsanghchalak of the RSS in 1940 after the death of its founder Keshav Baliram Hedgewar and remained at the post till his death on 5 June 1973. See, Mukhopadhyay (2019).

61 Mukhopadhyay (2019), p. 89.

62 Ibid.

63 To understand the ideological changes during Deoras time, see, Dubey (2019); to know about his life and RSS related activities, see, Mukhopadhyay (2019), pp. 247–337; also see, Chauthaiwale (2014).

64 Ladha (2013), p. 39.

65 Mall (2019), p. 32.

66 See Dubey (2019), pp. 33–105.

67 In the meeting, the VKA's workers from Bihar, Madhya Pradesh and Odisha discussed the issues related to the expansion of their organization. Senior activists like Krishna Damodar Sapre and Bhimsen Chopra, organization secretary from West Bengal, Rambhau Godbole, activists from Uttar Pradesh, Maharashtra and Andhra Pradesh, attended the meeting. Jagdamba Mall represented the eight states of the North-East. See Mall (2019), p. 32.

68 Ibid., p. 33.

69 Ibid., pp. 32–33.

70 Mahakaushal area is a geographical area of Madhya Pradesh, which is situated in eastern part of Narmda river valley. The region is also known as the Jabalpur Division. Jabalpur Division is geographically situated in the Central part of the state. It consists of Eight Districts—Jabalpur, Katni, Narsinghpur, Seoni, Chhindwara, Balaghat, Mandla and Dindori. This region is commonly known as Mahakoushal region.

71 Discussion with Girish Kuber, 'Hit Raksha Vibhag Pramukh' (President, Interest Protection Department) VKA, New Delhi, 25 July 2021.

72 At present, Atul Jog is the Organization Secretary and Ramchandra Kharadi is the president of the VKA. Discussion with Girish Kuber 'Hit Raksha Vibhag Pramukh' (President, Interest Protection Department) VKA, New Delhi, 25 July 2021

73 Discussion with Girish Kuber 'Hit Raksha Vibhag Pramukh' (President, Interest Protection Department) VKA, New Delhi, 25 July 2021.

74 Chapter 6 discusses the works of the JSM and DJS and shows with examples how some activists of the VKA have been working in JSM and DJS.

75 See *Van Bandhu* (2021, January), pp. 13–14; Kale (2021); Judev (2021). The mainstream political figures of the RSS–BJP paid their respects to Jagdev Oraon after his demise. Condoling the death of Oraon, Prime Minister Narendra Modi tweeted that '[A]nguished by the passing away of Shri Jagdev Ram Oraon Ji, President of the Vanvasi Kalyan Ashram. His was a life devoted to serving the tribal communities. He was known for his kind and hardworking nature. Om Shanti'. See Mishra and Rai (2020).

76 Vaid (2011).

77 Discussion with Girish Kuber, 'Hit Raksha Vibhag Pramukh' (President, Interest Protection Department) VKA, New Delhi, 25 July 2021.

78 Discussion with Girish Kuber, Hit Raksha Vibhag Pramukh (President, Interest Protection Department), VKA, New Delhi, 25 July 2021.

79 Anderson and Damle (2018).

80 Discussion with Girish Kuber, Hit Raksha Vibhag Pramukh (President, Interest Protection Department) VKA, New Delhi, 25 July 2021. This aspect is discussed in more detail in chapter 6.

81 Sundar (2006).

82 This aspect will be discussed in detail in chapter 4.

83 For example, during my fieldwork in the Surajpur District of Chhattisgarh, Dudhwa National Park of Lakhimpur Khiri (Uttar Pradesh) or Rajaji National Park (Uttarakhand), I did not see any presence of the VKA. One can list many such places where the VKA is not present, or not very active.

84 Sundar (2006), pp. 380–382.

Chapter 3: The Core Pillars of the VKA : Spread of Hindu Values, Opposition of 'Adivasi', and Proselytization

1 Interest protection works are related to the protection of the rights of tribals over forest land and its resources. This aspect is discussed extensively in chapter five.

2 Chapter 4 discusses the education-related works of the VKA in detail.
3 Ladha (2013), p. 24.
4 However, he also emphasized the need to provide medical facilities to the tribal people. This aspect is discussed in chapter 4.
5 Ladha (2013), pp. 24–25.
6 Discussion with a senior activist of the VKA, Suresh Kulkarni, on 20 October 2019 at the central office of the Vanvasi Kalyan Ashram in Delhi.
7 Sundar (2006).
8 Babu (2020), p. 5.
9 This aspect is discussed in the last section of this chapter.
10 *Van Bandhu* (2019a, February), p. 10; this report by *Van Bandhu* underlines the VKA's plans for the Prayagraj Ardh-Kumbh; for the reporting of Janjati Samagam (Tribal Communion) in the Prayagraj, see Awasthi (2019), p. 7.
11 Babu (2023a); (2023b).
12 *Van Bandhu* (2019a, February), p. 9.
13 See, *Van Bandhu,* (November 2023c), pp. 67–68.
14 Sundar (2006), pp. 387–388.
15 Sundar (2006).
16 Markam (2021a), pp 10-11.
17 Markam (2021a), pp. 10-11; (2021b), p. 19.
18 Tripathi (2021), pp. 12–13.
19 For example, see, Ladha (2020), pp. 10–14.
20 Badri Narayan also underlines that through the VKA, the RSS has succeeded in Hinduizing tribals, Narayan (2021); however, he does not present any extensive description of this process.
21 *Van Bandhu*, (November 2021), p. 18.
22 To comprehend the different arguments of the UCC debate see, Menon (2012); Roy (2013).
23 Pandey (2023).
24 To understand the key features of the Uttakrahand Uniform Civil Code Act, see Mishra (2024).
25 For detailed discussion, see chapter 6.

26 For the VKA's description of some of the key tribal figures, see Kharwar (2020); Dr. Sonkar (2020); Sharma (2020); and *Van Bandhu* (November, 2023).
27 Longkumer (2022), p. 215.
28 Interestingly, whereas in other sources the name is mentioned as Andna Panre, in Mandal's article published in *Van Bandhu*, the name is mentioned as Anand Pande. See, Ranjan (2022), p. 11; Mandal (2019), pp. 6–7.
29 Singh (1983); Ranjan (2022), p. 13.
30 *Van Bandhu*, (November 2020), pp. 6–7. The VKA's activists always present Birsa as a follower of rituals close to Hinduism. See Mandal (2019), pp. 6–7: Vijay (2023), pp. 12–13.
31 Mahashweta Devi's book *Jangal Ke Dawedar* was inspired by K.S. Singh's book. See Singh (1983); Devi (1998).
32 English translation of the message and poster released by the VKA on 9 June 2020.
33 Mandal (2019), pp. 6–7.
34 Mall (2014) quoted in Longkumer (2022), p. 196.
35 Longkumer (2022), pp. 193–194.
36 Ibid., p. 196.
37 Ibid., pp. 198–199.
38 Ibid., p. 199.
39 Ibid., pp. 200–201.
40 Ibid., pp. 203–204.
41 Mall (2014) quoted from Longkumer (2022), p. 208.
42 Ibid. Though the RSS and the VKA present her as a tribal icon of the North-east, she is not popular in Nagaland, primarily due to her opposition to Phizo and NNC and her birth in Manipur. See, Longkumer (2022), p. 213.
43 For understanding this controversy, see Mahaprashasta (2023).
44 To understand the life and politics of Jaipal Singh Munda see, Choubey (2021); Kiro (2018).
45 This issue is discussed in detail in chapter 6.
46 Pandey (2019).
47 Vijay (2019).
48 Xaxa (1999), p. 3590.

88 Ibid., pp. 220–21.
89 Deshpande (1986a) in Saxena (2004), p. 222.
90 Deshpande (1986b) in Saxena (2004), p. 213.
91 Ibid., pp. 214–15.
92 ABVKA (2018b).
93 This aspect will be discussed in detail in chapter 6.
94 Mall (2019), pp. 40–41.
95 Ladha (2013), p. 30. It is also notworthy that Deshpand always gave the works of the VKA more imortance than his personal health or family life. In the early years of the 1980s he faced several health related problems. In 1984, Deshpande suffered a personal loss, when his wife, Prabhavati, passed away. However, he tried to give his best to expand the works of the VKA.
96 Ibid., pp. 30–32.
97 Jamatia (2011), pp. 21– 22.
98 See Kamei (2002), p. 10.
99 Mall (2014).
100 Bahuguna (2022).
101 These organizations have mobilized the 'delisting' movement to exclude those tribals from the list of STs who converted to some other religion like Christianity. The issue of delisting will be discussed in detail in chapter 6.
102 Most of the grassroots activists of the VKA, with whom I interacted, defined all tribals as Hindus. Also see Longkumer (2022), p. 173.
103 Interestingly, all this information was given to me by P. Suryanarayan, who is an Organization Secretary of the Janjatiya Dharam Sankriti Suraksha Manch (JDSSM). The JDSSM is not directly affiliated with the VKA. It was formed in 2002 when seventy tribal religious organizations came together to protect their tribal religion from the proselytization attempt of Christian missionaries (Babu 2023a). After the request of the senior activist of the VKA Organization Secretary, Atul Jog, Suryanarayan gave me an interview regarding the works of the VKA in the North-east region. It also underlines the inseparable relationship between the VKA and many non-affiliated organizations

like JDSSM. Discussion with P. Suryanarayana, Organizing Secretary (Sangathan Mantri) of the Janjatiya Dharm Sanskriti Suraksha Manch, on 27 July 2021 through Zoom.

104 Ibid.

105 Ibid.

106 Longkumer (2022), pp. 223–24.

Chapter 4: Politics of Service: Key Aspects of the Vanvasi Kalyan Ashram

1 Deshpande (1990), p. 7.

2 Hari (2019), pp. 113–14

3 Many senior activists accepted this limitation of the Ekal Vidyalaya and claimed that the VKA's leadership is working to overcome this problem.

4 Sundar (2006).

5 Deshpande (1990), p. 17.

6 Atul Jog's Interview with Atul Singhal in the programme titled 'Swayamsevak' for the YouTube Channel NamoImpact TV on 6 June 2020, https://www.youtube.com/watch?v=_nUX84wt7Ys&t=6s, viewed on 20 January 2021.

7 Sundar (2006); Joshy (2011).

8 Chattopadhyay (2020).

9 Ibid.

10 Ibid., Sundar (2006).

11 Indeed, the VKA has always presented both Christian missionaries and Naxals as serious problems for tribal society, and it emphasizes this aspect in the activities of its hostels too. See Sundar (2006); Chattopadhyay (2020).

12 *Van Bandhu* (2021, April), p. 6; Shukla (2021).

13 Sundar et al (2018).

14 Some of the former residents of the VKA hostels are doing fairly well in their lives. I met some of such former residents in Delhi. They requested not to mention their name and profession.

15 Sundar (2004), p. 1608.

16 I met students during my visit to Dumka, Jharkhand in July 2023.

17 ABVKA (2023b).

18 Vaid (2011), p. 56. It seems that four-year sports festivals have not continued at a fixed interval after 2015 because the VKA website does not provide information regarding such events. See, ABVKA (2025).

19 The *Times of India* (2024).

20 ABVKA (2015).

21 Ibid., p. 46.

22 Ibid., p. 47.

23 Ibid., pp. 47–48.

24 Ibid., p. 48.

25 Ibid., p. 49.

26 See Petkar (2022); Kaul (2019a August) (2019b September); (2020 October).

27 The VKA magazine *Van Bandhu* published (or republished from other sources) articles, presents a critical evaluation of the NEP for not including many aspects of tribal life, and particularly for not making clear budget provision for its implementation, and excluding the right to education. For example, see Rampal (2020), pp. 15–16; For understanding of NEP, see Choubey (2023a); Government of India (2020).

28 Here it is necessary to understand the full impact of the judgment of the Allahabad High Court. The SCs and STs are entitled to get 15% and 7.5% reservations respectively both at the first stage of recruitment and promotions for the posts of faculties treating University/College as one unit; while the OBCs were to provide 27% reservation at the first stage only and not in promotions. The 200-point roster system treats different departments of the institution as separate units, but the thirteen-point roster system curtailed the scope of reservation for marginalized sections, including STs. In simple terms, in a thirteen-point roster system while filling vacancies for the first thirteen recruitments, 1 OBC candidate shall be recruited on the fourth vacancy and one SC candidate on the seventh vacancy; the ST candidate will not get any post and will get a reservation only on the fourteenth vacancy. Under the old formula carving out half of thirteen, i.e. seven, for the unreserved category, three posts go to OBC, two to SC and one post to ST.

29 The Modi government changed the name of MHRD to the Ministry of Education (MoE) on 18 August 2020. It is noteworthy that from independence till 1985 the name of this ministry was Ministry of Education, but Rajiv Gandhi changed it to Ministry of Human Resource Development in 1985. See *The Hindu* (2020).

30 Press release by the ABVKA on 1 March 2019.

31 For the news related to the ordinance, see The *Indian Express* (2019); To understand the new law regarding roster system in educational institutions, see Government of India (2019).

32 Vaid (2011), p. 34.

33 Atul Jog's Interview with Atul Singhal in the programme titled 'Swayamsevak' for the YouTube Channel NamoImpact TV on June 6, 2020, https://www.youtube.com/watch?v=_nUX84wt7Ys&t=6s, viewed on 20 January, 2021.

34 Ladha (2013), p. 26.

35 Ibid., pp. 26–8.

36 Bhatia (2019), p. 8.

37 Ibid.

38 Ibid.

39 Ibid.

40 Pankaj Kumar Bhatia informs about many doctors, who go to these hospitals for the surgery of poor tribal persons due to their relations with the VKA (and RSS). See Ibid., p. 9.

41 Ibid., p. 9.

42 To understand the politics and importance related to ayurvedic medicines and the current state of legal and political debates related to medicinal plants in India, see Banerjee (2009); Handa (2022).

43 Bhatia 2019, p. 9.

44 The Vision Document underlines that according to estimates based on the Census of 2001, infant mortality rate (IMR) for scheduled tribes in India was 88 per 1,000 live births compared to the national average (including scheduled tribes population) of 68 per 1000. See ABVKA (2015), p. 49.

45 ABVKA (2015), pp. 49–50.

46 Ibid., p. 50.

47 Choubey (2021c).

48 For the description of the VKA's women's work see the website of the VKA: https://kalyanashram.org/women_activity/, viewed on 7 September 2024.

49 Vaid (2011), pp. 44–45.

50 Dhingra (2023).

51 Ibid.

52 The VKA's website presents a list of many programmes run by it to empower tribal women. One can find a list of such programmes here: https://kalyanashram.org/women_activity/, viewed on 7 September 2024.

53 *Van Bandhu* (2019, September), p. 22.

54 Ibid., p. 22.

55 Chapter 3 has discussed the life and struggle of Rani Gaidinliu. Also see Longkumer (2022).

56 Venugopal (2022).

57 Discussion with Girish Kuber, Hit Raksha Vibhag Pramukh (President, Interest Protection Department) VKA, New Delhi, 25 July 2021.

58 ABVKA (2023a).

59 Ibid.

60 Mall (2019), pp. 45–50.

61 Ibid., pp. 45–50.

62 Interestingly, when some female workers decided to free themselves from the work of the VKA and get married, the senior office-bearers played the role of a 'father figure' and helped them find a suitable partner. Jagdamba Mall gives an example of the woman activist Neeta, who was a teacher and worked in different areas of Nagaland. When her father died, senior VKA activist Vasantrao himself made all arrangements for her to visit Pune. After a few years of work in Nagaland, Neeta wanted to get married and two senior activists of the VKA, Vasantrao and Bhaskar Rao, arranged her marriage with another activist, and now Neeta is living a happy married life. See Mall (2019), p. 50.

63 Choubey (2020b), pp. 132–134.

64 Singh (2021), p. 30.

65 ABVKA (2015), p. 59.

66 Ibid., p. 60.
67 Ibid., p. 62.
68 Vaid (2011), p. 71.
69 Ibid., p. 69.
70 Goel (2019), p. 19; To understand the different aspects of the Delhi Vanvasi Kalyan Ashram, See *Van Bandhu* (May, 2019), pp. 18–19.
71 *Van Bandhu*, (May, 2019), p. 20.
72 Ravi (2019), p. 18.
73 Vaid (2011), pp. 70–71.
74 Ibid., p. 73
75 *Van Bandhu*, (July, 2019), p. 20.
76 Anand (2023), pp. 114–115.
77 Bhattacharjee (2019), p. 10.
78 Deshpande (1986b) in Saxena (2004), pp. 214–15.
79 Chapter 6 consists of a more detailed discussion of this aspect.

Chapter 5: Forest Resources, Tribal Rights and Vanvasi Kalyan Ashram

1 Vaid (2011), p. 11.
2 Choubey (2015a).
3 Many senior activists of the VKA emphasize that though the HRV was formed in 1990, Balasaheb Deshpande always tried to help vanvasis and protect their interests, and he even provided legal help on different issues. There are many examples where the VKA successfully pressurized local FD officials and other departments to work for the benefit of the tribal people. In some places, it created an alternate system so that tribal people could get more benefits. Vaid (2011), p. 61.
4 Interestingly, Abhay Xaxa has argued that most activists who fought for tribal land rights were educated at Christian institutions. He has also underlined that in the colonial period, some priests had contributed to making tribal people aware of their land rights. However, VKA senior activists argued that the formation of the 'Hit Raksha Vibhag' had nothing to do with the

influence of activists educated at missionary schools. Girish Kuber termed the formation of the 'Hit Raksha Vibhag' as a natural extension of the VKA's work. Discussion with Girish Kuber, (Hit Raksha Vibhag Pramukh (President, Interest Protection Department) VKA, New Delhi, 25 July 2021. For Abhay Xaxa's view see Sundar et al (2018).

5 Apart from focussing on the PESA and FRA, the VKA and its affiliated organizations have done some tremendous work in enhancing cooperative works in certain tribal areas. For example, its state-level affiliated organization in Rajasthan, Vanvasi Kalyan Parishad (VKP), a constituent state-level organization of the VKA, helped tribal people of Devla (tehsil: Kotada, district: Udaipur), Bichhiwada (tehsil: Jhadol, district: Udaipur), and Kumbhalgarh (district: Rajsamand) to form a cooperative committee to sell forest produce. In the North-east states, particularly in Tripura, the VKA and its affiliated organizations helped local communities document their customs and laws, which helped them assert their rights over natural resources. For a detailed discussion, see Vaid (2011), pp. 62–64.

6 It is interesting to note that the VKA office-bearers remember B.D. Sharma and his works with respect. See Petkar (2021), pp. 12–13.

7 Government of India (1996); Savyasaachi (1998); Choubey (2015b) (2016).

8 Choubey (2015a).

9 ABVKA (2002), in Saxena (2004), p. 316.

10 Ibid.; Other tribal organizations vehemently criticised the decision of the FD in sending a circular. See CSD (2004); Choubey (2015a).

11 ABVKA (2002), in Saxena (2004)

12 For analysis of the issues of adivasis and other tribal communities in the election manifesto of various national political parties in the general election of 2009, 2014 and 2019, see Choubey (2021a).

13 Discussion with Girish Kuber, 'Hit Raksha Vibhag' pramukh (President, Interest Protection Department) VKA, New Delhi, 25 July 2021.

14 Few things should be clear about the 'patta' related to Individal Forest Rights (IFR) given by the FRA: first, it is related to the recongnition of maximum four hectare of 'encroached' forest land for a nuclear family, which means that if a family has less than 4 hectares of encroached land, it would get 'patta' for the 'encroached' land only. Simillary if a family has more than 4 hectares of encroached land, in that case too, it would get ownership only for four hectares. Second, though it is ownership rights, an important condition on this rights is that the family cannot sell its land. See Government of India (2007).
15 Government of India (2007); Choubey (2013a); (2013b); (2014); (2015a), pp. 116–180.
16 Choubey (2015b); Dandekar and Choudhury (2010).
17 ABVKA (2015), p. 12.
18 However, Chhattisgarh also made PESA rules in 2022. Since the ABVKA's Vision Document was published in 2015, it could not include this fact. See *The Hindu* (2023)
19 ABVKA (2015), p. 12.
20 Ibid.
21 Ibid., p. 13.
22 Ibid.
23 Choubey (2015b).
24 ABVKA (2015), p. 13; For the critical evaluation of this Bill, see Choubey (2015c).
25 ABVKA (2015), p. 13.
26 Ibid.
27 For a detailed discussion on the Pathalgadi movement and the stand of the VKA, see chapter seven.
28 Choubey (2017); (2020a); (2020b).
29 Choubey (2015a), Chapter 5.
30 ABVKA (2015), pp. 19–20.
31 Nevertheless, it praises Narendra Modi, and mentions that 'in April 2015, the Prime Minister, Shri Narendra Modi, called for the implementation of Forest Rights Act by the states in mission mode following which the Ministry of Tribal Affairs asked all states to implement the Act as soon as possible'. Ibid., p. 20.

32 Ibid.

33 Ibid., pp. 20–21.

34 Ibid., p. 21.

35 Discussion with Girish Kuber, president of 'Hit Raksha Aayam' of the VKA on 21 September 2021; Indeed, its Vision Document (2015) emphasizes its stand against displacement, but does not mention any mobilization by the tribals to oppose forced displacement. See ABVKA (2015).

36 Sethi (2019).

37 Rajagopal (2019).

38 ABVKA (2019a).

39 Ibid.

40 Kaul (2019a); (2019b); (2019c).

41 Ibid., p. 24.

42 Ibid., p. 26.

43 Kaul (2019c), p. 27.

44 Ibid., p. 28.

45 Ibid.

46 Ibid., p. 27.

47 Kukreti (2019).

48 This committee comprised the then Inspector General of Forests (IGF) Rekha Rai; the then Deputy IGF (forest policy) Noyal Thomas, Assistant Director General (Wildlife) M.S. Negi and principal chief conservators of the four states—Madhya Pradesh, Chhattisgarh, Maharashtra and Manipur. The three non-government members were also not related to the tribal communities or members of tribal organizations. Following were their non-government members: Ravi Singh, secretary general World Wide Fund for Nature, Shankar Shirivastav, MoEFCC counsel in the Bhopal branch of the National Green Tribunal, and Sanjay Upadhyay, a Supreme Court lawyer. (See Mohanty 2019).

49 Ibid.

50 Ibid., *Van Bandhu*, Editorial, (June 2019).

51 Kuber (2019).

52 Pratinidhi (2019); Kuber (2019); ABVKA (2019b).

53 Pratinidhi (2019), p. 13.
54 For the views of other environmental and tribal organizations see Kukreti (2019).
55 Kuber (2019), p. 12; Kukreti (2019).
56 ABVKA (2021).
57 ABVKA (2015), p. 2.
58 Ibid., pp. 7–9.
59 Ibid., p. 29.
60 See, Government of India (2014); ABVKA (2015), p. 63.
61 ABVKA (2015), p. 64.
62 Ibid., p. 64.
63 Ibid., pp. 55–57.
64 Ibid., pp. 53–54.
65 Ibid., p. 51.
66 Bhardwaj (2020); *Van Bandhu* (2019b, February); *Van Bandhu* (2019, March)
67 See Joy (2023); Lakshman (2023).
68 Discussion with Rajnish Gambhir (a senior member of the AIUFWP), 13 August 2018.
69 Some of the key slogans mentioned in the pamphlets of the AIUFWP are 'we have birthright over natural resources' (Prakritik Sampadano Par Hamara Janamsidhh Adhikar Hai), 'forest is our own property, not anyone else's,' (Jangal Apne Aapka, Nahin Kisi ke Baap Ka) etc.
70 In its erstwhile form as NFFPFW, the AIUFWP worked extensively for the rights of Van Taungya villages, and continues to do so. Van Taungya villages are those villages in the different forest areas of the country, which were earlier mobile villages. They were formed by the colonial administrators to plant and protect new trees in those forest areas which were destroyed due to overexploitation. Most people who formed such villages were landless lower backward caste or Dalit people of different villages. After independence this system continued, and later in mid-1980s it was discontinued by the government of India. So, the mobile villages became settled villages, but their rights were not recognized by the government. Though the FRA makes

a provision to recognize their rights, in most of the cases they could get rights according tot the provisions of the FRA. The key reason behind non-recognition of their rights is that they belong to the category of OTFDs, and to get rights according the provsions of the FRA, they must prove that they have been living on forest land for three generations and seventy five years. See Choubey (2015a), pp. 289–92.

71 Discussion with the leader of AIUFWP, Roma, 2 August 2014.

72 During my fieldwork in DNP, I found that the men and women of the Tharu community had a deep understanding of their rights over the forest. Though they were not able to describe all aspects of the FRA, they were aware of its key provisions. When the DNP administration did not permit them to enter the forest, they argued that they had the right over forest resources given by the FRA.

73 This aspect will be discussed in detail in chapter 6. Also see Choubey (2018).

74 See Choubey (2019), pp. 75–95.

75 Kale (2018).

76 Choubey (2015a), Chapter 6; Also see, Choubey (2021b).

Chapter 6: Vanvasi Kalyan Ashram and Hindutv a: Ruptures in the Vision of a Hinduized Tribal Society

1 Many scholars have also underlined a sensitivity towards nature and tribal way of life in the demand of Sarna Code. For the views of some (tribal and non-tribal) scholars, see Kukreti (2020).

2 For example, the state general secretary of Adivasi Adhikar Manch, Praful Linda, argues that 'this is a matter of historical injustice. Before Independence, we had a place in the census stipulated as indigenous populations. This changed post-1961; in 1971, the Supreme Court ruled that under the Sixth Schedule of the Constitution, tribals could practice any religion. Tribals across India practice different religions and the Sarna population amounts to approximately 20 lakh'. See Paul (2020).

3 Angad (2020).

4 Pandey (2020).
5 See Hansda (2023), pp. 12–13.
6 ABVKA (2018a).
7 *Organizer*, (3 November 2018).
8 Many other articles published in *Van Bandhu* expressed a similar argument. See Vaidya (2021); Bastariya (2021).
9 Hemant Soren told reporters that 'we have already sent all the papers (related to the demand for a separate Sarna religious code for tribals) to him. Now he has to take a decision on it'. Before that, he wrote a letter in September 2023 to the prime minister and demanded the recognition of the Sarna Code for tribals. See, *Deccan Herald* (10 November 2023).
10 Deogharia (2024); Bisoee (2024). Interestingly, in 2024 the BJP lost all five constituencies reserved for STs in Jharkhand. Some political commentators argued that overlooking the demand for the Sarna Code was one of the key factors in the defeat.
11 *Hindustan Times* (10 May 2019).
12 See Chatterji (2009), pp. 111–112.
13 Janjati Suraksha Manch (2022), p. 23.
14 Singh (2021); *Van Bandhu*, (November 2023), p. 111.
15 Janjati Suraksha Manch (2022).
16 I had extensive discussion with many senior office bearer of the VKA (including Suresh Kulkarni, Girish Kuber etc.). Though they discussed Harsh Chouhan's work with pride, the did not mention JSM and his earlier role in this organization.
17 Tiwary (2023). There is a similar organization in the North-east region with a slightly different name, i.e. Janjati Dharm Sanskriti Suraksha Manch (JDSSM), which works in the whole North-east region on the issues related to the faith and cultural awakening among the different tribal communities of the North-east. It opposes conversion by Christian missionaries and demands the delisting of those tribes who converted to Christianity and Islam. P. Suryanarayana is the Organization Secretary (sangathan mantri) of the JDSSM. He is from Andhra Pradesh and till 2010 he worked in the ABVP and then began work with the VKA in the North-east region. Discussion with

P. Suryanarayana, Organization Secretary (sangathan mantri) of the Janjatiya Dharm Sanskriti Suraksha Manch, on 27 July 2021 through Zoom.

18 Ibid., p. 12; *Van Bandhu* (November 2023a), pp. 106–7.

19 The Bill was introduced in Lok Sabha on the 12 August 1967. The motion for reference of the Bill to a Joint Committee of the Houses was moved in the Lok Sabha by Asoka Mehta, the then Minister of Petroleum and Chemicals and Social Welfare, on 26 March 1968, which was discussed and adopted the same day. See Lok Sabha Secretariat 1969.

20 See, Lok Sabha Secretariat (1969), p. 29. It is noteworthy that in the JPC, there was a Rajya Sabha member from Meghalaya, Emonsing M. Sangma who gave his dissent in the JPC against the proposal of delisting tribals who converted to Islam or Christianity (Janjati Suraksha Manch 2022, pp. 16–17).

21 See Janjati Suraksha Manch (2022), pp. 16–18. Referring to Kartik Oraon's book *Bees saal ki kaali raat* (20 Years of a Dark night), his daughter Geeta Shree says those invoking his idea for their demand did not completely understand what he was seeking regarding justice for tribals. 'While he said that benefits reserved for tribal communities should be given to them and not others, he did not ask for the rights of others to be taken away. He called for reservation to be given to the backward among the converted too. Now, RSS-backed organizations, which consider tribals as Hindus, are trying to polarise the community electorally'. (Angad 2023).

22 Janjati Suraksha Manch (2022), pp. 7–10.

23 Ibid., p. 5.

24 Tiwari (2023).

25 Singh (2023).

26 For example, see *Van Bandhu*, (January 2021, p. 13); Chauhan (2022); Pratinidhi (2023), p. 21.

27 It is interesting to note that the daughter of Kartik Oraon, Geeta Shree Oraon, has also questioned the demand of delisting converted tribals by the VKA, JSM and other RSS-affiliated organizations. She argued that 'the identity and entity of tribal

communities is Sarna religion', she added that 'an adivasi adopting any religion, including Hinduism, is a convert'. (Angad 2023).

28 See Xaxa (2009), pp. 31–32. Indeed, many civil society groups also reiterate the same view. For example, Jharkhand Janadhikar Mahasabha has argued that 'there is a clear provision under the Constitution that any tribal group can be considered a "Scheduled Tribe". There is no mention of religion anywhere in these sections. (There is an attempt) to create communal divide in tribal society on the basis of baseless facts related to religion and reservation'. See Angad (2023).

29 Tiwari (2023).

30 Angad (2023).

31 Das and Thirumalai (2023).

32 To understand the history and politics of the Naxal and Maoist movements, see, Banerjee (1980); Dubey (1989); Paul (ed,) (2013).

33 For detailed discussion, see chapter 1.

34 It is interesting to note that within the VKA even senior office-bearers do not differentiate between the term Maoism and Naxalism. However, the term Naxal/Naxalism came from the Naxalbari movement that started in 1967. It largely focused on peasant mobilization, which was not against the use of violence but did not use it as its primary tool. On the other hand, the CPI (Maoist) emphasizes the politics of 'class annihilation', i.e. killing those people who belong to the class of exploiters.

35 Mall (2019), p. 114.

36 Discussion with Pramod Petkar (managing editor of *Van Bandhu* and senior activist of the VKA) at the Delhi Office of the VKA on 20 October 2020.

37 Ibid.

38 Sundar (2016b).

39 Rambhau Mhalgi Prabodhini (RMP), Development and Internal Security in Chhattisgarh: Impact of Naxalite Movement: A Report (Mumbai, 2005-6), p. 47 quoted from Sundar (2016b), p. 34.

40 Sundar (2016b), p. 228.
41 Ibid. Also see, Choubey (2018).
42 *Organizer* (2011).
43 Choubey (2015b).
44 Roy and Singh (2022).
45 *Organizer* (2018).
46 Ibid.
47 Kaul (2020a).
48 Discussion with Suresh Kulkarni at the VKA office in Delhi on 23 October 2019. Many other activists of the VKA also express the same kind of view in informal discussions.
49 Sundar (2019).
50 Chatterji (2009), p. 161.
51 Ibid., p. 291.
52 Ibid., pp. 290–291.
53 It is true that tribal Christians have not faced large-scale violence like the 2008 Kandhamal riots. Post 2014, there were several reports on lynching of Muslims and small-scale violence by cow vigilante groups. However, in many areas, tribal Christians also faced sporadic violence in the form of attacks on churches, especially in the tribal and Dalit pockets of Chhattisgarh, Maharashtra, Madhya Pradesh and Odisha. Most of these have been sporadic and small-scale and therefore escape widespread outrage. Churches have been destroyed, pastors attacked, a nun sexually assaulted, etc. See World Watch Monitor (2017); Sundar (2019); Mathew (2016).
54 Jaffrelot (1996), p. 322; Jaffrelot (2005), p. 8.
55 Chatterji (2009), pp. 263–264.
56 For Dileep Singh Judeo's obituary, see *Van Bandhu* (August 2019), p. 8.
57 See Arnimesh (2024). The BJP-ruled nine state governments have enacted anti-conversion laws, these include: Uttar Pradesh, Madhya Pradesh, Uttarakhand, Chhattisgarh, Haryana, Jharkhand, Karnataka, Himachal Pradesh and Gujarat. BJP-ruled states like Haryana, Uttarakhand, etc., have already passed

stringent laws against conversion. The Bhajanlal Sharma-led BJP government of Rajasthan is also planning such a law. Also see, Anand (2024); Scroll staff (2023).

58 John (2014).

59 Mathew (2022).

60 Das (2023).

61 Banerjee and Mishra (2024).

62 All World Gayatri Parivar is a Hindu organization that Shriram Sharma formed. It focuses on the spread of Hindu religious values, and it claims to promote unity, knowledge and harmony among people and societies. To understand the different facets of its works, see Heifetz (2021).

63 Das and Thirumalai (2023).

64 Chatterji (2009), pp. 263–264.

65 Nandini Sundar argues that while the Hindutva onslaught is overpowering there are also a few signs of resistance, both on the cultural and political fronts. The assertion is particularly marked among some communities like the Santhals and Bodos, who have developed their own script and are publishing extensively in these languages, but the spread is slow. Of late, Mahisasur/Mahishasura has become something of an icon of resistance against Hindutva, see, Sundar (2019), pp. 253–54. According to Hindu mythologies, Mahishasura was a demon and Devi Durga killed her. However, many activists and scholars have started to claim that Mahishasura was a ruler from the lower strata of the society. Some have argued that he was a Buddhist ruler not a demon. See Dev (2018); Jothe (2017).

66 Choubey (2024b); *Deccan Herald* (2024).

67 Discussion with Girish Kuber, president of Hit Raksha Aayam of the VKA on 21 September 2021.

68 Dhingra (2023).

69 Discussion with senior activist Suresh Kulkarni at the VKA office in Delhi on 23 October 2019.

70 On 23 October 2019, I was in the central office of the VKA in Delhi to discuss about its works with its senior activists. A person came with lots of fruits and sweets and told Suresh Kulkarni that

he wanted to greet him for the forthcoming Diwali festival and also mentioned that he wanted a BJP ticket to fight the Delhi Assembly election. Later, Kulkarni informed me that he was a local leader who wanted their 'good words' to get the ticket. This incident underlines that the voice of the VKA's senior activists has at least some 'moral authority' in the selection of the candidates in the BJP. Of course, it is not the sole or most important element in candidate selection. To understand the RSS and VKA's role in BJP's candidate selection at the grassroots level, see Thachil (2014), p. 162.

71 Dhingra (2023).

72 Thachil (2014), p. 162.

73 Chatterji (2009), pp. 183–184.

74 It should be noted that a separate National Scheduled Tribes Commission was formed in 2004, when the Constitution (89th Amendment) Act, of 2003 came into effect. See the website of the National Scheduled Tribes Commission: https://ncst.nic.in/?lang=en

75 Thachil (2014), p. 161.

76 To understand the RSS and VKA's works in the North-east region, see Longkumer (2019); (2022); Mehta (2023); Kashyap (2017).

77 Longkumer (2019).

78 Agarwala (2023).

79 See Kumar (2017); Halliday (2015). However, Rijiju retracted his statement after criticism within the BJP. Since he was part of the Central Government, his statement was problematic for the larger pro-Hindutva narrative of the BJP in other parts of the country. See the *Economic Times* (2015).

80 Sundar (2016), p. 245.

81 Jaffrelot (1996), p. 322.

82 Harsh Chouhan was appointed as the chairman of NCST in February 2021 and he resigned from this post in the last week of June 2023. See Joy (2023); Lakshman (2023).

83 See *Organizer* (2019); Pandey (2019).

84 Pratinidhi (2021).

Chapter 7: Conclusion: Is VKA a Robust Ambassador of Hindutva Politics?

1 Discussion with Girish Kuber 'Hit Raksha Vibhag' pramukh (president, Interest Protection Department) VKA, New Delhi, 25 July 2021.

2 However, Girish Kuber argued that the formation of 'Hit Raksha Vibhag' was related to the natural expansion of the VKA's work. Since its work expanded in new areas and many new tribal activists became part of this organization, it started to take on new issues related to the lives of tribal communities. Discussion with Girish Kuber 'Hit Raksha Vibhag' pramukh (president, Interest Protection Department) VKA, New Delhi, 25 July 2021

3 Ashis Nandy has used this term to evaluate the limitations of those revolutionary Indian freedom fighters, who wanted to use arms to defeat the armed might of Britain to achieve Indian Independence. The British were the intimate enemy of the Indian armed revolutionaries, who wanted to be like Britishers to defeat them. It means that the Britishers had strong armed forces, and their rule was based on violence or fear of violence, and revolutionaries wanted to defeat them by using the method of violence and armed struggle. Nandy argues that Gandhi followed a different path, that of non-violence and Satyagraha. See Nandy (1983).

4 Abhay Xaxa has made an important point on the background of land rights activists. He argues that he studied 25 such activists, and out of them, twenty were educated in educational institutions run by Christian missionaries. He also underlines that the educational system of Christian missionaries' played a crucial role in developing consciousness in the minds of tribal youths about land rights. Historically, the famous priest Father Hoffman prepared the first draft of the Chota Nagpur Tenancy Act of 1909. See Sundar et al (2018).

5 To read the full script of Rajendra Prasad's letter and the reply of Thakkar Bapa, see Choudhary (1984).

6 Thakkar Bapa himself formed organizations like Bhil Seva Manda (1922), and Bharatiya Adimjati Sevak Sangh (1948). The

latter organization was more active on tribal issues till the 1970s, and it did many commendable works for tribal welfare with the help of the government of India. However, it could not provide a clear vision on ideological issues and was primarily limited to some kind of welfare work with the help of the government. For a brief and lucid understanding of Thakkar Bapa's life and work, see Tiwari (2017).

7 This aspect is discussed in chapter four.

8 The idea of Hindutva in this form can be discerned from the writings of its two crucial propagators, namely Savarkar and Golwalkar. To understand their ideas regarding Hindutva, see, Savarkar (1989; First Publication 1923); Golwalkar (2000; First Publication 1939); To understand the exclusionary and majoritarian nature of Hindutva, see, Joshy and Seethi (2015), pp. 89–99; Vanaik (2017); Ashutosh (2019), pp. 8–13.

Bibliography

ABVKA (Akhil Bharatiya Vanvasi Kalyan Ashram) (1999). 'U.N. Draft Declaration on Rights of Indigenous People: Memo to Prime Minister'. In Saxena, Surya Narayan (2004). *Wide Wings of Vanvasi Kalyan Ashram: A Tale of Service and Struggle*. Delhi: Suruchi Prakashan, pp. 141–167.

ABVKA (2002). 'Resolution: Akhil Bharatiya Vanvasi Kalyan Ashram, Karyakari Mandal Baithak 26 September 2002'. In Saxena, Surya Narayan (2004). *Wide Wings of Vanvasi Kalyan Ashram: A Tale of Service and Struggle*. Delhi: Suruchi Prakashan, pp. 313–320.

ABVKA (2015). *Bharat Mein Janjatiyon Hetu ek Neeti Drishti-Patra*. (Also available in English as *Vision Document for Janjatis of India*) Ramabhau Mahalgi, Mumbai.

ABVKA (2018a). 'Demand for Separate Religion Code in Census is Misleading and Illogical' Karyakari Mandal of Akhil Bharatiya Vanvasi Kalyan Ashram in Shirdi, September 29.

ABVKA (2018b). 'Prastav Sankhya 7: Andaman Nicobar ki Suraksha Vyavashta Mabjoot kar Dharmantaran

Gatividhiyan Roki jayen', Kendriya Krayakrini ki 19 December 2018 ki Biathak mein Yavatmal mein Parit Prastav, 19 December.

ABVKA. (2019a). Press Release: Resolution Passed by the Central Executive Board Meeting, Satna, 24 February.

ABVKA (2019b). Tweaks in the new draft of the Indian Forest Act, 1927, give power to forest officials to shoot tribals for 'violation of laws'. *Van Bandhu*, June 44 (1), pp. 6–7.

ABVKA (2021). Akhil Bhartiya Vanvasi Kalyan Ashram: Kendriya Karyakarini Mandal ki Baithak 19 July 2021—Jashpur mein Parit Prastav. Press Release 19 July.

ABVKA (2023a). Kalyan Ashram Believes, Janjati Women MPs and MLAs will become the voice of society. Press Release 30 September.

ABVKA (2023b). Karyavrit, November, Bhagyanagar, Telangana. *Van Bandhu* (November 2023), p. 60.

ABVKA (2025). Website of Akhil Bhartiya Vanvasi Kalyan Ashram. https://kalyanashram.org/sports/, viewed on 5–28 February 2025.

Agarwala, Tora (2023). Meghalaya BJP Chief: No one in the Party tells us don't have that (beef). It's our lifestyle, BJP has nothing to do with it. The *Indian Express*, February 23, https://indianexpress.com/article/political-pulse/meghalaya-bjp-chief-earnest-mawrie-party-beef-lifestyle-8459622/, viewed on 4 June 2024.

Ambagudia, J. and Xaxa, V. (2021). *Handbook of Tribal Politics in India*. Delhi: Sage.

Ambekar, S. (2019). *The RSS: Roadmaps 21st Century*. Delhi: Rupa.

Amin, S. (1995). *Event, Metaphor, Memory: Chauri Chaura 1992–1992*. Berkeley: University of California Press.

Anand (2020). Kalyan Ashram Ko Janana hai to Bala Saheb ko Jaan Lo. *Van Bandhu*, December, 46 (7), pp. 12–13.

Anand (2023). Vartman Vimarsh ko Jane aur Dhridta se Aage Badhen. *Van Bandhu*, (November), 48 (6), pp. 114–115.

Anand, U. (2024). New BJP govt in Rajasthan to introduce fresh law on religious conversion. *Hindustan Times*, June 19, https://www.hindustantimes.com/india-news/new-bjp-govt-in-rajasthan-to-introduce-fresh-law-on-religious-conversion-101718737347994.html, viewed on 27 June 2024.

Anderson, W.K. and Damle, S.D. (1987). *The Brotherhood in Saffron: The Rashtriya Swayamsevak Sangh and Hindu Revivalism*. Delhi: Penguin Viking.

Anderson, W.K. and Damle, S. (2018). *The RSS: A View to the Inside*. Delhi: Penguin Viking.

Angad, A. (2020). Explained: Why Jharkhand wants a separate religious code for the Sarna tribals? The *Indian Express*, 18 November, https://indianexpress.com/article/explained/why-jharkhand-is-seeking-a-separate-religious-code-for-sarna-tribals-7048700/, viewed on 5 May 2020.

Angad, A. (2023). RSS affiliate on one side, lines sharpen between tribal, 'converted' section in Jharkhand The *Indian Express*, 27 December, https://indianexpress.com/article/political-pulse/rss-tribals-converted-section-in-jharkhand-9083357/, viewed on 5 May 2020

Arnimesh, S. (2024). 60-day notice, DM verification, jail threat in Chhattisgarh conversion bill—but not for 'ghar wapsi'. *The Print*, 23 February, https://theprint.in/politics/60-day-notice-dm-verification-jail-threat-in-chhattisgarh-conversion-bill-but-not-for-ghar-wapsi/1975167/, viewed on 10 May 2023.

Awasthi, A. (2019). Prayagraj Kumbh Mein Janjati Ka Samagam. *Van Bandhu*, March, 43 (10), p. 7.

Babu, R. (2020). Janjati Dharm-Sanskriti-Parmpra ke Saath ho rahi Chhedchhad Band ho. *Van Bandhu*, March, 44 (10), pp. 5–6.

Babu, R. (2023a). Shradha Jagran Aayam: Ek Laghu Parichay. *Van Bandhu*, February, 47 (9), pp. 10–12.

Babu, R. (2023b). Shradha Jagran Aayam: Ek Laghu Parichay Prishthbhumi. *Van Bandhu*, February, 47 (10), pp. 10–12.

Bahuguna, V. K. (2022). Tribals and their Religion: The Sanatan Dharma has ingredients of tribal worship, *Van Bandhu*, February, 46 (9), p. 34.

Banerjee, A. and Mishra, A. (2024). 'Akbar is Satyam': How One Man 'Re-Converted' 1,650 in 4 'ghar wapsis' as BJP Won Chhattisgarh, *News18*, January 31, https://www.news18.com/politics/akbar-is-satyam-how-one-man-re-converted-1650-in-4-ghar-wapsis-as-bjp-won-chhattisgarh-exclusive-8760608.html, viewed on 18 March 2024.

Banerjee, S. (1980). *In the Wake of Naxalbari: A History of Naxalite Movement in India*. Calcutta: Suvarnrekha.

Bastariya, R. (2021). 'Janjati Samaj aur Alag Dharm Code ki Maang: Ek Sameeksha', *Van Bandhu*, January, 46 (8), p. 10.

Baviskar, A. (2005). Adivasi Encounters with Hindu Nationalism in MP. *Economic and Political Weekly*, 40 (48).

Baviskar, A. (1995). *In Belly of the River: Tribal Conflict over Development in Narmada Valley*. Delhi: Oxford University Press.

Bhagat-Ganguly, V. and Kumar, S. (eds). (2019). *India's Scheudled Areas: Untangling Governance, Law and Politics.* London and New York: Routledge

Bharat Sarkar (Government of India). 1989. *Anusuchi Jatiyon aur Anusuchit Janjatiyon ke Aayukat ki Report, Unatiswi Report.* New Delhi.

Bhardwaj, R.K. (2020). Janjatiyon ke Kanooni Adhikaron Par Karyashala Sampann. *Van Bandhu*, 44 (8), pp. 11–13.

Bhatia, Dr P. (2019). 'Dur Khade Rahkar Darshak Na Bane, Seva ke Liye Aage Aayen', *Van Bandhu*. 44 (7), pp. 7–9.

Bhattacharjee, M. (2019). *Disaster Relief and the RSS: Resurrecting 'Religion' through Humanitarianism.* Delhi: Sage.

Bijoy, C.R. 2012. *Policy brief on Panchayat Raj (Extension to Scheduled Areas) Act of 1996*. Delhi: UNDP.

Bisoee, A. (2024). Congress leader Rahul Gandhi pledges Sarna Code and forest rights for tribals. The *Telegraph*, 8 May, https://www.telegraphindia.com/elections/lok-sabha-election-2024/congress-leader-rahul-gandhi-pledges-sarna-code-and-forest-rights-for-tribals/cid/2018360, viewed on 25 June 2024.

Broom, N.P. et al (2019). The Indian Forest Act's proposed amendments are dangerous and fanciful. *Down to Earth*, 3 May, https://www.downtoearth.org.in/blog/forests/the-indian-forest-act-s-proposed-amendment-is-dangerous-and-fanciful-64319, viewed on 2 July 2019.

Campaign for Survival and Dignity (CSD) (2004). *Endangered Symbiosis: Evictions and India's Forest Communities, Report of the Jan Sunwai, 19–20 July* 2003.

Chandra, B. et al (1989). *India's Struggle for Independence.* Penguin: Delhi.

Chatterjee, P. (1993). *The Nation and Its Fragments: Colonial and Postcolonial Histories*. Delhi: Oxford University Press.

Chatterji, A.P. (2009). *Violent Gods: Hindu Nationalism in India's Present; Narratives From Orissa*. Gurgaon: Three Essays Collective.

Chattopadhyay, S. (2020). Inside A Hindutva Hostel: how RSS is Rewriting the tribal mind. Catchnews, 4 May, https://www.catchnews.com/india-news/exclusive-inside-a-hindutva-hostel-how-rss-is-rewiring-the-tribal-mind-1450354461.html, viewed on 21 June 2024.

Chaturvedi, A. (2024). Jharkhand Mein Ghuspaithiyon ne Adivasi Sanskriti aur Bahnon aur Betiyon ki Surkasha ko

Khatre Mein Daal Diya hai. *Prabhat Khabar*, May 29, https://www.prabhatkhabar.com/prabhat-khabar-special/prabhat-khabar-interview-pm-narendra-modi-said-infiltrators-endangered-tribal-culture-sisters-daughters-safety-in-jharkhand-grj, viewed on 21 June 2024.

Chauhan, S. (2022). Delisting-Delisting, Bas! Ek Hi Naara Delisting. *Van Bandhu*, June, 47 (1), pp. 6–7.

Chauthaiwale, M.K. (2014). *Maine Dekhe Hue Balasaheb Deoras*. New Delhi: Shri Bharti Prakashan (an RSS publication).

Choubey, K.N. (2013a). Do 'Pragtisheel' Kanonon ki Dastan: Rajya, Jan-Andolan aur Pratirodh. *Pratiman: Samay Samaj Sankriti*, 1 (1), pp. 149–177.

Choubey, K.N. (2013b). *Jungal ka Sangharsh, Pragtisheel Kanoon aur Rajya.* Samayik Prakashan, Samaj aur Itihas, Naveen Srinkhla 3, Nehru Samrak Sangrahalya aur Pustkalya, Delhi.

Choubey, K.N. (2014). *The Forest Rights Act and the Politics of Marginal Society.* NMML Occasional Paper: Perspectives in Indian Development, New Series 31, Nehru Memorial Museum and Library.

Choubey, K.N. (2015a). *Jungle ki Haqdari: Rajniti Aur Sangharsh*. Delhi: Vani Prakashan.

Choubey, K.N. (2015b). The Public Life of a 'Progressive' Law: PESA and 'Gaon Ganarajya' (Village Republic). *Studies in Indian Politics*, 3 (2), pp. 247–259.

Choubey, K.N. (2015c). Enhancing PESA: The Unfinished Agenda. *Economic and Political Weekly*, 50(8), pp. 21–23.

Choubey, K. N. (2016). The state, Tribals, and Law: The Politics Behind the Enactment of PESA and FRA. *Social Change*, 46 (3), pp. 355–370.

Choubey, K.N. (2017). Turning the Tide in Forest Rights. *Economic and Political Weekly*, 52(1), pp. 21–23.

Choubey, K. N. (2018). Salwa Judum: Rajya, Maowad Aur Hinsa ki Anthin Dastan. *Pratiman: Samay Samaj Sanskriti*, 6 (12), pp. 187–208.

Choubey, K.N. (2019). Adivasi Jeevan Aur Vanvasi Kalyan Ashram. *Paratiman: Samay, Samaj, Sanskriti*, 7 (14), pp. 75–95.

Choubey. K.N. (2020a). Protected Areas, Forest Rights, and the Pandemic. *Economic and Political Weekly*. XL (51), pp. 10–12.

Choubey, K.N. (2020b). Indian Forest, Tribal Life, and Intricate Legal Structure: From Subjecthood to Quest for Citizenship Rights, *Studies in Humanities and Social Science*, XXVII (2), Winter 2020, pp. 122–139.

Choubey, K.N. (2021a). Adivasi Issues and the Elections Manifestos of National Political Parties. In Ambagudia, J. and Xaxa, V. (ed.), *Handbook of Tribal Politics in India*. Delhi: Sage.

Choubey, K.N. (2021b). Forest Governance, Tribal Rights and state: A Study of Third Layer of Federal Structure in India. In Saxena, R. (ed), *New Dimensions in Federal Discourse in India*. New York: Routledge, pp. 106–119.

Choubey, K.N. (2021c). Jaipal Singh Munda Aur Adivasi Rajniti. *Pratiman: Samay Samaj Sanskriti*, 9 (17–18), pp. 1–32.

Choubey, K.N. (2023a). Adivasi, Shiksha ka Prashn Aur Rashtriya Shiksha Neeti. *Pariprekshya: Shaikshik Yojna Aur Prashasan ka Samajik-Arthik Sandarbh*, 30(1), pp. 135–152.

Choubey, K. N, (2023b). Birsa Munda and the Politics of Memory. *The Book Review*, XLVII (7): 24–25.

Choubey, K.N. (2024a). Understanding Tribal India: Constitutional Rights, Issues and Challenges. In Jha, M.K. and Choubey, K.N. (eds), Indian Politics and Political Processes: Ideas, Institutions and Practices. New York: Routledge. pp. 318–341.

Choubey, K.N. (2024b). 'Chunavi Rajneeti, Adivasi Hit Aur Bhajpa ka Varchasv', *Sablog-127*, 15 (3), pp. 14–17.

Choudhary, V. (ed.) (1984). *Rajendra Prasad: Correspondence and Select Documents* (Volume 3). Delhi: Allied Publishers Private Limited.

Citizen's Inquiry Committee. (2006). *Untold Story of Hindukaran (Proselytisation) of Adivasi (Tribal) in Dang: A Report.* http://indianculturalforum.in/2016/10/14/untoldstory-of-hindukaran-proselytisation-of-adivasi-tribal-in-dang-a-report/, viewed on 25 May 2024.

Dandekar, A. and Choudhury, C. (2010). *PESA, Left-Wing Extremism and Governance: Concerns and Challenges in India's Tribal Districts.* Anand: Institute of Rural Management.

Das, M. (2023). Inside 'ghar wapsi' of Chhattisgarh Tribals: RSS women priests reach out, royal washes feet. The *Print*, 27 February, https://theprint.in/politics/inside-ghar-wapsi-of-chhattisgarh-tribals-rss-women-priests-reach-out-royal-washes-feet/1398989/, viewed on 24 June 2024.

Das, M. and Thirumalai, N. (2023). Ghar wapsi trumps Gober Economy: How Vishnu Deo Sai Turns the Tables on Bhupesh Baghel. *New18*, 11 December, https://www.news18.com/elections/ghar-wapsi-trumps-gobar-economy-how-vishnu-deo-sai-turned-the-tables-on-bhupesh-baghel-in-chhattisgarh-8698992.html, viewed on 24 June 2024.

Deccan Herald (2023). Decision on Sarna religious code for tribal pending with Centre: Soren. 10 November, https://www.deccanherald.com/india/jharkhand/decision-on-sarna-religious-code-for-tribals-pending-with-centre-soren-2765333, viewed on 10 June 2024.

Deogharia, Jaideep (2024). If we form the govt, Sarna code will be implemented. The *Times of India*, May 25,

https://timesofindia.indiatimes.com/city/ranchi/if-we-form-govt-sarna-code-will-be-implemented-kharge/articleshow/110410035.cms, viewed on 24 June 2024.

Deshpande, B. (1986a). 'Kalyan Ashram (A letter of Prime Minister Rajiv Gandhi)'. In Saxena, Surya Narayan (2004). *Wide Wings of Vanvasi Kalyan Ashram: A Tale of Service and Struggle*. Delhi: Suruchi Prakashan, pp. 221–223.

Deshpande, B. (1986b). 'Presentation of Akhil Bhartiya Vanvasi Kalyan Ashram to President of India, Shri R. Venkataraman'. In Saxena, Surya Narayan (2004). *Wide Wings of Vanvasi Kalyan Ashram: A Tale of Service and Struggle*. Delhi: Suruchi Prakashan, pp. 213–217.

Deshpande, B. (1986c). 'An Open Letter to Pope John Paul II On the Eve of His First Visit to India'. In Saxena, Surya Narayan (2004). *Wide Wings of Vanvasi Kalyan Ashram: A Tale of Service and Struggle*. Delhi: Suruchi Prakashan, pp. 217–221.

Deshpande, B. (1990). *Sanstha, Shasan aur Karyakarta*. ABVKA, Delhi.

Deshpande, B.V. and Ramaswamy, S.R. (1981). *Dr. Hedgewar, The Epoch Maker: A Biography*. Bengaluru: Sahitya Sindhu.

Dev. A. (2018). Clearing a 'Good Demon's' Name. The Quint, 17 October, https://www.thequint.com/news/india/mahisha-dasara-mysuru-durga-puja, viewed on 28 July 2024

Devi, Mahashweta (1998). *Jangle Ke Davedar: Adivasi Sangharsh Ki Mahagatha*. Delhi: Radhakrishna Paperbacks.

Deccan Hearld (2024). Lok Sabha Elections 2024: A Close Look at Scheduled Tribes (ST) Constituencies. *Deccan Herald*, 6 June, https://www.deccanherald.com/elections/india/lok-sabha-elections-2024-a-close-look-at-scheduled-tribe-st-constituencies-3050049, viewed on 24 June 2024.

Dhingra, S. (2023). How did BJP pull off tribal turnaround in Chhattisgarh? Inside RSS's 'apolitical' Vanvasi Kalyan

Ashram. The *Print*, 29 December, https://theprint.in/india/how-did-bjp-pull-off-tribal-turnaround-in-chhattisgarh-inside-rsss-apolitical-vanvasi-kalyan-ashram/1903917/, viewed on 5 June 2024.

Sonkar, D. (2020). 'Sant Gahira Guru: Vanvasi Samaj ke Adwitiyak Sadhak'. *Van Bandhu*, October, 46 (5), p. 23.

Dubey, A.K. (2019). *Hindu Ekta Banam Gyan ki Rajneeti*. Delhi: Vani Prakashan.

Dubey, A.K. (1989). *Kranti ka Aatm-Sangharsh: Naxalwadi Andolan ke Badlte Chehre Ka Adhyayan*. New Delhi: Vinay Prakashan.

Eschmann, A. (ed.) (2005). *The Cult of Jagannath and the Regional Tradition of Orissa*. New Delhi: Manohar.

Froerer, P. (2008). *Religious Division and Social Conflict: The Emergence of Hindu Nationalism in Rural India*. New Delhi: Social Science Press.

Furer-Haimendorf, C.V. (1982). *Tribes of India: The Struggle for Survival*. Delhi: Oxford.

Ghurye, G.S. (1963). *The Scheduled Tribes*. Bombay: Popular Publishers.

Goel, R. (2019). Swatantrata Senani Birsa Munda Ham Sabhi ke Adarsh: Delhi Mein Manaya Gaya Janjatiya Gaurav Divas. *Van Bandhu*, December, 44 (7), p. 19.

Golwalkar, M.S. (2020; first publication 1939). *We or Our Nationhood Defined*. Delhi: Global Vision Publishing House.

Government of India (1996). *The Provisions of Panchayats (Extension to the Scheduled Areas) Act, 1996*, No. 40 of 1996.

Government of India (1972). *Wild Life (Protection) Act*. New Delhi: Ministry of Law and Justice.

Government of India (1980). *Forest (Conservation) Act*. New Delhi: Ministry of Law and Justice.

Government of India (2007). *Scheduled Tribes and Other Traditional Forest Dwellers (Recognition of Forest Rights) Act 2006*. Ministry of Law and Justice.

Government of India (2014). *Report of the High-Level Committee On Socio-Economic, Health and Educational Status of Tribal Communities of India*. New Delhi: Ministry of Tribal Affairs

Government of India (2020). *The Central Educational Institutions (Reservation in Teachers' Cadere) Act, 2019*. New Delhi: Ministry of Law and Justice.

Government of India (2020). *New Education Policy*. New Delhi: Ministry of Human Resource and Development, .

Government of India (2024). *Government of India Committed to Tribal Welfare: PM JANMA (Pradhan Mantri Janjati Adivasi Nyay Maha Abhiyan)*. Delhi: Ministry of Tribal Welfare.

Government of Madhya Pradesh (1956a). *Report of the Christian Missionary Enquiry Committee, Madhya Pradesh*. Volume I, Nagpur: Government Printing Press.

Government of Madhya Pradesh (1956b). Report of the Christian Missionary Enquiry Committee, Madhya Pradesh. Volume II, Nagpur: Government Printing Press.

Graham, B. (1990). *Hindu Nationalism and Indian Politics: The Origin and Development of Bharatiya Jan Sangh*. New Delhi: Foundation Books.

Goyal, D.R. (1979). *Rashtriya Swayamsevak Sangh*. Delhi: South Asia Books.

Gramsci, A. (1971). The Intellectuals, in *Selections from the Prison Notebooks*. Translated and Edited by Q. Hoare and G.N. Smith. New York: International Publishers, page 3-23, Marxist Internet Achieve, https://www.marxists.org/archive/gramsci/prison_notebooks/problems/intellectuals.htm, viewed on 5 Jan 2025

Halliday, A. (2015). Kiren Rijiju gives it back to Naqvi: 'I eat beef, can somebody stop me?' The *Indian Express*, May 28, https://indianexpress.com/article/political-pulse/kiren-rijiju-gives-it-back-to-naqvi-i-eat-beef-can-somebody-stop-me/, viewed on 6 March 2024.

Handa, A. (2022). The Politics of Knowledge of Medicinal Plants in India: Corporations, Collectors and Cultivators as Constituents. *Studies in Indian Politics* 10 (1), pp. 1–14.

Hansda, Dr R.K. (2023). Janjati Samaj Ko Alpsankhyak Banakar Anusuchit Janjati Ke Aarakshan Se Vanchit Karne Ka Shdyantra. *Van Bandhu*, November, 48 (6), pp. 12–13.

Hansen, T.B. (1990). *The Saffron Wave*. New Delhi: Oxford.

Hari, R. (2019). *Bhaskarrao: Pracharak-karmyogi* (Part:1). (Translation: Ramesh Babu). Jashpur: Akhil Bhartiya Vanvasi Kalyan Ashram.

Heifetz, D. (2021). *The Science of Satyug: Class, Charisma, and Vedic Revivalism in the All World Gayatri Pariwar*. New York: state University of New York Press.

Hoare, Q. and Smith, G.N. (1971). *Selections form the Prison Notebooks of Antonio Gramsci*. London: Lawrence and Wishart. Delhi: Bloomsbury.

Hoare, Q. and Sperber, N. (2015). An Introduction to Antonio Gramsci: His Life, Thought and Legacy. London: Bloomsbury.

Jaffrelot, C. (1996). *The Hindu Nationalist Movement and Indian Politics: 1925 to the 1990s*. London: Hurst & Company.

Jaffrelot, C. (ed.) (2007). *Hindu Nationalism: A Reader*. Princeton: Princeton University Press.

Jamatia, B.B. (2011). *Religious Philosophy of Janjatis of Northeast Bharat*. Guwahati: Heritage Foundation.

Janjati Suraksha Manch (2022). *Change in Faith is Change in Culture: Tribal Cultural Identity is embodied in their deities and their Faith*. Bhopal: Janjati Suraksha Manch.

July, https://countercurrents.org/2016/07/21/voices-from-the-ruins-of-kandhamal-and-why-i-cried-after-watching-the-film/, viewed on 10 March 2024.

Mathew, L. (2022). BJP banks on the late 'ghar wapsi' campaigner, Judeo, to revive fortunes in Chhattisgarh. The *Indian Express*, November 13, https://indianexpress.com/article/political-pulse/bjp-dilip-singh-judeo-revive-chhattisgarh-8264929/, viewed on 11 March 2024.

Mehta, A. (2023). RSS, BJP have come a long way to win over the Northeast. The *Sunday Guardian*, 4 March, https://sundayguardianlive.com/news/rss-bjp-have-come-a-long-way-to-win-over-the-northeast, viewed on 18 June 2024.

Mehta, S. (Compilation) (2002). *Gandhiji On Religious Conversion*. Mumbai: Mani Bhavan Gandhi Sangrahalya.

Menon, N. (2012). *Seeing Like a Feminist*. Delhi: Penguin–Zubaan.

Mishra, I. (2024). President Approves Uttarakhand UCC Bill. *The Hindu*, March 13, https://www.thehindu.com/news/national/president-approves-uttarakhands-ucc-bill/article67947099.ece, viewed on 20 June 2024.

Mishra, R. and Rai, A, (2020). Tribal Leader Jagdev Ram Oraon dies, PM Modi expresses grief. *Hindustan Times*, July 15. https://www.hindustantimes.com/india-news/tribal-leader-jagdeo-ram-oraon-dies-pm-modi-expresses-grief/story-1D2999bN2efCKPOHClhtKN.html, viewed on 20 June 2024.

Mohanty, P. (2019). Draft Indian Forest (Amendment) Bill 2019: Arming state to Undermine the rights and wellbeing of tribals. *India Today*, 7 August, https://www.indiatoday.in/news-analysis/story/draft-indian-forest-amendment-bill-2019-arming-state-to-undermine-rights-and-wellbeing-of-tribals-1578054-2019-08-07, viewed on 1 July 2021.

Mouffe, C. (1979). *Gramsci and Marxist Theory*. London: Routledge and Kegan Paul.

Mukhopadhyay, N. (2019). *The RSS: Icons of the Indian Right*. Chennai: Tranquebar.

Nandi, R.N. (1973). *Religious Institutions and Cults in the Deccan, C. A.D. 600–A.D. 1000*. Delhi: Motilal Banarsidas.

Nandy, A. (1983). *The Intimate Enemy: Loss and Recovery of Self Under Colonialism*. Oxford: Oxford University Press.

Narayan, B. (2021). *Republic of Hindutva: How the Sangh is Reshaping Indian Democracy*. Delhi: Penguin.

Narayanan, D. (2025). *The RSS And the Making of the Deep Nation*. Delhi: Penguin.

Nartam, V. (2021). Revered Jagdev Ram Jee's Life, Work and His Legacy. *Van Bandhu*, October, 46 (5), pp. 27–29.

Noorani, A. G. (2020). *The RSS: A Menace to India*. Delhi: Leftword Book.

O'Neill, D. and Wayane, M. (2017). On Intellectuals. Historical Materialism. 8 October, https://www.historicalmaterialism.org/on-intellectuals/, viewed on 1 January 2025.

Organizer: Voice of the Nation (2011). Supreme Court verdict on Salwa Judum: Can Courts enforce ideology? July 11, https://organiser.org/2011/07/24/47390/general/rcaf263f5/, viewed on 10 December 2020.

Organizer: Voice of the Nation (2018). Separate Religious Code not acceptable, Vanvasi Kalyan Ashram raises concerns with the Home Minister. https://organiser.org/2018/11/03/121888/bharat/separate-religious-code-not-acceptable-vanvasi-kalyan-ashram-delegation-raises-concerns-with-the-home-minister/, viewed on 14 December 2022.

Organizer: Voice of the Nation (2018). Cover Story: Manipulating Monoliths. May 17, https://organiser.org/2018/05/17/120530/bharat/manipulating-monoliths/, viewed on 10 December 2020.

Organizer: Voice of the Nation (2019). 'Felicitation of Scheduled Tribe MPs', July 11, https://organiser.org/2019/07/11/124300/bharat/felicitation-of-scheduled-tribe-mps/, viewed on 10 December 2020.

Pandey, Dr, B.M. (2019). 'Arya Bahar Se Aaye'- Ek Sampoorn Asatya Sidhant. *Van Bandhu*, January, 43 (8), pp. 10–13.

Pandey, N. (2020). Jharkhand resolution allowing tribals to identify as non-Hindus a conspiracy—RSS affiliate. 16 November, The *Print*, https://theprint.in/india/jharkhand-resolution-allowing-tribals-to-identify-as-non-hindus-a-conspiracy-rss-affiliate/545515/, viewed on 5 December 2020.

Pandey, N. and Arnimesh, S. (2023). 'UCC should not undermine tribals' customary laws', RSS affiliate tells Law Commission. The *Print*, 17 July, https://theprint.in/india/ucc-should-not-undermine-tribals-customary-laws-rss-affiliate-tells-law-commission/1673160/, viewed on 20 June 2024.

Pandey, S. (2019). Vanvasi Ashram Ne Pratibhaon Ko Ubharane ka Kaam Kiya: Arjun Munda. *Amar Ujala*, 29 December, https://www.amarujala.com/uttar-pradesh/kanpur/arjun-munda-said-vanvasi-ashram-worked-to-attract-talent, viewed on 21 June 2024.

Paul, S. (2020), 'Adivasis Not Hindus': Protests Demanding Sarna Code intensify in Jharkhand. *News Click*, 24 September, https://www.newsclick.in/adivasis-hindus-protests-demanding-sarna-code-intensify-jharkhand, viewed on 21 June 2024.

Pankaj, A.K. (2015). *Marang Gomke Jaipal Singh Munda*. Delhi: Vikalp Prakashan.

Paul, S. (ed.) (2013). *The Maoists Movements in India: Perspectives and Counter-Perspectives*. New Delhi: Routledge.

Petkar, P. (2021). Samvedansheel Sarkari Adhikari Evam Samajik Karyakartta: Dr B.D. Sharma. *Van Bandhu,* 46 (7), pp. 12–13.

Petkar, P. (2022). Nai Shiksha Neeti Mein Asha ki Kiran-Matribhasha. *Van Bandhu* February, 46 (9), pp. 12–14.

Pratinidhi (2019). Akhil Bhartiya Vanvasi Kalyan Ashram: Kendriya Karyakarini Mandal Ki Baithak, Dinank 19 September 2019—Haridwar mein Parit Prastav. *Van Bandhu*, October, 44 (5), pp. 12–13.

Pratinidhi (2021). Janjati Samaj Ke Vikas Ke Bina Desh Ka Vikas Adhura. *Van Bandhu*, April, 45 (11), p. 6.

Pratinidhi (2023). Delisting Janjati Samaj Ke Jeevan Maran Ka Prashn hai : Rajkishore Hansda. *Van Bandhu*, 47 (10), p. 21.

Rajagopal, K. (2019). SC stays Feb 13 order of eviction of tribals, forest dwellers. *The Hindu*, 28 February, https://www.thehindu.com/news/national/sc-stays-feb-13-order-for-eviction-of-tribals-forest-dwellers/article61537784.ece, viewed on 4 June 2024.

Rampal, A. (2020). NEP: Reads like an impressive wish list but barters right to education. *Van Bandhu*, September 46 (4), pp. 25–26.

Ranjan, R. (2022). *The Political Life of Memory: Birsa Munda in Contemporary India*. UK: Cambridge University Press.

Ravi (2019). Amritsar Mein Vanvasi Kalyan Ashram—Punjab Ne Manaya Pratham Varshikotsav. *Van Bandhu*, September, 44 (4), p. 18.

Roy, A. (2013). *Gendered Citizenship: Historical and Conceptual Explorations*. Delhi: Orient Blackswan.

Roy, A. and Singh, U.K. (2022). Pathalgadi Movement, Self-Governance, and the Question of 'Weak statehood' in Neubert, Diter et al (eds.), Local Self-Governance and Varieties of statehood: Tensions and Cooperations, Cham: Springer, pp. 117–138.

Roychaudhuri, T. (1995). Shadows of the Savarkar: Historical Reflections on the Politics of Hindu Nationalism. *Contention*, 5: Fall. pp. 141–62.

Sampath, V. (2019). *Savarkar: Echoes from Forgotten Past: 1883–1924*. Delhi: Penguin.

Sapre, K.D. (1999). *Shri Bala Saheb Deshpande: Jeevan Aur Karya*. Jabalpur: Van Sahitya Akedemy

Sapre, P.D. (1991). *Hamre Vanvasi aur Kalyan Ashram*. Lucknow: Lokhit Prakashan.

Savarkar, V.D. (1940). *Hindu Sangathan: Its Ideology Immediate Programme*. Bombay: Hindu Mahasabha Presidential Office.

Savarkar, V.D. (1989). *Hindutva: Who is a Hindu?* (First Publication: 1923) New Delhi: Bharati Sahitya Sadan.

Savyasaachi. 1998. *Tribal Forest-Dwellers and Self-Rule: The Constituent Assembly Debates on the Fifth and Sixth Schedules*. New Delhi: Indian Social Institute.

Saxena, S.N. (1993). *Friends or Foes of Adivasis and Dalits*. Delhi: Publicity and Publication Division-ABVKA.

Saxena, S.N. (1994). *Vanvasi Kalyan Ashram: Kya Aur Kyun?* Delhi: ABVKA.

Saxena, S.N. (2004). *Wide Wings of Vanvasi Kalyan Ashram: A Tale of Service and Struggle*. Delhi: Suruchi Prakashan.

Scroll Staff (2023). Anti-Conversion laws in India enable discrimination, vigilante violence, says US Panel. *Scroll.in*, April 7, https://scroll.in/latest/1047002/anti-conversion-laws-in-india-enable-discrimination-vigilante-violence-says-us-panel, viewed on 10 June 2024.

Seshadri, H.V. (ed.) (1998). *RSS: A Vision In Action*. Bangalore: Sahitya Sindhu Prakashan.

Sethi, N. (2019). SC Orders Forced Eviction of More Than 1 Million Tribals, Forest Dwellers. The *Wire*, 20 Feb, https://thewire.in/rights/sc-orders-forced-eviction-of-more-than-1-million-tribals-forest-dwellers, viewed on 4 June 2024.

Sharda, R. (2018). *RSS 360 degree: Demystifying Rashtriya Swayamsevak Sangh*. New Delhi: Bloomsbury.

Sharma, B. D. (1998). *The Little Lights in Tiny Mud-pots Defy 50 Years of Anti-'Panchayat' Raj*. New Delhi: Sahyog Pustak Kuteer.

Sharma, B.D. (2010). *Unbroken History of Broken Promises: Indian state and the Tribal People*. New Delhi: Freedom Press and Sahyog Pustak Kuteer.

Sharma, J. (2003). *Hindutva: Exploring the Idea of Hindu Nationalism*. New Delhi: Penguin.

Sharma, M.C., (2014). *Builders of Modern India, Pandit Deendayal Upadhyaya*. Delhi: Publication Division.

Shukla, S. (2021), UP: President Ram Nath Kovind calls for including tribals, forest dwellers in India's inclusive growth. The *Free Press Journal*, 14 March, https://www.freepressjournal.in/india/up-president-ram-nath-kovind-calls-for-including-tribals-forest-dwellers-in-indias-inclusive-growth, viewed on 15 March 2021.

Singh, K.S. (1983). *Birsa Munda and His Movement 1874–1901: A Study in the Millenarian Movement in Chotanagpur*. Calcutta: Oxford University Press.

Singh, K.P. (2021). Village Development. *Van Bandhu*, October, 46 (5), pp. 30–31.

Singh, P. (2020). Delisting: Demand grows to strip ST status to converts. *Organizer: Voice of the nation*, February 22, https://organiser.org/2023/02/20/108789/bharat/delisting-demand-grows-to-strip-st-status-of-converts/, viewed on 18 June 2024

Singh, S. (2021). Neev ke Pathar Moru Bhaiya Ketkar. *Van Bandhu*, 46 (5), pp. 15–17.

Smith, B. (1989). *Reflections on Resemblance, Ritual and Religion*. New York: Oxford University Press.

Sundar, N. (1999).The Indian census, identity and inequality. In Guha R. & Parry, Jonathan P. (eds), *Institutions and*

Inequalities: Essays in Honour of André Béteille, New Delhi: Oxford University Press.

Sundar, N. (2005). 'Verrier Elwin and the 1940s missionary debate in central India', in Subba, T.B. and Som, S. (eds), *Between Ethnography and Fiction: Verrier Elwin and the Tribal Question in India*, Himayatnagar: Orient Longman, pp. 86–127.

Sundar, N. (2006). Adivasi vs. Vanvasi: The Politics of Conversion in Central India, pp. 357–90. In Saberwal, S. and Hasan, M. (eds.) *Assertive Religious Identities*. New Delhi: Manohar.

Sundar, N. (2004). Teaching to Hate: RSS' Pedagogical Programme. *Economic and Political Weekly*, 39(16), pp. 1605–1612.

Sundar, N. (2019). Hindutva Incorporation and Socioeconomic Exclusion: The Adivasi Dilemma. In Chatterji, A.P., Hanse, T.B. and Jaffrelot, C. (eds.), *Majoritarian state: How Hindutva Nationalism is Changing India*. New York, Oxford University Press, pp. 249–258.

Sundar, N. (ed) (2016a). *The Scheduled Tribes and Their India: Politics, Identities, Policies and Work*. Delhi: Oxford.

Sundar, N. (2016b). *The Burning Forest: India's War In Bastar*. New Delhi: Juggernaut.

Sundar, N. et al. (2018). Adivasi Bharat: Parikalpna, Rajniti, Mudde Aur Chintayen. *Pratiman: Samay Samaj Sanskriti*, 6 (12), pp. 149–186.

Sundar, N. (1997). *Subalterns and Sovereigns: An Anthropological History of Bastar*. Delhi: Oxford University Press.

Swartz, C. (2019). After 30 Years Only 23 Countries Have Ratified Indigenous and Tribal Peoples Convention 169, *Cultural Survival*, June 5, https://www.culturalsurvival.org/news/after-30-years-only-23-countries-have-ratified-indigenous-and-tribal-peoples-convention-ilo, viewed on 12 June 2021.

Thachil, T. (2014). *Elite Parties, Poor Voters: How Social Services Win Votes in India*. New York: Cambridge University Press.

Thakur, N. and Kranti, V. (eds) 2015). *About RSS (Rashtriya Swayamsevak Sangh)*. Delhi: Vichar Vinimay Prakashan.

The Constitution of India. Diglot Edition, Allahabad: Central Law Publication, 2008 (Fourth Edition).

The *Economic Times* (2015). I don't eat beef; media 'twisted' my statement: Kiren Rijiju. 29 May, https://economictimes.indiatimes.com/news/politics-and-nation/i-dont-eat-beef-media-twisted-my-statement-kiren-rijiju/articleshow/47474809.cms?from=mdr, Viewed on 4 June 2024.

The Hindu (2020). HRD Ministry is now officially Education Ministry, as President Approves name change. Delhi, 18 August, https://www.thehindu.com/news/national/president-gives-nod-to-hrd-ministry-name-change/article32380281.ece, viewed on 4 June 2024.

The Hindu (2022). Chhattisgarh government implements PESA Rule- 2022. 10 August, https://www.thehindu.com/news/national/other-states/chhattisgarh-govt-implements-pesa-rule-2022/article65751589.ece, viewed on 5 July 2024.

The *Indian Express* (2019). Union Cabinet okays proposal for ordinance restoring 200-point roster in faculty jobs. 7 March, https://indianexpress.com/article/education/union-cabinet-approves-hrd-ministrys-proposal-to-bring-ordinance-to-restore-teacher-quota-5615374/, viewed on 5 May 2024.

National Scheduled Tribes Commission (2005). Website, https://ncst.nic.in/?lang=en viewed on 25 Jan 2025.

The *Times of India* (2024). National Tribal Sports Fest begins in Raipur with 800 participants. 29 December, https://timesofindia.indiatimes.com/city/raipur/natl-tribal-sports-fest-begins-in-raipur-with-800-participants/articleshow/116751290.cms, viewed on 5 February 2025

Tiwary, D. (2023). Slowly and steadily, RSS groups prepare ground for 'delisting' of converted tribals. The *Indian Express*, December 28. https://indianexpress.com/article/political-pulse/slowly-and-steadily-rss-groups-prepare-ground-for-delisting-of-converted-tribals-9085831/, viewed on 7 May 2024

Tiwari, S. (2017). Kasht-Nivarak Thakkar Bapa: Samaj Seva Ko Samarpit Jeevan Par Ek Vihangam Drishti. *Pratiman: Samay Samaj Sanskriti*, 5(10), pp. 278– 96.

Tople, L. (2011). *Han! Hum Hindu hain* (Translation: Prasann Damodar Sapre), New Delhi: Suruchi Prakashan.

Tripathi, Dr R. (2021). Aham Ramah Asmi-Main Ram Hum. *Van Bandhu*, July 46 (2), pp. 12–13.

Trivedi, V. (2020). *Sangham Sharanam Gachchami: RSS ke Safar ka Ek Imandar Dastavej*. Chennai: Eka.

United Nations (2007). *United Nations Declarations on the Rights of Indigenous Peoples*. https://www.un.org/development/desa/indigenouspeoples/wp-content/uploads/sites/19/2018/11/UNDRIP_E_web.pdf, viewed on 2 November 2023.

Vaid, S. (2011). *Vanvasi Kalyan Ashram: Karya Parichay*. Jashpur Nagar: Akhil Bhartiya Vanvasi Kalyan Ashram.

Vaidya, Dr M. (2021). Kaun Si baat Sarna Dharam Code Samarthkon ko Swikar nahi hai? *Van Bandhu*, 46 (8), pp. 6–9.

Van Bandhu (2019, November). 'Kalyan Ashram- Jashpur ne Manaya 'Karma Utsav', 44 (6), p. 18.

Van Bandhu (2019, September). 'Ati Pichhdi Janjati Mahila ka Sshaktikaran', 44 (7), p. 22.

Van Bandhu (2019, May). 'Delhi Ke Badhte Charan: Delhi Ne Prastut Kiya Apna Varshik Vrit', 43 (12), pp. 18–19.

Van Bandhu (2019, July). 'Delhiwasi Kalyan Ashram Ko Sahyog Karne Aage Aayen: Indresh Kumar', 44 (2), p. 20.

Van Bandhu (2019, May). 'Haryana ke Chhatron Ki Nagar Yatra', 43 (12), p. 20.

Van Bandhu (2019, May). 'Janjati Samaj ka ek Veer: Raghoji Bhangre', 43 (12), p. 15.

Van Bandhu (2019a, February). 'Prayag Kumbh Mein Vanvasi Bandhuon Ka Pavitra Snan', 43 (9), pp. 6–10.

Van Bandhu (2019b, February). National Workshop on Effective Implementation of PESA Act. 43 (9), pp. 28–29.

Van Bandhu (2019, March). Van Adhikar Kanoon ke Antargat Dawe Wali Vanbhumi Se Kabja Hatane Sambandhi Uchchtam Nyayalay ke Aadesh Par Avilamb Hastkshep kare Sarkar. 43 (10), pp. 16–17.

Van Bandhu (2019, September). Pujya Swami Amranandji. 44 (7), p. 6.

Van Bandhu (2020, November). Birsa Munda Angreji Shasan Ewam Dharmantaran ke Virodhi (Avran Katha). November, 46 (6), pp. 6–7.

Van Bandhu (2021, April). Janjati Samaj ke Vikas ke Bina Desh ka Vikas Adhura: Rasthrapati Ram Nath Kovind. 45 (11), p. 6.

Van Bandhu (2021, January) Diwangat Karyakartaon ka Karya Aage Badhane ka Nischay Karen: Vanvasi Kalyan Ashram ki Akhil Bhartiya Baithak Bengaluru mein sampan. 45 (8), pp. 13–14.

Van Bandhu (2023a November). Karmyogi Vaktitv: Kartik Uraon. 48 (6), pp. 106–7.

Van Bandhu (2023b November). Karmyogi Vyaktitv: Moren Singh Poorti. 48 (6), p. 111.

Van Bandhu (2023c November). Ek Baar Rohtasgarh Avashy Padharen. 48 (6), pp. 67–68.

Van der Veer, P. (1994). *Religious Nationalism*. Berkeley: University of California Press.

Van Bandhu (August 2019). Ghar Vapsi Abhiyan ke Senani Dilip Singh Judeo. 44 (3), p. 8.

Vanaik, A. (2017). *Hindutva Rising: Secular Claims, Communal Realities*. Delhi: Tulika Books.

Venugopal, V. (2022). RSS-backed tribal wing to Highlight fight against Muslims, British regimes. The *Economic Times*, August 7, https://economictimes.indiatimes.com/news/politics-and-nation/rss-backed-tribal-wing-to-highlight-fight-against-muslim-british-regimes/articleshow/93415202.cms?from=mdr, viewed on 4 June 2024.

Vijay, T. (2019). Naam mein Bhala kya Rakha hai. *Van Bandhu*, January 2019, 43 (8), pp. 8–9.

Vijay, T. (2023). Janjatiya Yodha Jinhone Bharat Swatantra Karaya. *Van Bandhu*, June, 48 (1), pp. 12–13.

Vishnudas, S. and Ursula M. (2012). In the Jungle of Law: Adivasi Rights and Implementation of Forest Rights Act in Kerala. *Economic and Political Weekly*, 47 (19), pp. 38–45.

Vskteam (Vishwa Samwad Kendra Team) (2018). 'Katre Guruji: A Saint Who Walked Over Leporsy', https://vsktelangana.org/katre-guruji-a-saint-who-walked-over-leprosy, April 14, viewed on 27 May 2021.

Wintage, A. (1997). *The Church and Conversion*. Delhi: ISPCK.

World Watch Monitor, 'Indian Christians faced almost as many attacks in first half of 2017 as all of 2016', 8 Aug. 2017, https://www.worldwatchmonitor.org/2017/08/hinduisation-of-india-leads-to-more-anti-christian-viol, viewed on 6 June 2024.

Xaxa, A.F. and Devy, G.N. (2021). *Being Adivasi: Existence, Entitlements, Exclusion*. Delhi: Penguin.

Xaxa, V. (1999). Tribes as Indigenous People in India. *Economic and Political Weekly*, 34 (51), pp. 3589–3595.

Xaxa, V. (2001). Protective Discrimination: Why Scheduled Tribes lag behind Scheduled Castes? *Economic and Political Weekly*, 36 (29), pp. 2765–2772.

Xaxa, V. (2005). Politics of Language, Religion and Identity: Tribes in India. *Economic and Political Weekly*, 40 (13), pp. 1363–1370.

Xaxa, V. (2009), 'Tribes, Conversion, and the Sangh Pariwar', in Dharmendra Kumar and Yemuna Sunny (ed.), *Proselytization in Hindi: The Process of Hinduisation in Tribal Society*. Aakar: Delhi, pp. 19–36.

Zeliang, N.C. (2012). *Glimpses from the Life of Rani Gaidinliu*. Guwahati: India Heritage Foundation.

Index

Scan QR code to access the
Penguin Random House India website